ANIMAL DREAMING

the spiritual and symbolic language
of the australasian animals

scott alexander king

BLUE ANGEL®
PUBLISHING

Animal Dreaming:
The Spiritual and Symbolic Language
of the Australasian Animals
- Revised and Expanded -

Second edition
Copyright © 2007 Scott Alexander King

This printing 2016

First edition originally published in 2003

Published by Blue Angel Publishing
80 Glen Tower Drive, Glen Waverley
Victoria, Australia 3150
E-mail: info@blueangelonline.com
Websites: www.blueangelonline.com

Cover illustrations by Karen Branchflower and Toni Carmine Salerno
Book illustrations by Scott Alexander King
Design & layout Copyright © 2007 Blue Angel Publishing
Edited by Tanya Graham

Blue Angel is a registered trademark of Blue Angel Gallery Pty. Ltd.

ISBN: 978-0-9803983-0-4

"*A human being is part of the whole called by us 'Universe,' a part limited in time and space. He experiences himself, his thoughts and feelings as something separated from the rest, a kind of optical delusion of his consciousness. This delusion is a kind of prison for us, restricting us to our personal desires and to affection for a few persons nearest to us. Our task must be to free ourselves from this prison by widening our circle of compassion to embrace all living creatures and the whole of nature in its beauty.*"

— Albert Einstein

acknowledgements

To my beautiful wife Trudy and our three amazing children. You are my angels and my anchors. I love you so much.

With thanks to Mark Baldock for bringing the first two print-runs of this book to fruition, (the first being way back in 2003), to Roz Tilley (www.beyondblueprint.com) for suggesting I write it in the first place and to Susan Oliver for unconditionally supporting the process from the start.

With much love to my 'spirit family': Maws, the Dales, the Campbells, the Olivers and the Hawkins, Raven, Marlene, Christian and Ghinni, Ronnie and Maggie Burns, Maria Elita and Lucy Cavendish. And my actual family: Leita, Len, Jake, Charley, Demi and Dylan; Joy, Harry, Kris, Rob, Nick, Ava and Scott. Thank you all for being there.

And humble gratitude to Toni Carmine and Martine Salerno for republishing *Animal Dreaming* and to Maria Elita for introducing us. It means a lot to know that this, my first book, which was written years ago from the heart and self-published (complete with editing mistakes and badly structured sentences), will remain intact, but revised and re-edited, as a legacy to my children, the animals and the Earth Mother herself. Thank you.

contents

preface

From as early as eight years of age I have been aware of animal spirits.

It was not unusual for me to regularly see and feel the energy of Cats, Rats and Rabbits in and around my home. No one questioned me when I spoke of them, and no one seemed to be concerned by their presence. I therefore grew up believing it was natural, like breathing. I honestly thought everyone could see them. It was not until later that I realised they couldn't. As I matured, my ability to see the animals came and went, until my mid-twenties when I was forced to notice, listen and honour them as my personal Dreaming and a way for me to follow my path and celebrate my connection to Spirit.

I have since discovered that there are animals in Spirit with the acumen to assist us in every aspect of our lives: as teachers, totems and guides. Similarly, the animals that physically share our Earth with us are equally imbued with wisdom potent enough to navigate us successfully and abundantly through life. They can, for example, bring about healing for ourselves and others. They can return a traveller safely home or ensure a safe passage for someone about to embark on a journey. They can ease a mother's pain as she watches her children leave home or ensure health, peace and happiness when a new baby enters the world.

No matter what the scenario or circumstance, there is an animal in existence permeated with the symbolic medicine to aid and support us in every single aspect of our lives. I know this to be true because I call upon them on a daily basis and they have never let me down, and I promise that when you begin to integrate their good judgment into your life, you too will celebrate this ancient notion as your truth.

introduction

The Dreamtime

The Dreamtime was the time before time, when the world was new and the Ancestor Spirits still wandered the Earth (often in human shape, sometimes not), helping to bring form to the land, the plants and the animals. It was when everything on the horizon was being created and when everything was getting used to existing. Some indigenous people refer to this time as 'The Dreamtime', while others refer to their personal spiritual connection to the Ancients and the land as 'The Dreaming'.

As the Ancestor Spirits roamed the Earth, they set about forming links between groups and individuals, some of which were human and some not. As they travelled, they fashioned the ground by creating mountains and valleys, rivers and streams. Places marked by the Ancestors held great spiritual significance to the people, with stories and legends related to their Dreaming emerging as a way of explaining this sacred time of Creation.

After the Ancestors had finished influencing the land, some returned to the stars or the earth, while others became animals and other things. This was a sacred time, alive with the magick of Creation; a time now gone, but which still holds great power for the people who continue to believe that the Spirits are still here, disguised in the forms they took when the Earth was new.

The term 'Dreaming' could relate to a person's spirituality or 'medicine', or the belief system held by their family or clan as a whole. Every clan member was allocated an animal totem at their birth: an animal spirit that not only offered the individual the strength of its wisdom, but that also protected them as they explored life, by perhaps warding off illness or removing obstacles and impending danger. They would carry this animal's Dreaming as part of their knowledge and their gift to the rest of the people. The animal Dreaming carried by an individual often held sanctified relevance to the geographical area their people called home.

For reasons known only to those concerned, a rule was enforced that determined marital rites and strict expectations relating to the joining of members of different tribes or family clans. Among minority groups, it was stipulated that individuals born into tribes governed by the Dreaming of certain family or ancestral totems were only permitted to marry others born into clans governed by the Dreaming of complimentary totems. For example, it was considered only right and proper for a Dingo clan member to marry an individual from a Water Hen tribe, and vice versa. This was perhaps enforced to honour ancient tribal blood relationships or the Ancestors that originally birthed the Dreaming of the land inhabited by the tribes concerned. Whatever the reasoning behind the rule, the stories associated with the birth place, the land, the animals and the Ancestors were passed down from one generation to the next, with each passing forming the integral basis of the individual's Dreaming, that of their family group and the people as a whole.

Throughout this book the word 'Dreaming' denotes the wisdom and symbolic interpretation of the animals listed and has intentionally been used slightly out of context; the word referring more to the 'medicine' of the animal rather than its customary 'Dreaming'. To the western mindset, the word 'medicine' automatically inspires visions of pharmaceuticals prescribed by a doctor with the intention of making ill people well again. To experience an animal by chance, and to have that animal share its wisdom on a spiritual level, is like absorbing aspects of its strength and power, or its *medicine*: energetic knowledge that can inspire change and healing within an individual. To experience a live Eagle, for example, could suggest the embracing of a spiritual life and the true, heartfelt honouring of Spirit's ways. The finding of a feather or a dead Eagle could possibly imply the opposite or reverse – an understanding obtained in much the same way as tarot cards are often interpreted. The viewpoint from which the word 'Dreaming' should be respectfully examined therefore, while referring to the animals in this book, should be in the context of 'medicine', wisdom or teachings as outlined above, as the word 'Dreaming' actually refers to the very deep, ancient relationship between an individual or family group and an animal that cannot be understood after just one brief encounter, unless one has a solid understanding of one's traditional family ancestral knowledge, as do the indigenous people of Australia. The word 'Dreaming', like the word 'totem', refers to ancient knowledge and ancestral lineage that outlines the family tree of a person, their family and their homeland while also helping to explain the Creation of the Earth and everything on it.

Power of Seed

Australia today is like a giant 'Noah's Ark' of people and animals. We are lucky to have representatives from all corners of the world here, including our own indigenous people, living side by side and, to a large degree, in peace and unity. With each ambassadorial group of people has come a plethora of spiritual beliefs and religions. To be born 'Australian' has meant that many individuals have gone 'the way of the Horse' and have had to form a spiritual path based on the collective teachings of one or more of these cultures. Australia is still such a young country and everything within it has been born from the teachings and customs of the mothers and fathers who 'founded' the country and originally 'shared' the land with the first Aboriginal people. Some of us, as Australians by birth, are, however, finding that we are becoming increasingly confused by the vast array of religions and teachings that suggest that their's is the one true path. We are now beginning to go back further in our personal search for the truth: to the teachings of the Ancients that relied on the language of nature, spoken in symbolic tongue by the animals, the plants and the stones: the sacred Earth Teachings that formed the basis of many beliefs, including the roots of the country we call home – Australia. It is with this sense of returning to the heart of spirituality that Ancient Earth Wisdom clearly illustrates the understanding of our relationship to all things as being equal.

The indigenous people of Australia viewed Creation as based on a sacred 'power of seed' which was deposited deep in Mother Earth at the beginning of her Dreaming. With the power of this seed, every worldly event or life progression that occurred left behind a residue of its energy within the Earth, a record or memory of its existence. This belief was seen to relate to the principle that plants leave an image of themselves within the Earth as seeds. The very makeup of the landscape – every mountain, rock, river, and tree and the vibrational memory of their forming – endorsed the proceedings that birthed that place within Creation. Everything of the natural world was read as a symbolic diary, acted out in the beginning by Spirit Beings – the Ancestors – that formed the world. As with the tiny seed, the fertility of a place was weighed against the memory of its origin. This was called 'The Dreaming', which represented the sacred core of Mother Earth. Always in the oral tradition, legends of the Dreamtime explained daily phenomena. Some stories were meant for initiated men's ears and very few, if any, white men would ever hear any of these 'secret' stories in their true form (and rightly so). As a result, it has been difficult for non-Aboriginals searching for the true spiritual basis of Australia to connect. Many stories, designed to explain and educate the ways of the people, Spirit and Creation, were meant for the children: to explain the Dreaming of the animals and the people's relationship to them, as well as for entertainment. Many of these stories have been shared and we should consider ourselves lucky to have these stories to pass onto our children. Much of the true essence of these stories, however, has been lost over time in translation, misinterpretation and in the blending of one tribe's legend with the next by non-Aboriginal authors. Therefore I have deliberately excluded tribal or Ancestral names, precise story outlines and spiritual associations shared with the animals by any particular people for fear of dishonouring their heritage and of 'getting it wrong' by ignorantly recording false information and labelling it as truth. It is not my intention, with the writing of this book, to humiliate, anger or distress any of Australia's indigenous people. Rather, it is my intention to value and record the primal connection that we, as a united people, have with our animal brothers and sisters.

The Circle of Compassion

What may be, at first glance, perceived as inert, ancient teachings portray as 'a person'. It is said that all things of nature, ultimately created from the One Source, are living, and thus, deserving of equal respect and honour. As a result, the traditions of many indigenous people encompass nature as a whole, with the understanding that Spirit dwells within all things. 'Mi taku oyasin', for example, is a well-known Native American phrase that means 'We are all related' – that is, EVERYTHING of nature – the stones, trees, people, mountains, animals – everything. And, in my opinion, this is a principle that we must all embrace if we, as a race, are ever to enjoy a truly interrelated existence with each other and the world around us.

Ancient cultures viewed our planet as a living, breathing entity. They revered her as our Mother and believed that from her we came and to her we shall return – a philosophy echoed by Grandfather HawkOwl (my Elder's elder) who once said, 'teach the people that it is the mud of this Earth that makes up the clay of their body, and it is to this Earth that they belong'. The ancients considered the Earth Mother as being no different from them. They viewed her as their equal. And if we take a close look, even today there are many similarities. The trees, for example, act as the Earth Mother's lungs. Like the average human adult, she is 70% water. Her average temperature is 35°C, exactly the same as the typical human being. And, to complete the correlation, the curative response to fever in humans typically consists of sweating, diarrhoea and vomiting, which, when you look at the state the Earth Mother is in at the moment, could easily be compared to the tsunamis, storms and heavy rains, the mudslides or the lava currently spewing from the volcanoes that form the 'Ring of Fire'. Mother Earth has been cautioning us for ages that she is not well. She has been warning that if something is not done to support her (and soon), she will pull in all her known resources to help herself and that, if her hand is forced, things will seriously change for humankind as a whole. She has been creating mudslides, earthquakes, floods, droughts and strong winds for centuries, but in recent years there has been an increased number of occurrences, with each major event proving more devastating than the last.

If you were to ask any doctor, they would tell you that the term 'fever' is to the immune system's response to a need to expel pathogens and toxins from the body. And, in a frightening way, global warming could be seen as Mother Earth's response to expel the pollution, toxins and pathogens currently scourging her system. Put simply, a pathogen is a 'life form' that causes infection and plague. It upsets me to ask the question, but, could it be that humanity has become nothing more than a pathogen? I don't like to believe it, but our planet is sick, and she is getting sicker ... and, I am sorry to say, it is happening largely because of us. How could we do this to her? Even worse, how can we allow it to continue?

As a people, we need to find a cure; a real, tangible cure. It's like we've disconnected from the Earth Mother on an emotional level. We've literally turned our backs on her. There's no other explanation. Mother Earth supplies us with everything we need – she clothes us, feeds us and provides for us in every way. She cradles us when we are despaired, feeds us when we are hungry and shelters us when we are vulnerable. She loves unconditionally as mothers do. She scolds too, when we disrespect her, by lashing us mercilessly with storms and drought. She instructs us well in all of life's lessons – of giving and taking, of love and war, of birth, death and rebirth. She teaches symbolically – her lessons clearly marking our rites of passage with the changing of the seasons, the transition of day into night and night into day, the waxing and waning of the moon and the ebb and flow of Grandmother Ocean's tides. She gifts us with healing herbs, medicine stones and vibrational wisdom hidden deep within her heart, made available to us as needed. She employs the animals to act as our teachers, healers and guides; each metaphorically gifted with a unique and sacred 'message' potent enough to guide us, spiritually, along even the rockiest of roads.

The animals present themselves to us when we need them most. They share their knowledge unconditionally – even if we do not consciously heed their wisdom at the time. The animals, when celebrated as 'creature-teachers', can assist us in the manifesting of positive change. They can help us to bring about healing for ourselves and others; they can return a traveller safely home, or ensure a safe passage for someone about to embark on a journey. They can ease the pain a Mother feels as she watches her children leave home, just as they can ensure health, peace and happiness when a new baby enters the world. There is an animal imbued with the symbolic wisdom to help us with every aspect of our physical lives.

Essentially, this understanding lies at the heart of the ancient spiritual path known as 'animism'; a path very similar to that of shamanism, but more generic and open to personal interpretation. Animism espouses the belief that all objects and living things are imbued with a soul which, in turn, is permeated with wisdom, insight and choice. Put simply, animism advocates that everything is alive, conscious and has a soul, and should be treated with respect. It also says that the world is a community of living 'persons', only some of which are human and it portrays all things as equal: the humans, rocks, plants, animals, birds, ancestral spirits, etc. Animism offers a 'belief in spirits', be they mystical, paranormal, unseen or illusory beings. Animism, as a spiritual path, celebrates all of life. It celebrates beings for their own sake, regardless of whether they are living 'persons' or have passed on and become souls. Shamanism, on the other hand, is the oldest known practiced faith; the foundation of many of the world's most respected religions. It refers to a range of traditional beliefs and practices that claim the ability to diagnose and cure human suffering by forming a special relationship with 'spirits' and those of the Spiritual Realms. Shamans (those who practise shamanism) are believed to control the weather, exercise divinatory arts, interpret dreams, astral travel and drift between the upper and lower worlds. Shamanism, as a tradition, has existed since prehistoric times. Shamans are said to form a bridge between the natural and spiritual worlds and to travel between worlds in a trance state, where they call upon the spirits to help with healing and hunting. Shamanism champions the belief that the tangible world is infused with invisible forces or spirits that influence the lives of the living. Unlike animism, shamanism requires specialized training, initiation, knowledge and ability. Shamans, it could be said, are the 'experts' employed by animists when necessary, especially when beneficial change on behalf of the wider community is required.

The ancients viewed Mother Earth as the 'Great Provider'. Their culture and philosophies were based on a deep respect for her. In our 'modern' world, connecting again with her is imperative – for her survival ... and ours. We, as living organisms, rely on a larger, living host which is, of course, the Earth Mother herself. It is important that we to make an effort to stop draining our host of life-force. We, as a race, need to shift from our current position as negative 'free radicals' that are driven by self-attainment and self-satisfaction and return to the original and true plan for humanity, which is to be aware of our intimate connection with the world around us. Humanity has become a kind of 'pathogen' which is draining the health and resources of the Earth Mother, rather than working with her in a more balanced way and assisting in the natural evolution of the planet. We need to move into the positive by broadening our 'circle of compassion' and shifting our mind-set into the 'right place' – a positive, united state of being. We need to think globally, while acting locally. We need to rid ourselves of the pathogens that plague and infect our bodies. We need to heal ourselves, tend to our own backyards and become fully conscious beings before we point a reproachful finger at anyone else. And when we have taken responsibility for our own healing, we can then heal our kids. Only when we have healed ourselves, can we hope to heal the planet.

We must embrace the 'Law of One', which states that when everything is in true frequency, then all is in peace and harmony. We need to break away from our 'robot mindset', ruled by the collective unconscious and social conditioning, and return, as a people, as free-thinking, fully conscious beings who operate in a interrelated network or 'animist' community that is populated by all 'persons', whether they be human or not. By respecting the Earth Mother, the animals and all her inhabitants as equals, we will ultimately learn to respect ourselves. And by making the effort, we might just save this jewel of a planet and all her wondrous creations – including you, me and humanity itself.

Animal Dreaming

And it is with this conviction that I present this uniquely Australian compilation of Animal Dreaming to you, the seeker. It is intended as a spiritual handbook; a field guide of sorts, which offers clarity, wisdom and guidance to all who consult its pages.

The sacred understanding that Spirit lives within all things of nature and that the animals metaphorically speak to those who listen forms the hub of spiritual belief for many indigenous cultures all over the world, including the Aboriginal people of Australia.

Every animal, as our brother or sister, figuratively presents us with messages or lessons as a sacred aspect of their Dreaming – a gift to us that combines its symbolic wisdom with its tangible ways of being. To determine these messages and lessons so that I might present them in the pages of this book, I set about combining my own observations and intuitive insights with common understandings and traditional reflections to form a single reference; a generic yet relevant list of life lessons for a nation of people who yearn to 'walk as one', charged with the knowing that 'we are all related' – physically, emotionally and spiritually.

Australia's Wheel of the Year

The four seasons govern much of our life – symbolically, spiritually, physically and even emotionally. They are nature's timepiece. They mark the moment we enter the World and will do so again when we shed our robes and leave. They represent every aspect of our journey through the great Wheel of Life, while also governing the four directions, the elements and even the guardian spirits that protect them.

Ancient Earth wisdom depicts all things as living, and deserving of equal respect – even those things we might see as inanimate or invisible – due to the belief that everything was created from the One Source. This wisdom is based on the sacred understanding that Spirit lives within all things of nature. Within this tradition, life is viewed as a great wheel, developed around the ancient symbol of the circle, with a cross in the middle, which forms the spokes that divide our lives into four main growth stages. The paths within represent our life on Earth and the paths of our Ancestors. Each of the four directions, starting with the East, represents a season, and with each come the teachings of the corresponding minerals, plants and animals, as well as the elemental creatures and spirit beings that govern them. Beginning with new life in the Spring, to the height of fullness and energy in Summer, from the inward contemplative energy of Autumn, Winter's wisdom of old age and finally to the passing over to begin a new life once again in the East, it can be said that the seasons aim to remind us of our mortality and our immortality while instilling within each and every one of us a greater understanding of Mother Earth and the forces of nature that surround us every day.

The Teachings of the East

Each morning the sun rises in the East – the direction of the greatest light, and the light of wisdom and consciousness. As the Kookaburra chuckles, heralding a new day, the promise of a new beginning is realized by all. As the morning sun banishes the dark mysteries of night, birthing the new day, potential is ripe and opportunity is there for the taking. The East symbolically represents the energies generated by Spring – the season of new growth and fertility. In the Spring the countryside is dotted with baby animals, the air is warm and the fields are being sown. It is a time of balance and harmony, when light and dark stand equal. It is a time to celebrate life and what it means to be alive by playing musical instruments such as the didgeridoo, the flute, the panpipes and other wind instruments. The male in all things is recognized and the Goddess is in her maiden stage. Spring and its correspondences are masculine in nature, being dry, expansive and active, being represented by the topaz, yellow fluorite, quartz crystals, amethyst, citrine, tin and copper, by pansies, primroses, vervain, violets, yarrow, dill, wattle blossom and bracken fern, daffodils and lavender, and creatures such as the Palomino Horse, the Sunbird, the Eagle, the Hawk and the Owl. Spring is also represented by kernels, seeds, eggs, the yellow of the sun and the sky at dawn, the element of air, the intellect, the realm of thought and symbolic items such as the incense stick, smudge wand, the boomerang, the stone knife, the Woomera and the spear, the sword, the dagger and other phallic objects. It also governs the zodiac signs of Gemini, Libra and Aquarius.

The energies of Spring and the East, in the form of Eurus, the East Wind, bring with them the projective energies of change by invoking a desire to seek knowledge pertaining to abstract learning, breath work, inspirational arts, clear hearing and inner harmony through activities such as Zen Meditation and brainstorming. It encourages us to travel, to find inner peace and outer freedom prompting us to reveal hidden truths, to find lost things, to study herbalism, to develop psychic abilities, to undertake instruction of any kind, to enhance memory and to find personal illumination by remembering long lost dreams and acting upon them.

In accordance with the teachings of the Wheel of Life, during Spring we find ourselves symbolically back in infancy, ready to start life over again with the innocence of childhood. The gifts of illumination and intuition are ours for the taking, and our path toward the North is governed by the spirits of the Air – the sylphs, zephyrs and faeries who inhabit the world of trees, flowers, winds, breezes and the mountains, the Goddess Aradia and the God Thoth.

Guided Visualisation: Journeying to the East

Visualise yourself walking with the sun rising on the horizon. You can feel its warmth on your back. In the distance, visualise a Circle of Stones. Make your way towards it. As you get closer you become aware that this Circle of Stones is actually a Sacred Circle and so, out of respect, you do not enter.

Make your way to the stone directly in front of you. It sits in direct alignment with the sun behind you. The stone embodies the energies of the East. In the East we discover our strengths, sources of personal power, confidence, joy and excitement. It is where we start life, and where we commence all of life's journeys. In the East we are encouraged to play like children and see the world through their eyes. It is Spring on the Wheel of Life – everything is new and life is rich with potential.

Place both your hands on the East stone. You notice a brilliant yellow glow emanating from it. Feel a rush of energy as it begins to flow through your fingertips, up your arms and into your shoulders. The yellow glow trickles down to your toes and gradually begins to fill your body, from the feet upwards.

In the East, we play and laugh as the new born baby and the innocent child. We are encouraged to investigate life and to see the new dawn as a chance to start afresh. Whenever we have a new idea, or start a project from scratch, we are symbolically standing in the East. Just as the sun's first rays appear on the horizon, banishing the darkness of night, we embrace potential and the will to consider. It embodies all new beginnings: the commencement of a new job, embarking on a journey, initiating a new relationship or realising a new idea.

In your mind's eye, envision a golden Lion with a lean, muscular body and huge paws. Notice its mane flowing behind it as it walks off into the distance. Picture a Wedge-tail Eagle soaring high above your head. Notice the way its wing feathers spread like outstretched fingers. Visualise it swoop down and stand on the rock in front of you. Look into its eyes and become one with the Eagle. Attune with its consciousness and listen to what it has to say.

As this happens, remember the innocent joy and excitement of childhood. Picture a sunrise, dewdrops on a Spider's web and sunflowers in a field. Listen for the sound of a Rooster crowing and smell breakfast cooking in the kitchen. Visualise yourself running barefoot along the beach, with your pants rolled up to your knees. Feel the wet sand as its squelches between your toes, smell the crisp beach air and hear Seagulls bickering overhead. Taste the salty water and hear yourself squeal with delight as you play chicken with the incoming waves. Do you remember the first birthday party you ever had? Who was there helping you celebrate? What did your cake look like? How many candles are there? Hear the laughter. Feel the excitement. This is the innocent, expectant energy of the child.

Enjoy the inner strength and confidence you feel with each of these positive memories. Think of a word that describes what these feelings mean to you. How do they make you feel? Relish in these feelings, and give thanks for them.

The Teachings of the North

At approximately 12.00 pm each day, the sun is directly overhead and the plans for the day's events are usually fairly well established. The afternoon still holds untold mysteries, but with the strength and warmth of the sun streaming down, life's possibilities feel limitless and we are confident in our abilities to face everything with a degree of success. When the sun is at its peak, as it is at midday, we symbolically find ourselves at the time of the longest day and the shortest night, it is Summer and we are standing in the North – the direction of the greatest heat. During Summer, when the Goddess is in her pregnant phase, the World is thriving, happy and at peace. It is at this point that we begin to realize our connection to the world of Nature, and we take full advantage of her by camping in the bush and taking trips to the ocean.

Summer is cleansing, energetic, sexual and forceful in nature and is represented by fire spirits such as Salamanders and Fire Dragons. Summer is the Lion, the Chestnut Horse, the Snake, the Bee, the Scorpion, and the Phoenix, the Coyote, the Dingo, the Red Wolf and the Fox. Summer is symbolized by cinnamon, juniper and garlic, the Koori 'fighting stick', burning incenses, lamps, candles, wands and torches, lightning, volcanoes, red jasper, lava and gold, as well as the zodiac signs of Aries, Leo and Sagittarius. Summer is the time to learn the guitar and other stringed instruments, and to study the lessons of power that are offered there – the lessons of innocence and passion.

It is a time to go within and to confront our inner child face to face, to remember the dreams of youth and to bring them to the forefront so that they may be remembered, realized and finally brought to fruition.

When the sun is at its fullest, it is representative of the element Fire. Fire is the element of great change. It is the element that represents will and passion and it is the most primal of the all the elements – and an element not unknown to the Australian landscape. It governs the realms of sexuality and innocence, growing within all at a great pace. According to the teachings of the Wheel of Life, we find ourselves working with the element of fire when we are standing symbolically at the peak of Summer in our youth, when we think we know everything but in fact we know nothing. Still, at that time, the potential to learn is ripe and we are more than willing to try everything that life offers. Summer represents not only the 'sacred fire' of sex, but also the spark of divinity that shines within all living things. It is both the most physical and spiritual of all the seasons, as it represents growth and maturity, connection and wisdom.

Summer symbolically invokes the projective energies within each of us, the energies which promote the masculine powers of spirit in its physical forms: the heat of the naked flame and of blood and sap, the God Vulcan and the Goddess Pele, deserts, hot springs, volcanoes and fireplaces. It is indicative of one's primal life-force, one's pure intent and will in its rawest form, the ability to heal and destruct, the act of purification, bonfires, hearth fires, candle flames, Grandfather Sun, the colours orange, crimson and red, the colour of golden flames, and of eruptions and explosions.

Guided Visualisation: Journeying to the North

Visualise yourself walking with the sun rising on the horizon. You can feel its warmth on your back. In the distance, visualise a Circle of Stones. Make your way towards it. As you get closer you become aware that this Circle of Stones is actually a Sacred Circle and so, out of respect, you do not enter.

Make your way to the stone directly in front of you. It sits in direct alignment with the sun behind you. The stone embodies the energies of the East. Approach the stone and place both your hands on it. You notice a brilliant yellow glow emanating from it, which instantly fills your entire body. Now take your hands off the East stone and feel the energy dissipate from your body. Make your way in an anticlockwise direction to the stone standing in the North. In the North, we realise our personal power and tap into what inspires passion. We discover what it means to experience emotional ups and downs and catch glimpses of our potential future and the sense of freedom that accompanies it. In the North, we are encouraged to make mistakes. It is where we learn many of life's lessons and where we discover who we truly are, where our faith is tested and proven and where we explore sexuality and find the confidence to make life-affecting decisions for the first time. The North here in Australia is the point closest to the Equator. The air is humid and the land is tropical. It is Summer on the Wheel of Life, and the world is warm and inviting. Place your hands on the North stone and notice a rich red glow radiating from it. Feel a rush of energy as the glow begins to flow through your fingertips, up your arms and into your shoulders. The red glow trickles down to your toes and gradually begins to fill your feet and the rest of your body. As this colour flows into your body, notice the difference between the self-empowering energy of the North and the illuminating energy of the East.

In the North, the passion and enthusiasm of youth rises in our stomach. We feel excited, driven and sure. We deem ourselves invincible and believe ourselves to be full of knowledge. We know everything, but nothing at the same time. It is here that we confidently make plans for our future, anchoring them with statements like 'When I grow up, I want to be...'. We are encouraged to make mistakes because we are still discovering who and what we are. Whenever we put thought and planning into our new ideas, or take a fresh project to the next level, we are symbolically standing in the North. As the sun sits directly overhead (at noon each day), we embrace the determination and will to dare. It is when our naivety and excitement merge to form a solid foundation on which endurance can establish itself.

In your mind's eye, envision an auburn Coyote howling, its body silhouetted against a blood red moon. Picture a Fire Dragon spewing raging flames and a herd of Chestnut Stallions galloping toward you. As they come to a halt, froth dripping from their mouths, their hooves impatiently pawing the ground and their nostrils flared wide, look deep into their wild eyes and become one with them. Attune with their consciousness and listen to what they have to say.

As this happens, remember the passionate confusion and growing maturity of the adolescent, when, for the first time, you realised were not completely reliant on your parents. Picture a field of red soil, a red fire truck and a bunch of red balloons. Remember when you received your first pay cheque and how proud that made you feel. Remember back to the first time you realised you had stepped out of childhood and into puberty; your first moon flow; your first crush. Embrace the way you felt as a youth; the awkwardness, the infatuation, the inner confidence. Do you remember how you considered yourself to be grown up? Do you remember your body responding to grown up things in a grown up way? Do you remember the pimples and the frustration of feeling 'held back' by your mother's love and your father's protective ways? Embrace the energy of the Chestnut Horses, and the passion and desire to gallop. This is the energy that once raced through your veins; the power that once roared loudly in your heart. This is the energy of the teenager.

At what point did you realise you were a young adult? How did you know? How did you feel? Enjoy the inner strength and confidence you feel with each of these positive memories. Think of a word that describes what these feelings mean to you. How do they make you feel? Relish in these feelings, and give thanks for them.

The Teachings of the West

The spirits of water; the undines, nymphs, mermaids and mermen who live in the sea, lakes, streams and springs, and the fairies of the lakes, ponds and streams, govern and protect Autumn – the season of Great Change when rain showers the Earth. Autumn is a time of contemplation and introspection and of reaching the point in one's life when we ask ourselves, 'Is this it...?' . It is the time when all that has been sewn is now ripe for the harvest. Autumn, by its very nature, is flowing, purifying, healing, soothing, nurturing and loving. The Goddess is in her mothering phase, the animals are preparing for hibernation and the approaching winter, and the land is preparing the fruits of our labour for harvest. It is a time for acknowledging that the end of the cycle of growth is fast approaching – that all that is born must also die, and eventually, perhaps, be reborn. It is a time for personal growth, for realisation and personal illumination before the approaching darkness.

According to the teachings of the Wheel of Life, during Autumn we are symbolically standing in the West – the place of the setting sun and the home of Zephyrus the West Wind, the Goddess Aphrodite and the God Neptune. It is twilight, or dusk, on an energetic level, and while standing in the West we are in the phase of life dedicated to parenthood, the gaining of maturity and the knowledge that all the wisdom we seek is within us instinctively. Autumn is feminine and receptive in nature, as are the calming, inward energies of the West. During Autumn we are encouraged to explore our emotions, our feelings, and our concepts of love. Governed by the element of Water and therefore the zodiac signs of Cancer, Scorpio and Pisces, Autumn is represented by the colours silver, blue, indigo and black; by symbolic correspondences such as silver chalices, black cast-iron cauldrons, pewter goblets, ornate mirrors, fishing nets and fishing baskets, the moonlit sea, Serpents, Dolphins, Koalas, Fish, Seals, Sea Birds, Frogs, Turtles, Otters, Platypus, Swans, Crabs, Bears and Black Horses; by gems and semi-precious stones such as aquamarine, amethyst, blue tourmaline, pearls, coral, blue topaz, lapis lazuli and sodalite; as well as by herbs and plants like myrrh, willow, the boab and eucalyptus trees, chamomile, seaweed and water lilies.

Autumn tests our courage and daring, intuition, and the subconscious mind by raising questions of fertility, awareness of the womb, of healing, purification, pleasure, friendship, partnership and our immediate happiness. As Autumn is the time when the animals start to consider hibernation, our sleep patterns and the rate at which we dream is also a factor during this time. Fall is also an excellent period to investigate the psychic planes and to begin communicating with the spirit realms, because at this time, with its association with the West and the Moon, the veils between the Worlds are rapidly thinning. Vision Quest and traditional-style journey work are best done during Autumn as it is a fine time for the investigation of the inner self, inner knowing, self-healing, inner vision, and one's sense of security, sympathy and love.

Guided Visualisation: Journeying to the West

Visualise yourself walking with the sun rising on the horizon. You can feel its warmth on your back. In the distance, visualise a Circle of Stones. Make your way towards it. As you get closer, you become aware that this Circle of Stones is actually a Sacred Circle and so, out of respect, you do not enter.

Make your way to the stone directly in front of you. It sits in direct alignment with the sun behind you. The stone embodies the energies of the East. Approach the stone and place both your hands on it. You notice a brilliant yellow glow emanating from it, which instantly fills your entire body. Now take your hands off the East stone and feel the energy dissipate from your body. Move in an anticlockwise direction to the stone standing in the North and place both your hands on it. You notice a brilliant red glow emanating from it, which instantly fills your entire body. Now take your hands off the North stone and feel the energy dissipate from your body.

Make your way in an anticlockwise direction to the stone standing in the West. In the West, we find inner silence and the chance to cease the inner chatter. It is the place of introspection – of going within to find the answers to our questions. It is a place of rebirth, the moon and all nocturnal creatures. It symbolises the point in life where we are forced to make decisions for ourselves and others; the point in life where we perhaps find ourselves married with a family, heavily mortgaged but settled in a job or career. It is a time of great fertility, a chance for us to make something of our lives. It is where we stop and ask questions about life, our happiness and our true purpose; when we contemplate our choices and 'mistakes' and ask, 'Is this really my life?' It is Autumn on the Wheel of Life, and the world is cool and sleepy. Place your hands on the West stone and notice a midnight blue glow radiating from it. Feel a rush of energy as the glow begins to flow through your fingertips, up your arms and into your shoulders. The deep blue glow trickles down to your toes and gradually begins to fill your feet and the rest of your body. As this colour flows into your body, compare the self-empowering energy of the North and the illuminating energy of the East with the introspective energy of the West.

In the West, we find ourselves pondering life as the adult or parent. We find ourselves contemplating life, asking ourselves the tricky questions like, 'Is this it?'. In the West, we are encouraged to seek our own counsel and to do what feels right for us. Whenever we doubt ourselves, or question our integrity or that of those around us, we are symbolically standing in the West. It is here that we take ideas formulated earlier and perhaps dismissed as pointless, and adjust them, affording them greater chance of being brought to fruition in the future. Just as the sun goes down and the day comes to an end, our vision becomes clear and we embrace the wisdom of introspection and the will to dream. It is when we reassess life and make necessary adjustments and changes, while acknowledging the value of past decisions and seeing how they have contributed to our lives.

In your mind's eye, envision a Barn Owl ruffling its feathers, looking from side to side. Picture a pod of Dolphins leaping, playing and chattering, their heads held high, staring at the full moon, its light shining on the ink-black water and their mouths wide open in ecstasy. Imagine a Koala lazily wedged in the fork of a tree as if contemplating life. Look deep into its eyes and become one with it. Attune with its consciousness and listen to what it has to say.

As this happens, feel the confident security and knowing that comes with adulthood. Embrace the joy of seeing your children grow, of watching your house become a home and of fulfilling some of your childhood dreams. Acknowledge, too, the doubts and fears that come with being an adult – the insecurities and regrets of not reaching all your goals or of not becoming the person you thought you would be. Journey back to when you were a teenager and recall the things you wanted to achieve. Take pleasure in seeing how far you have come and how much you have accomplished, and celebrate what you may yet achieve and the dreams you can still bring to fruition. Now, formulate a question you would normally ask someone else. Make it a personal question, a question centred on your secrets and aspirations for the future. Without calling in your guides or totems, this is your chance to once again seek and trust your own counsel.

Imagine yourself standing in the entrance hall of a large house, with stairs to your left leading down to a dark cellar. The stairs represent the inevitable journey you must take into your inner self, while the cellar represents your inner voice. While standing at the top of the stairs, concentrate on stilling your mind of all internal chatter and enjoy the silence. Now, ask your question and with each step down into the cellar, allow the answer to formulate in your conscious mind. As you reach the final step, the answer will be clear in your mind. Know that this answer represents your truth, and make every effort to live by it.

Enjoy the inner strength and confidence you feel as you begin to trust your inner voice. Think of a word that describes what these feelings mean to you. How do they make you feel? Relish in these feelings and give thanks for them.

The Teachings of the South

According to the traditions of Ancient Earth Wisdom, we symbolically visit the South as a Grandmother or a Grandfather – an elder with much knowledge to share and acumen to pass on to the younger members of the family. South, on the Wheel of Life, speaks of great wisdom, abundance, prosperity and wealth. It can be relied upon to be stable, solid and dependable. It is represented by the element of Earth and all percussion instruments, such as the drum and hitting sticks. South is seen as the place of the greatest darkness, as is Winter, the season energetically associated with the South.

Winter is feminine and receptive in nature and vibrates to the zodiac signs of Taurus, Virgo and Capricorn. She teaches those who are ready to listen the lessons of personal and physical growth and the surrendering of the self-will, of sustenance, material gain, prosperity and abundance, creativity, fertility, birth and death, inner silence, compassion, grounding, mystery, industry, personal possessions, conservation, business and employment, stability, success, healing and strength, all of which are lessons of maturity and wisdom, often learnt best through experience, hardship and, at times, through grief and loss.

Winter, governed by the Earth spirits that inhabit the interior of the Earth, the gnomes, dwarfs and trolls, is represented on the Wheel of Life as the period in our life when we have reached advanced age, and it is, on a symbolic level, midnight, when the sky is at its darkest. During Winter, the veils between the Worlds are at their thinnest and it is a time of great transformation. The seeds shed during the fertile months are germinating under the ground, even if the earth above lies dormant, frozen and barren. They are preparing to burst through the surface of the land as new life and the crops of the New Year, completing the Great Cycle of Life – birth, death and rebirth. The Goddess is in her Crone stage, when she realizes her purpose and is able to see and understand better the complexities of life due to her wisdom and experience.

Winter, being fertile, nurturing, stabilising and grounding in nature, and typified by the Goddess Rhiannon and the Gods

Cernunnos, Dionysus and Pan, is represented symbolically by objects such as rocks and gemstones, mountains, open plains, fields, caves and mines, rock salt, coal, emeralds and peridot, onyx, jasper, amethyst, tourmaline, iron and lead; by herbs, such as benzoin, comfrey, ivy, grains, oats, rice, rye, wheat, patchouli, vetivert, moss, lichen, nuts, roots and oak trees; by the colours brown, green and white and by the animals which govern the Earth element; White Horses, Kangaroos, Emus, Bulls, Bison, Stags, Dogs, Ants, Polar Bears and White Wolves. The lessons learned during Winter leave us complete and whole, with nothing left to do but to return to the East, and the freshness of spring, to start life over again. We can 'shed our robes' as an Elder in Winter to be reborn as the infant in the Spring and to relearn life's lessons all over, or to 'polish up' on the lessons learned last time.

We visit the four seasons physically, emotionally and spiritually many times over countless lifetimes, and each time we do so, we find greater harmony within ourselves, and all the things around us. We come to better understand the significance of life and the four sacred Gifts of Power – illumination, innocence, introspection and wisdom – with the hope of becoming a more compassionate, prudent, confident and healthy person.

Guided Visualisation: Journeying to the South

Visualise yourself walking with the sun just rising on the horizon. You can feel its warmth on your back. In the distance, visualise a Circle of Stones. Make your way towards it. As you get closer, you become aware that this Circle of Stones is actually a Sacred Circle and so, out of respect, you do not enter.

Make your way to the stone directly in front of you. It sits in direct alignment with the sun behind you. The stone embodies the energies of the East. Approach the stone and place both your hands on it. You notice a brilliant yellow glow emanating from it, which instantly fills your entire body. Now take your hands off the East stone and feel the energy dissipate from your body. Move in an anticlockwise direction to the stone standing in the North and place both your hands on it. You notice a brilliant red glow emanating from it, which instantly fills your entire body. Now take your hands off the North stone and feel the energy dissipate from your body. Continue around the circle in an anticlockwise direction to the stone standing in the West and place both your hands on it. You notice a cool, midnight blue glow emanating from it, which instantly fills your entire body. Now take your hands off the West stone and feel the energy dissipate from your body.

Make your way in an anticlockwise direction to the stone standing in the South. In the south we develop greater understanding of why things are. We reach a place of maturity and inner peace, acceptance and gratitude to surrender fear and impatience. We just know and trust unconditionally. The South offers great wisdom, a place to see people, places and things as they are and to reject the need for explanations of why, how and when. The South here in Australia is the point closest to the South Pole. The air is cold and the land is frozen hard, covered in snow and ice. It is Winter on the Wheel of Life, and the world is dormant and still, but opportunity is imminent. Place your hands on the South stone and notice an apple green glow radiating from it. Feel a rush of energy as the glow begins to flow through your fingertips, up your arms and into your shoulders. The green glow trickles down to your toes and gradually begins to fill your feet and the rest of your body. As this colour flows into your body, compare the self-empowering energy of the North, the illuminating energy of the East and the introspective energy of the West with the fertile energy of the South.

In the South, we find contentment and security. We sit comfortably in our own skin, confident that we have fulfilled our dreams and realised our potential. We can look in the mirror and smile, certain that we have done all we could, safe in the knowing that we have reached our life destination. Just as midnight arrives, affirming the day's close, we realise there is nothing more we can do; our hands are tied and we find the strength to surrender our fears and trust. We find peace, maturity and the will to do. It is here that we see our dreams come to fruition, and the fruits of our labour are ready for harvest.

In your mind's eye, envision a herd of Bison grazing, a wise old Elephant showing her calf how to pull branches from a tree and a healthy mob of Grey Kangaroos huddled together against the chill of the night. Look deep into their eyes and become one with them. Attune with their consciousness and listen to what they have to say.

As this happens, feel the rewarding feeling of contentment that comes with being an Elder. Your energy is pure, balanced and whole, and your heart is wise. Realise that you have reached an age and a point in life where you have done and achieved all you possibly can. It is now that you get to see your children fully grown, possibly with children of their own. You can now enjoy the bounty of new life, but remain free of its responsibility. As grandparents we sit in the South, as spiritual teachers and tribal leaders. Celebrate this time as a chance to pass your knowledge on to someone else, for now you are the Wise One and Teacher. The South represents maturity and completion of life's cycle. We may walk the wheel symbolically many times over in this lifetime, but to physically reach the South as an Elder is an accomplishment in itself.

Enjoy the inner strength and confidence you feel as you begin to believe in your wisdom. Think of a word that describes what these feelings mean to you. How do they make you feel? Relish in these feelings and give thanks for them.

THE KINGDOM OF THE FOUR-LEGGED ONES

Most mammalian species are earthbound. Simple and down-to-earth in their approach, mammals generally carry the medicine of emotion, in a plethora of ways. They demonstrate how our emotions may manifest, and why. They embody those aspects of life that trigger our emotions — aspects that must be addressed by demonstrating how to bring them into our lives, how to deal with them later or how to abandon them completely.

native / indigenous mammals

Antechinus
Inevitability

The Antechinus looks like a Mouse, but with a longer nose and very sharp teeth. A nocturnal, ground-dwelling marsupial, the Antechinus eats insects, flowers and nectar. It also hunts small reptiles, birds and mammals, neatly turning their skins inside out as it feeds. Its pelt colour ranges from dark grey to near black.

While the female Antechinus may seem to hold the key to resilience, the male understands that life is way too short. He packs in as much activity as he can: he feeds ferociously, eating everything he can get his paws on. For him, nothing is off the menu. Antechinus Dreaming encourages us to relish in new things and not limit our potential with doubt or 'what ifs'. Even the chance to make love is snatched passionately in the Antechinus community. During the mating season, for example, the male Antechinus couples with any female that happens by; the mating process being quick and aggressive. He knows that he must live life to the fullest, work quickly and spread himself as thinly as possible, because he accepts that soon after mating, the males of the species usually die. No one knows why for sure, but it is believed that the little animal's heart gives out, unable to cope with the stress and the physiological changes sustained by the mating experience. Antechinus Dreaming augers inevitable change on a tangible or conscious level; a symbolic 'death' of sorts of a relationship, perhaps, a change of career or residential address; a chance to change direction and refocus energy in a more fruitful way so that a stable future can be assured for all. A symbol of certainty, Antechinus Dreaming indicates the necessary closing of one door whilst heralding the opening of another. It reminds us that all things must end or figuratively 'die', either physically or metaphorically, and that things deemed 'good' must come to an end some day, usually to make way for something 'better'. Antechinus Dreaming embodies the one thing of which we can be sure – the inevitability of change. He encourages us to live life richly and to the fullest, to avoid stagnation and see change as improvement. Antechinus helps us surrender our fears regarding the outcome of necessary change. He espouses the idea that life is short – too short to worry, but long enough to live entirely and abundantly.

Bandicoot
Industry

Often mistaken for rodents, Bandicoots are small, omnivorous marsupials found throughout Australia. Nocturnal marsupials, Bandicoots have long pointy noses, used to sniff the ground for food. Very vocal animals, Bandicoots dig 'scrapes' in the ground in search of insects, grubs and worms. They build their nests in shallow holes lined with grass and leaves, hiding the entrance with ground litter.

According to Aboriginal legend, the Bandicoot is said to have birthed itself from the body of an Ancestor Spirit as he slumbered underground, leaving in its place a cavity filled with honeysuckle buds and nectar. Such association suggests that when we honour our heritage and ancestry, live in harmony with the land and show respect for Spirit, our life will be rich, abundant and whole, especially when we physically set about doing what we can to match and maintain that support. The Bandicoot's inquisitive nose explores every window of opportunity, for instance, busily unearthing insects, worms, insect larvae and spiders, as well as rhizomes, roots and fungi. Such behaviour has afforded it the affectionate title of 'gardener's friend'. The early European settlers labelled the Bandicoot a thief and nuisance. Caught stealing flowers and vegetables from their gardens, the Bandicoot was both admired and condemned as an enterprising risk-taker; an animal that did what was necessary to survive. Such strength of mind earned it the repute of being both ambitious and industrious because it mirrored the opportunistic mindset, endurance and stamina the pioneers required to survive their strange new home. The Bandicoot is therefore considered a productive and worthy role model: a creature always on the go, always searching for food and always looking for ways to make its life richer and more abundant. If Bandicoot has appeared in your life, expect to 'birth' something agreeable in the near future, or to be rewarded for your hard work and level of industry. You may be supported as you struggle to fulfil a goal, or recompensed favourably for your time and effort. Bandicoot Dreaming warns against being tempted to 'borrow' resources that do not belong to you or overstay your welcome in your quest for achievement and attainment. Such behaviour, even if unintentional, will bring with it the labels of 'thief' and 'pest'. Although the Bandicoot helps the gardener by eating pesky grubs and insects, for example, it also samples food items not intended for its larder, while leaving shallow but unsightly holes in manicured suburban lawns as it goes about its business – its good intentions thus foiled by over-familiarity and insensitivity. Bandicoot endorses reliability and frankness, hard work and staying power. After all, only when we are prepared to knuckle down in an honest and unified way can we truly expect to enjoy the sweet smell of success in all that we do.

Bat
Rebirth

Bats hang upside down when roosting, wrapping their wings around their bodies. They hunt insects at night by means of echolocation. The Bat is the only mammal truly capable of flight. Other mammals, like the Sugar Glider, only glide from one branch to another. Bats, however, have a thin skin membrane stretched from their front legs to their back legs that performs in much the same way as a regular pair of wings. Bats flap these wings in order to fly.

According to superstitious interpretation, finding a Bat physically roosting under the eaves of your home is an admonition of gossip and jealousy, while a Bat appearing in the home is an inauspicious warning of 'ill-wishing' or unrest aimed at the household, sometimes believed to result in illness or disharmony if the one responsible for the unrest is not confronted immediately and if the issues are not resolved. Some indigenous groups, though, believe Bats to be the embodiment of male souls. They are considered sacred because, as the souls of men, they are essentially our brothers and, in turn, our brothers are essentially Bats. Generically, though, Bats remind us that, in similar fashion to how babies rest upturned in the birth canal waiting to be born, the Bat hangs inverted in its cave (the quintessential womb of the Earth Mother herself), waiting for the right moment to emerge from the darkness into the next phase of its life. The Bat, as it flies out of the cave, symbolically invites the people to follow its lead: to regenerate and rebirth in one or more area of their lives. Although many view the act of rebirth as a figurative process, renewal of life energy can be achieved on all levels with favourable and lasting effects when approached with pure intent and strength of mind. Bat inspires us to start from scratch when the need to begin a new life is realised, to shed and release all that limits, binds or holds us back so that we may walk into the future as new beings free of fear, anger and constraint. In order to open new doors, it must be understood that old ones must be allowed to close. We must be prepared to surrender those aspects of our life that no longer serve us. We must surrender our 'familiar self' and allow it to die a metaphoric death so that we may rebirth and breathe life into our true self and the life we were meant to live.

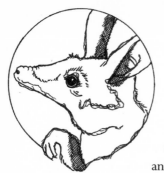

Bilby
Harnessing Fear

Bilbies are gentle, nocturnal mammals that grow to roughly the size of a rabbit. They have a pointy snout, large, erect rabbit-like ears, a long, fluffy-tipped tail and soft, silver-grey fur. Bilby numbers have dropped so dramatically in the wild that the species now sits teetering on the edge of extinction. Fear surrounds this unassuming marsupial, demonstrated by both their nervy disposition and the concerns the authorities hold for its survival in the wild.

When wildfire strikes, it ruthlessly razes everything in its path to the ground. Fear is no different. It is equally destructive and unbiased. When left unchecked, it cripples the mind, envelops the soul and diminishes our ability to see clearly and think rationally. Sustained by a nervy disposition and super-sensitive ears, Bilby metaphorically 'listens' for, harnesses and carries the burdens of our fears so that we don't have to. It provides assistance by teaching us how to control our fear so that the energy we would otherwise waste may be transmuted and channelled into more productive means, such as the manifestation of abundance, love, happiness and good health. Trepidation can be a positive influence when perceived as a warning or as a prompt to look before we leap, but when allowed to become fear and worse still, panic, it is capable of influencing us and deluding us from our true destiny. Bilby warns the more you focus on fear, the more you draw what you fear most into your life. To worry about the negative is to ensure its endurance. But when you shun fear and focus only on the positive, you render fear powerless, thus ensuring that faith and promise reign triumphant.

Cuscus
Calmness

The Cuscus is a shy, arboreal mammal that inhabits the rainforests of northern Queensland and New Guinea. Very rare in Australia, the Cuscus is active at night, spending the day asleep on a podium of leaves and twigs high in the forest canopy. It is a sluggish, slow-moving creature that ensures its foothold by means of a naked, prehensile tail that acts as a fifth hand, and an opposable thumb on each of its hind feet. The Cuscus feeds mainly on fruit, insects and eggs.

Trees like the Tasmanian Huon Pine and the Californian Red Wood take centuries to reach maturity. They take their time, savouring the growth process with awe-inspiring persistence. The giant Galapagos Tortoise, too, takes life slowly, moving about with incredible apathy. Like the trees, the Tortoise lives to a ripe old age. It has no need to rush and, for this reason, doesn't know stress or anxiety. The Galapagos Tortoise has been known to live for hundreds of years. They are considered sacred because of their antediluvian knowledge (having witnessed pretty much everything worth seeing), and the wisdom that comes with realising that what cannot be achieved today can be tackled tomorrow. Both the trees and the Galapagos Tortoise endorse the saying that 'all good things take time' and are, generally, worth waiting for. The Cuscus, a gentle, unimposing creature, also embraces this relaxed attitude – so much so, though, that it has been likened to the South American Sloth on more than one occasion, an animal known for its lethary. Classified as one of the seven principal sins (according to Christian belief), 'sloth' denotes opposition to labour or physical exertion of any sort. Some see it as being nothing more than a lack of caring. In everyday terms, the description can be attributed to those within the community who choose not to participate in making society a better place for all. They usually exhibit the attitude of 'Why should I?' followed by the comment, 'They have never done anything for me'. Such individuals fail to see any advantage in trying.

They would rather discount the option and divert their energy into other things. South American Sloth Dreaming therefore, encompasses laziness and idleness and can be seen as a physical reminder of what the principal sin describes. Unlike the South American Sloth though, Cuscus resonates a sense of calm rather than lethargy. It endorses approaching life at a pace that suits and not being unnecessarily rushed into making decisions that could later seem rash. Cuscus says that to take slow, purposeful steps is a sure fire way of ensuring a long, safe, bountiful trip, as is embarking optimistically on life's journey with a clear view of your destination. To know one's heart and one's soul, while being true to one's self, one's journey, one's relationships and one's inherent values, is the best medicine according to the Cuscus. He ignores the urgency of everyday life, choosing to dedicate quality rather than quantity to everything he does. It is the way of Cuscus to tackle all tasks with a sense of calmness even if it takes all day. To do something constructive, even if it takes a while, is far better than doing nothing, or worse still, expecting someone else to do it for you; a tactic endorsed by the lazy Sloth. Cuscus rejects laziness and believes that everything in life is worth considering – and if it is worth doing, it is worth doing well. Although Cuscus outwardly rebuffs the notion of physical exertion, he does apply solid effort when grasping new projects. Although the Cuscus' eagerness and enthusiasm may appear wanting to the incidental onlooker, the truth is he never jumps on board immediately or pushes anything away without first pondering the pros and cons. He takes his time and contemplates the best plan of attack. And then he commits – sooner or later. Cuscus reminds us that 'we will make it eventually'. Remain calm and trust that when the mental desire to move forward is there, all you have to do is wait for the physical body to catch up. When issues appear big or overwhelming, don't ignore them or file them under 'too difficult and time-consuming'. Cuscus suggests tackling them little by little – like moving a mountain a grain of sand at a time. It may take a while, but at least the desire to reach your goal will be achieved honourably. Simply remain calm and plod on. Being a Sloth gets you nowhere – fast. Being a Sloth is reminiscent of the little Mouse and its exercise wheel: always dreaming of moving forward while never taking a single productive step. Putting effort into doing nothing takes just as much energy as initiating the first steps forward. Getting other people to take responsibility for your life is equally as exhausting as getting out there and doing it yourself. Cuscus Dreaming affirms that there is an explicit distinction between laziness and carefulness, or sloth and calmness, with neither to be mistaken for the other.

Dingo
Trickster

The Dingo is believed to be a direct descendant of the wild Dogs of Asia and Thailand. The Aboriginal People are thought to have brought dingoes to Australia as companion animals around 40,000 years ago when the continents were still joined. Dingoes usually live by themselves or in small family groups. They are not fond of water and don't bark like regular dogs.

There are some Indigenous tribes who, during ritual and ceremony, danced in honour of the Dingo, an animal they revered as their totem. To invoke the spirit of the Dingo, the dancers would apparently howl and walk about on all fours in sacred recognition. Some tribes upheld a law, too, that ruled 'Dingo' People could only marry an individual whose family totem was the Swamp Hen. So, if you were drawn to seek the wisdom of the Dingo, you may also find it beneficial to research the complimentary significance of the Swamp Hen. Dingo is said to represent each of us symbolically as we 'step out' on our own. He supports each of us as we venture out, possibly for the first time or, alternatively, after a long time. Dingo is the young person setting out into the world to make their fortune; the recently single person who has just experienced a relationship breakdown; the (figurative or actual) captive released after a time of forced (or self-induced) segregation; the sufferer of depression; the victim of grief and the person returning to the workforce after years at home raising children or off work for some other personal reason. Dingo embodies those of us currently 'testing the waters' or deciding whether to dive (back) into the pool of life or not. In support, Dingo dares us to look at life through the eyes of a child again, to shun all adult, tainted cynicism and to start our journey over as a 'newborn babe'. He dares us to step out of our comfort zone, to explore and try new things, to laugh, have fun and to take risks and act spontaneously. Dingo Dreaming personifies our willingness to embrace whatever comes our way and to consider the world our oyster. Be warned, though; although obvious to everyone else, Dingo often appears blind to the perils that blatantly appear right in front of him, as well as the hardships he may face as he ventures out into the world. Although it may seem fun to laugh at ourselves and to live instinctively, Dingo readies us to learn from our mistakes before our artlessness turns and trips us up. Like a naïve child, Dingo's innocent ways coach us to learn from our mistakes while not taking life too seriously.

Dunnart
Preparation

Dunnarts feed largely on insects, but will supplement their diet with Mice and Lizards when available. Resembling a large Mouse or Antechinus, the Dunnart stores fat in the base of its plump tail (in much the same way as a Camel stores fat in its hump), to preserve necessary nutrients when food is scarce. The large, specialised ears of the Dunnart are infused with blood vessels that help to keep it cool by expelling excess body heat. The Dunnart's physical adaptations have assured its survival in an otherwise difficult habitat.

Groundwork, revision and practical forward planning are the keynote elements of Dunnart Dreaming. It lives a calculated, systematic life, for it knows that being ill-prepared can spell disaster, even downfall. Dunnart demonstrates that charting an intended path well in advance generally promises accomplishment, while being negligent or relying on uneducated guesswork frequently results in confusion and disappointment. Rushing into things or not thinking our actions through before embarking on a venture are tactics unendorsed by the meticulous Dunnart. It suggests we never move forward with any project, relationship or contractual agreement before first ensuring that we have carefully crossed all our t's and dotted all of our i's. By following Dunnart's fine example, we can rest assured that we are always fully prepared, no matter where we are heading in life or what we are hoping to achieve. In being prepared, the place we hold within our family, our relationships, community and even our culture will prove forever fruitful. In readying ourselves for success, we teach (by example) those close to us how the keys to abundance are found. Put simply, Dunnart demonstrates the importance of being personally prepared and self-sufficient. By listening with an intuitive ear to the wisdom of the Dunnart, we come to understand that sometimes we can only rely on ourselves to be there when we need support the most, despite the best intentions of the other people in our lives.

Echidna
Rebirth and Personal Protection

Echidnas (also called Spiny Ant-Eaters), are egg-laying marsupials that belong to the monotreme family (an elite club shared only by the Platypus). Echidnas have sharp quills covering the bulk of their body. They feed on ants and termites, which they catch by means of a sticky tongue. Echidnas, bearing no teeth, have little defence against their enemies, save for their quills which they raise when danger presents itself, and sharp claws which are used to bury themselves in the ground.

When threatened, Echidnas quickly dig themselves into the

ground, leaving no part visible except for their quills. Such a move precludes anyone from picking them up or altering their path. They effectively shut themselves off from the world, preventing anyone from interfering or getting too close. Such action not only protects them from predatory attack, but unfortunately also shields them from the assistance or support offered by those who would see no harm come to them. What if the Echidna's quest for food leads him onto a busy road, into oncoming traffic and inevitable danger, for example? What if a passing motorist stops and attempts to direct him off the road? What if the attempts prove futile, because the Echidna's obstinate character prevents him from realising the error of his ways?

Quickly agitated, Echidnas prey on Ants because they know they inherently hold a secret: patience and strength of character. Ant nurtures the collective powers of the mind, body and spirit. It expounds the strength found in community and unity. Open your heart to the needs of those around you and the nurturing they can offer. Stop shutting people out. You need to let down your guard, relax your sense of personal protection, develop tolerance and begin to trust. Shunning anything (or anyone) that may divert you from your path is great if you want to live an independent life, but Echidna warns against protecting yourself to the point that your heart becomes impenetrable to the possibility of change. Echidna helps us understand the fundamental distinction between denial and determination or, more to the point, the difference between not wanting assistance and not needing support. The idea of an independent lifestyle may appear attractive – free of the hassles of commitment and responsibility to others, but if you become too complacent you may accidentally find yourself exiled from social activity altogether. Your friends may wander away, for example, and your family may forget to invite you to family events. To stand rigid and distant from those in your life will eventually give rise to the general belief that you are unapproachable, ungrateful, aggressive and lacking in humility.

Glider
Trust

A member of the Possum family, the Glider is a shy, nocturnal creature that spends most of its time high in the forest canopy, only descending to the ground to drink. Species include the Greater Glider, Northern Glider, Yellow-bellied Glider, Biak Glider, Sugar Glider, Squirrel Glider and the Feathertail Glider. Not capable of true flight (the only mammal capable of this is the Bat), the Glider has a thin membrane of skin stretched between its front and back legs. As the Glider leaps, it flexes this flap of skin, trusting that it will create enough lift to support the weight of its body and carry it to the safety of the next tree.

Trust is the key word when looking to the Dreaming of the Glider, for it knows that without it, we may never take an educated risk again. Glider Dreaming nurtures the understanding that sometimes decisions must be made without the safety net of guarantee or foresight. Sometimes we must trust that our judgment alone will be prudent enough to ensure the avoidance of obstacles or failure during our resolution making and direction changing moments (especially those which are spontaneous and totally unplanned). Like a performing trapeze artist, Glider Dreaming validates the blind faith needed to release our grip on all that is definite and assured in our bid to nurture change, to sail unaided for a spell before being caught and carried to a vantage point of safety from where we may consider our progress and either 'fly blind' again or sit and contemplate our position. Glider Dreaming validates those moments when we know we must leave or move from one setting or set of circumstances before beginning something new, but we are afraid to shut the old door before having some idea of what the 'new' door will look like. For example: when we try to find a new job before leaving our current one; when we want to sell our house and buy a new one, but when we must sell first to ensure the funds for the next, or when we are falling out of love with a partner and simultaneously falling in love with someone new. Glider helps us to 'bridge the gap' by coaching how to 'fly by the seat of our pants' so that we may find the courage to temporarily face the unknown and trust that all will work out fine. Glider only asks that we follow a path that is right for us and demonstrate integrity in all that we do.

Honey Possum
Restoration

Also known as the Honey Mouse, the Honey Possum is neither a Mouse nor a Possum but a species unrelated to any other group of marsupial. Found only in the south-west of Western Australia (between Kalbarri and the South Coast, east of Esperance) the Honey Possum is equipped with a brush-like tongue designed to remove nectar from native flowers. Having little need for teeth, it obtains all the nutrients it needs from pollen and nectar.

When blended with salt, honey was revered by ancient cultures as a preservative, with some using the sticky fluid as an embalming agent believed to preserve and prepare the soul for reincarnation. Sacred to the Greek goddess, Pandora (the 'All-Giving One'), who was said to be able to restore life to dead men with a special honey-based balm, honey was so heavily linked with new life that it gave rise to the term 'Honey-Moon', a celebration of matrimonial union that traditionally lasted a full lunar month. The Honey-Moon was intended to encourage healthy marital relations and the successful (and expected) conception of offspring. The Honey Possum cultivates within us a desire to breathe life back into some lost, forgotten or stagnant aspect of ourselves. Pandora, whose name also means 'All Gifts', works with the Honey Possum to reinstate a sense of abundance, purpose and hope in the hearts and lives of those who embrace its Dreaming. Honey Possum (particularly when witnessed grasping things with its tail) primes us for rebirth, heightened awareness, a new attitude toward life, a reawakening of the self and a reclaiming of past values and beliefs previously put on hold for practical or emotional reasons. It promises new beginnings, a fertile future and the ability to turn dormancy into action. No matter how the animal manifests, its Dreaming is deeply rooted in the healing and restoration of the true essence of self.

Kangaroo
Family

Members of the macropod family (Kangaroos and Wallabies) travel on powerful hind legs, using their long, thick tails to balance their body while hopping. Some species can travel at up to 60 km/h and are capable of leaping over obstacles up to three metres high. Anything that looks like a Kangaroo, but weighs less than 20kg, is classified as a Wallaby. Wallabies prefer to lead a semi-solitary life, unlike Kangaroos that travel and live in 'mobs'. The Red Kangaroo stands taller than a man and weighs up to 85 kg. They are categorised as the largest marsupials in the world. Kangaroos rest in the shade during the heat of the day and feed from late afternoon until well into the night when it is much cooler. They feed mainly on grass and need very little water. They can actually survive without drinking for many months. So plentiful were kangaroos that they formed the staple diet of early Indigenous Australians.

Grey Kangaroo - *Abundance*
When questioned about what wealth means to you, would you say that having copious amounts of money would definitely seal the deal? If so, it would be a good answer – but a misguided one. To focus exclusively on the acquisition of money only amplifies how little you have. When you concentrate on your desire to attain money, you are effectively

nurturing poverty mentality; a state of mind supported by society and inherited ways of thinking. It feeds poverty mentality because it prevents you from seeing the wealth that surrounds you everyday; the wealth that comes with family and friends.

To know true love is to hold supreme wealth. When you know that wealth rarely takes the form of money or gold, you release the monetary mindset so fear of lack can be transmuted into trust. In doing so, the block preventing your stream of abundance may be removed forever and greater cash flow will result. Letting go of lack will essentially result in gain. Grey Kangaroo once offered its rich meat, warm pelt and strong bones, which were useful as cutting and digging implements. Prosperity meant healthy children, a full stomach and a warm, dry sleeping place to the people. They believed the land would provide all they needed and, if they lived in harmony with the Earth Mother, their life would be safe and plentiful as a result. So long as the Grey Kangaroo was there, the people knew they would never know hunger or suffering. Its mere existence promised true abundance. If Grey Kangaroo has vaulted into your life today, your life will soon be rich with productive emotion, thought and knowledge. These fundamentals will abundantly serve the personal needs of both you and your family. What you require is currently manifesting and your needs are soon to be met. Grey Kangaroo reminds us to always separate what we want from what we need, though, before commencing the hunt for either. To seek what we materialistically want above what we realistically need often results in continued stagnation. Getting what we want rarely shapes an abundant life, while securing the things we need does. Grey Kangaroo's appearance acts as a reminder that as children of the Earth, it is our birthright to have all our requirements fulfilled – so long as our requests are offered in a sacred way.

Red Kangaroo - *Responsibility*
The Red Kangaroo is unique in its ability to maintain three young at once: one at foot, one in the pouch, while a third develops in the womb. As the one at foot is weaned, the one in the pouch exits, making way for the partly formed sibling which instinctively climbs into the pouch directly after birth. With the womb now devoid of life,

the female will mate immediately, thus replacing the foetus. When environmental conditions are fertile and rain is abundant, the feed is lush and plentiful and the weather is benevolent, Red Kangaroos live a productive existence. If the conditions deteriorate however, bringing drought, fire or flood, the female Red Kangaroo will relinquish the infant in her pouch and put the foetus in the womb into a state of suspended animation. The infant remains nourished and is continually fed by the mother, but it does not develop physically. She can sustain the foetus in this way for quite some time, waiting for the conditions of the land to improve so that the Joey can be born into a time of plenty. By surrendering the existence of one Joey and by putting the other into a state of hold, she takes responsibility for her own survival and that of her family. Red Kangaroo prompts the question; do you feel as though you have sacrificed a large part of yourself for the benefit of the family? Maybe the time has come to reclaim these aspects instead of harbouring resentment and jealousy. Are you living in a constant state of stress, for example, barely surviving from one day to the next? If so, do you see this as taking sound responsibility? If you are a parent, remember that everything you do inherently instils itself in the consciousness of your children as acceptable behaviour. Ask yourself if you are taking your responsibility as parent, partner or principal person seriously. Are you honouring the pledge of responsibility you made to yourself growing up, or would you say that you were in an emotional drought or dormancy at the moment? If so, it may be time to reanimate some element of yourself, so that you can begin taking responsibility for your life and that of your children in a more productive, abundant manner.

Wallaby - *Progression*

After trauma, people often seek teachers and healers who claim to have the keys needed to help them regain peace and clarity. Despite leaving these sessions feeling confident and reassured, however, they often lose confidence in their inherent ability to maintain wellness, and gradually find themselves regressing into confusion and emotional darkness. It is never their intent to slip back, but rather a force of habit. This shadow space is familiar and feels safe, despite its negative pitfalls. They revert because they aren't born equipped with a clear understanding of how to turn darkness into light, or how to find sacredness in the horrors that haunt them; horrors that often hold within their recesses the keys to realising their Personal Power and Purpose. When confronted, we usually grit our teeth, swallow hard and push through the pain in order to move forward in the hope of finding light at the end of the tunnel. When we repetitively visit our shadow space or examine past experiences, people may suggest we are dwelling in the past. And in reality, we may be. It is sometimes necessary, if we are to heal fully and honourably. We must visit our shadow space in a sacred way if we are to learn from it and, in time, rebirth ourselves from its limiting clutches. Wallaby, because of its unusually shaped hind legs and bulky tail, cannot physically walk backwards. It rejects stagnation, therefore, and reluctant movement of any sort. Instead, it promotes progression, healing and growth – in forward leaps and bounds. Wallaby asks, 'Are you dwelling on some past event and using it as an excuse to linger in your shadow space? Despite good reason, you may be blaming the event for your lack of healing, growing or release of pain. Wallaby is priming you to leap into the future without regret with a healthy respect for your grief. Wallaby helps you move in a forward motion, to explore new horizons, take risks, avoid the temptation to look back with regret and never return to your comfort zone once you have left. Wallaby takes the pains from the past, dissects them and extracts their purpose to find their reason. This reason is the vital ingredient in realising your Personal Power; the ingredient that can be shared among the people to aid in their healing. 'Onwards and upwards' is a motto that champions the advice Wallaby offers those who seek its counsel.

Koala
Journeys

The closest relative to the Wombat, the Koala spends much of its time high in the canopy of eucalyptus forests, only coming down to move from one tree to another. The Koala will wedge its rump into a forked branch and sleep up to 18 hours a day. The Koala is a marsupial mammal, which means the female suckles her young and carries it in a pouch.

If you come across a Koala in the wild, you will find it in one of two states – awake, feeding and tending to its young, or dozing in a foetal position, its rump securely wedged into the fork of a tree. It is believed that the Koala slips into an altered state of awareness after ingesting the eucalyptus leaves that form the heart of its diet. Whilst in this state, it is mused that it can enter other realms of reality, or journey deep within the inner landscape. Once there, it is thought that the Koala gathers knowledge and is able to offer healing in ways not considered physically possible in the tangible world. Koala also fosters the notion that, as spiritual beings, we inherently know the answers to all of our questions, with the knowledge we seek stored deep within our consciousness. Koala demonstrates the healing flight we must take in our personal quest for answers. It embraces the inner journey to the core of the deepest self. To journey with the Koala is to quest for the ancient knowledge and spiritual awakening stored inherently within our consciousness. Koala represents a sacred journey that is unique for everyone, an expedition that supports the individual needs and requirements of all people. Koala reassures us that we inherently know the answers to our questions. Now is the time to start taking notice of your inner self, your innate connection to all the information of the Universe. Stop looking to others for corroboration, advice or wisdom. Take responsibility for your own life, your own path and your own destiny by listening to your heart of hearts. Koala says that you must start your own journey; a quest that will unlock the answers you seek from a place hidden deep within your essence. The journey must begin today. Koala's healing journey is an experience of unimaginary proportions; a flight beyond the boundaries of the physical body. With Koala, your potential for growth and transformation strengthens and your sense of self escalates. To fully embrace Koala Dreaming, you must first take responsibility for your own healing and trust that all will evolve as it is supposed to.

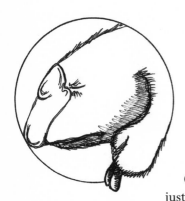

Marsupial Mole
Clairsentience

The Marsupial Mole is the only marsupial of its kind. Digging tunnels to depths of two and a half metres, the Marsupial Mole forages for food (earthworms, insect larvae and beetles) just under the surface of the ground leaving little ridges of dirt and sand in its wake. Largely golden-yellow in colour (though occasionally ranging from grey to a deep red/brown) the Marsupial Mole is blind, despite the fact that it does have very small remnants of eyes hidden under its skin. It is also devoid of external ear flaps. It has a short, naked tail and stumpy limbs equipped with two flat, powerful claws on each forefoot. Like the Wombat, the Marsupial Mole's pouch faces backwards to prevent it filling with soil as the animal burrows into the earth.

'Clairsentience' refers to the extra-sensory ability to 'sense clearly' the metaphysical world that exists simultaneously within and around the physical world. The expression 'clairsentient' applies to individuals who, when they have a thought, know it to be true. Their capacity to accurately 'know things', such as when the phone is about to ring or that a friend is about to visit unannounced, is dependent upon the level to which they have developed their abilities. They may experience precognitive hunches, visions and dreams. Often skilled in the art of psychometry, these individuals tend to rely heavily on their intuitive sense of touch and their ability to 'read' people by feeling what they feel on an emotional level, empathetically tapping into the pain, loss and grief of those around them. Being totally blind and having only limited hearing, Marsupial Moles must trust their other senses to find food, secure a mate and avoid predators. Having a strong sense of smell and a hypersensitive snout helps them determine 'beneficial' from 'detrimental' through touch alone. Marsupial Mole Dreaming inspires us to go within and trust blindly when there are no tangible triggers or 'sign-posts' suggesting options or alternatives when external direction is required. When life seems dark and directionless, Marsupial Mole is there to encourage us to close our eyes, shut our ears, swallow hard and listen intuitively to what our gut tells us. Its advice: silence the inner chatter, do not panic, and blindly look to the Void for inspiration, where we may spy an illuminating light breaking through the shadows, guiding us to a place of clarity and awareness. Trusting Marsupial Mole's acumen affords the ability to see when it appears dark and to hear when all seems silent. As a point of interest too (and as its name implies), Mole's unexpected appearance may betray the presence of an informant, or someone exposing secrets or things told in confidence to parties not privy to such information. So, when it comes to unearthing such a culprit, listen to your intuition and wait for them to make a mistake that will ultimately reveal their identity.

Numbat
Care

The Numbat, or Banded Ant Eater, is an elusive, diurnal, carnivorous marsupial found in dwindling numbers in south-western Australia. Numbats have rust coloured coats, black stripes across their back, a pointy nose and a large brushy tail typically carried in an arc over their back.

An engineer and planner, the Ant understands and celebrates the 'strength found in numbers' philosophy. By its very nature, it demonstrates that when individuals team up and work cooperatively toward a communal goal, they are more likely to achieve a rewarding outcome. So, when integrated as a way of life, Ant Dreaming affords strength of mind, body and spirit, patience, a sense of community and perseverance. Established by its wary and vigilant nature (coupled with its veracious penchant for Ants), Numbat suggests we take our time when initiating any forward movement. Not a procrastinator by any means, she simply warns against being imprudent or rash, particularly when caution and care are required. Resembling a feather duster poised for a session of spring-cleaning, Numbat's brush-like tail hints at the removal of energetic stagnation and unexpressed negativity, while her busy, probing nose prompts us to seek and unearth truth in all areas of life. Acknowledging the adage 'everything in its own time', Numbat affords quality time to prepare and build confidence before we step out of the shadows to reveal who and what we are. It encourages us to shun fear and hurriedness when it comes to seeking the support of others, especially when it becomes apparent we may not reach a set goal on our own. It also instils a sense of contentment when it comes to reaping the eventual rewards in a shared way.

Pademelon
Deflection

A member of the Wallaby family, the name 'Pademelon' is believed to have derived from a mistaken observation made by an early settler who thought he saw a 'PADdock full O' MELONs'. Following established tracks through the brushy undergrowth, Pademelons sleep all day and venture out at night to forage in grassed clearings. Once common in concentrated pockets along the southern coast of Australia, Pademelons are now only found in Tasmania, largely due to the lack of Foxes and other predators in that state. Although Pademelons are solitary and territorial by nature, it is not uncommon to witness small groups feeding in close proximity to one another.

Many fruits and vegetables, including melons, pumpkins, squash and cucumbers are actually members of the gourd family – a family that boasts hundreds of species of vines that bear curled, climbing tendrils and a plethora of fruit of varying shapes, colours and sizes. Gourds have been grown by people the world over to be used as musical instruments, pipes, masks, canteens, water jugs, dippers, birdhouses, bath sponges and even currency. Gourds were so valued by the Haitian people, for example, that in 1807 the gourd was declared the national currency by the governor of northern Haite, Henri Cristophe. To this day, the average coin of Haiti is known as a 'gourde'. While, the 'penis sheath gourd', an attachment worn over the genitals by some traditional tribal men of New Guinea, Africa and northern South America (arguably the most unusual use for a gourd), are still fashioned today for social and protective reasons. But the most fascinating use has to be that which lists the gourd as a powerful and protective talisman. Portions of dehydrated gourd, for example, were once carried in carefully sewn pouches as a means of deflecting evil, while hanging a gourd on both sides of the exterior side of a door was once thought to ward off unwanted negativity. In shamanic practice, dried gourds were filled with dried beans and used as rattles. It was believed that these rattles would worry malevolent spirits so they would return to whence they came. I had a dream once, not long before my first trip to Tasmania, in which I saw many Pademelons on a manicured lawn. I was standing on a porch at night, and a light was shining behind me. The light shone out so that the Pademelons could be clearly seen feeding on the lawn. I made a noise and all the Pademelons looked up at the same time and faced me and, as they did, the light sparkled in their eyes and bounced back at me as a red glow. Their eyes took on a red shine, and I knew, somehow, that they were sharing with me their protective, deflective 'medicine'. Ever since that dream, Pademelon Dreaming has championed (for me) the art of deflection; the ability to protect by averting or repelling negative interference, and sending it back from whence it came. Pademelon addresses the importance of setting boundaries by saying 'no' occasionally and meaning it. It also affords the strength to only go as far as you feel comfortable and to never compromise your values and beliefs. It talks of healing by encouraging us to speak up about past issues; of acknowledging and addressing negative or limiting experiences that bind and hold us in a place of lack and fear. It provides space for us to admit when we need help, or when we need support in surrendering our weaknesses and secrets to Spirit so that we may move forward more productively, free of the burdens of shame, regret, grief and pain. For me, Pademelon Dreaming assists in the deflection of negativity, the exorcism of emotional demons and guards against interference and abuse. And when we have addressed the need for healing and protection and dealt with the reasons why, Pademelon paves the way for a life rich in fun, fertility, abundance and fruitful progress, as indicated by the other traditional uses for the humble gourd.

Phascogale
Scapegoat

Phascogales usually give birth to eight young. Medium sized, arboreal, flesh-eating marsupials, Phascogales inhabit stands of she-oak, but generally nest in hollow eucalyptus trunks. Phascogales are best recognised for their brush-like tail and their habit of lining their nest with their victim's feathers. The word 'phascogale' is a derivative of the Latin word for 'pouched Weasel'.

Throughout Europe, Weasels have earned themselves the reputation of being cold-blooded killers and egg-thieves. Sneaking into hen houses at night and agitated by the flurry of feathers that ensues, Weasels are said to slip into a frenzied state, madly killing all the Hens as they hysterically flap about in a vain attempt to escape the onslaught. A vicious circle quickly develops: the more the birds flap, the more agitated the Weasels become, and the more they attack, the more the birds flap. When considering the whole scenario, the Weasel almost certainly enters the hen house initially with the intention of taking a few eggs. But, plans sometimes go askew, even for Weasels. So, after making its first unplanned kill, it is probably more than happy to leave with its victim firmly lodged in its mouth, to return home and feed its family. But because of its diminutive size and the heavy weight of the birds, it generally escapes empty handed totally forgetting about the eggs in the excitement, leaving the dead birds untouched. On waking the next morning, the keeper of the fowls is confronted with a gory scene, thus compounding the erroneous belief that Weasels kill for sport, driven by bloodlust; a shocking and unfair reputation indeed. Despite the fact that Weasels may never have it in mind to kill the Hens, they very often do. And so, because of an obscure physical resemblance to the European Weasel, the Australian Phascogale was ultimately tarred with the same brush by the early settlers who first encountered it. The Phascogale has become the totem of those who find themselves 'scapegoats'; unfairly held responsible for things they have not done. The term 'scapegoat' refers to an individual who is made to bear the blame of others. The expression comes from the biblical account of Aaron and the live Goat over whose head he confessed the sins of the Children of Israel on the Day of Atonement. Carrying their sins, the Goat was then released into the wilderness. Seemingly lining its nest with the 'proof of the crime', Phascogale walks with those who frequently find themselves in the wrong place at the wrong time. As unfair as it may seem, if there is trouble afoot, Phascogale people more often than not find themselves on the 'most wanted' list – even if they are innocent of any crime. If you are drawn to explore Phascogale Dreaming, you are being primed to take responsibility for your life, to pull your head in, disassociate yourself with people and activities classified as 'trouble' and to consider the consequences of everything you do before you do it. Phascogale offers council to those regularly in trouble with authority figures, namely those considered 'followers' and 'fall guys'.

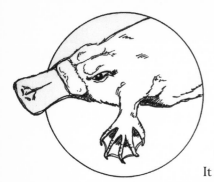

Platypus
Women's Wisdom

When a stuffed specimen was first taken to Europe, the people thought the Platypus too odd a creature to be true – and promptly declared it a hoax. It is indeed an unusual looking creature; it has a bill and webbed feet like a Duck, a tail like a Beaver and it lays eggs. The Platypus is a playful mammal known as a monotreme – a family name shared with their only cousin: the Echidna. They live in creeks and streams and can remain under water for up to five minutes, using their flat tail and webbed feet to move forward. They swim with their eyes closed, detecting the slightest disturbance in the water with their sensitive bill. Platypuses are born with a venomous spur on each of their rear ankles, but the females generally shed theirs at an early age. The Platypus builds its creek-bank nests in burrows with the entrance located just under the water's surface.

According to Aboriginal legend, the Platypus was birthed from the forbidden coupling of two souls joined by unlawful union. Out of vengeance for their reprehensible behaviour, the Elders transformed her into a Duck and him into a Water Rat. They were then exiled indefinitely from their respective clans. She eventually produced an egg, from which hatched a strange furry, duck-billed creature equipped with four powerful webbed feet: the Platypus. Those who have ever felt abandoned or rejected should investigate the wisdom of the Platypus. She was created under a blanket of dishonesty, judgement and betrayal, brought into this world as a result of true, honest but devastating love. No matter how old we are, we instinctively look to our parents, as our primary role models, for confirmation and guidance in all areas of our life. But what if that guidance is absent, or predisposed by traditional values or belief; values or beliefs inappropriate for today's world? Platypus is not only committed to honouring her parent's heartfelt desire to see the people merge with peace and love in their hearts, but also the empowerment of all women by reminding them of their worth, wisdom and their role as 'sorcerers', and individuals charged with the power to create within the dark recesses of their womb. She works to free all women of guilt and oppression and to reinstate their connection to 'the source'. Platypus prepares you to realise, understand and embrace the potency of your own intuition and higher levels of knowing. A creature that swims with her eyes shut, Platypus listens to the heartbeat of the Earth Mother for direction. She looks to her inner yin and yang for guidance, thus finding the strength needed to make her own decisions. She honours her innate masculine and feminine qualities, knowing that she is more than capable of navigating herself through life without the support of others. You are being urged to trust your own judgement, direction and endurance. This is the wisdom of all women – the ability to trust in their intuition and to consciously act with purpose. Women are natural dreamers, visionaries and mystics, but they must embrace their masculine aspects in order to realise the full potential of these gifts.

Possum
Opportunity

Australian Possums were so named because of their assumed relationship to the Opossums of South America. Apart from them both being arboreal marsupials, however, the two are completely unrelated. Opossum Bay in Hobart apparently takes its name from the misnomer. There are 23 known species of Possum in Australia, which are divided into three major families: the Ringtail Possum and Glider family; the Brushtail Possum and Cuscus family and the Pygmy Possum and Feathertail Glider family. All Possums are nocturnal, with some species sporting prehensile tails and powerful claws.

Possum inspires us to see opportunity in any condition and to productively harness all opportunities to our best advantage; to gently ride on the back of any circumstantial generosity afforded until we are comfortably established, after which retreat should be executed in an honourable and discreet manner. To take opportunity by the horns when it is offered is to believe one hundred percent in your total worth and life purpose. To act on every thought and to honour every possibility as potential for growth is what separates successful people from ordinary folk. Possum urges us to see our life as a foundation on which great things can be initiated. He encourages us to seek out new experiences and attempt new things. Although the Possum is ideally suited to living in the hollows of trees, the idea of squatting in the roofs of human dwellings poses no moral dilemma for him at all. Possum asks you to remember who you are and what agreements you made with yourself before commencing your Earth Walk. What did you want to achieve? Where did you see yourself ultimately? Pay close attention to the opportunities afforded you at this time, for new ways to develop your abilities and to enhance your growth are on offer right now. Identify and discard all self-doubt – they simply keep you from furthering your skills and employing your talents to the best of your abilities. Possum's appearance heralds the chance to better yourself and to take your knowledge deeper. Opportunity knocks for those aware of its presence. So long as you are willing to work hard and apply yourself, it is acceptable to gently ride on the back of any opportunity that is presented to you. The wealth locked within the authentic self is filled with great possibility and all it takes is the courage to access it and birth it into the light of day. Possum's appearance may also mean that you have a freeloader in your midst. The best way to expel a Possum from your roof is to install a sensor-light. Nocturnal by nature, Possums hate bright light, so with lights turning on at the slightest movement they quickly find an alternate dwelling. Using a similar approach, to illuminate your squatter's sponging ways, visualise their light turning on (and staying on) when ever they enter their bedroom. They will soon find it impossible to stay as a result.

Quokka
Assimilation

The Quokka was first described by Dutchman, Volkersen, as 'resembling an Asian Civet Cat, but with brown hair'. In 1696, de Vlamingh described the Quokka as 'a kind of Rat as big as a common Cat'. The island on which it was first discovered was so named Island 'Rotte nest' (meaning 'Rat's nest'), but was later renamed 'Rottnest'. A small member of the Wallaby family, the Quokka climbs small shrubs where it feeds on buds and foliage. A marsupial the size of a Hare, the female Quokka suckles her young in a pouch. Quokkas congregate under dense shrubs for shelter, and are less active during the day.

Under any other circumstance, to be mistaken for a Rat would normally prove quite devastating, as Rats are considered vermin by many, best eradicated at once. Luckily, however, people soon noticed the stronger semblance to the Wallaby, a close cousin of the Quokka, and put right their earlier mistake. Despite the identification mix up, being called names has never posed a problem for the Quokka, who lives by the adage 'sticks and stones may break my bones, but names will never hurt me' – good advice that the Quokka encourages us to integrate into our lives. In fact, the Quokka has come to assimilate the wisdom of Rat into its Dreaming as proof of its broad and progressive attitude. Combining the symbology of Rat with that of Wallaby, the Quokka effectively honours both its mistaken identity and its true ancestry. She suggests that we act on instinct, be mindful of when to advance and when to withdraw and to resist the urge to return to our comfort zones once we have plucked up the courage to leave them. She rejects pretence, withdrawing support from those who intentionally cut themselves short or rob themselves of choice and/ or opportunity to grow because of intolerance, fear or blinkered judgment. Acceptance and patience are keynotes of the Quokka, who demonstrates that life is too short to worry about what other people think, or to quibble over differences in attitude or choice. Quokka coaches us as we set about assimilating who we once were with who we are today, for example. If we have gay friends or family members, Quokka helps us come to terms with their different lifestyle and blend their values and beliefs with ours. It instructs us in being flexible enough to accept others' religious beliefs, even if they differ or clash with our own, and not to judge others for their perceived weaknesses or dependencies, but rather to work with them as they overcome them. Quokka Dreaming affords the confidence to assimilate to any group, new environment, family reshaping or alternative way of thinking, and it does in a way that allows our true character to remain intact, keeping personal compromise to a minimum.

Quoll
Wholeness

Captain Cook recorded 'Quoll' as the carnivorous marsupial's local Aboriginal name back in 1770 when he captured his first 'sample' on the east coast of Australia. The early settlers quickly became familiar with the Quoll, calling it 'Native Cat', 'Native Polecat' and 'Spotted Marten', names based on more familiar (though totally unrelated) animals back home. Australia boasts four species of Quoll: the Northern Quoll, Spotted-tailed Quoll, Eastern Quoll and Western Quoll. All four species were once common, but because of habitat loss and introduced predators such as Foxes, Dogs and Cats, their numbers have reduced dramatically. Quolls are primarily nocturnal, with pointed muzzles, long tails and ginger brown to black fur boldly spattered with white spots. They are vivacious, striking animals, with intense eyes, a pink nose and very sharp teeth. Quolls reach sexual maturity at one year, but experience a naturally short life of only two to five years (on average).

The Quoll, a mystical creature that combines an evolved sense of inner strength and self-love with a deeply psychic and spiritual disposition (evident in its nocturnal nature; the dark being symbolic of the unknown, the magickal and the unseen), when coupled with its tendency to hunt alone and its fastidious habit of grooming its stunning coat whenever it can, is an animal that relies on the light of the moon to guide its footsteps and inspire its journey. A proud, assured creature, the Quoll explains that the tangible and intangible worlds are not independent from one another, but united as a single entity. Quoll helps us find a balance between our spiritual life and our physical life by explaining that one is no more important than the other; that they must exist as one, creating a whole, interrelated way of life. When chatting about Quoll Dreaming once, not long after witnessing my first wild Quoll, my friend Maria Elita pondered, 'We have always been whole. We *will* always be whole. We are eternal beings of love, after all. The problem is, however, our human perception leads us to believe that we aren't. Social conditioning and 'lower vibrational' belief systems instil the belief that we are broken and incomplete. Perhaps the Quoll teaches wholeness by espousing that we are 'One'; the embodiment of what I call 'The Miracle'. If so, then you are perfect! At this point in time you may be feeling incomplete and imperfect. Honour this human perception by claiming that your Truth is whole, One *and* complete. In doing so, you may well reclaim your Truth, and when this happens you'll become an unstoppable force, invoking synchronistic experiences that enhance the human journey of your celestial spirit.' Thus, Quoll helps us remember that we are 'spiritual beings living a physical life', which is far more than simply being 'physical beings striving to live a more spiritual life': an assumption many of us make. A great deal of pressure is lifted when we embrace the difference; a realisation that enables us to approach our everyday, seemingly mundane life with a sense of sacredness, excitement and joy. To quote her once more, Maria contends: 'to say 'I'm on a spiritual journey' is really an unconvincing argument. It doesn't really say anything. To say 'I'm a divine being experiencing a human's journey', though, is far closer to the truth. It says what it is. Spirituality is everything. It is the air we breathe. The sights we see. The sounds we hear. The tastes we savour. The touch we feel. Spirituality is not a phase of life or a level to achieve. It is now; the dawning of our existence that has always been.

Waking up to this dawn, though, takes time for some of us. Many of us have experienced an awakening of some sort at some point in our lives. These awakenings, however, are simply our remembering a truth that transcends the physical world. At this point we surrender to our human existence and relish the blessings that come with living a physical life – be they deemed 'positive' or 'negative'. When we then go back over our lives, many people say, 'before I was spiritual I used to be …' which is a common statement riddled with flaws. The truth is, you and I have *always* been spiritual, because we are eternal spirits, with the concept of 'spirituality' just embodying the human perception of the awakening / remembering process. Whether the people around you are 'awake' yet or not, does not make them any less spiritual then you, because we are, in essence, all connected to the one Spirit anyway. Oneness is the Eternal Spirit, sourced by love. You are, therefore, we all are 'One'. You have always been and always will be whole - and with this in mind, there is essentially nothing to strive for and no level of achievement to work toward, just the remembering of who and what you truly are. Once realised, this Truth then assists your human journey and its evolutionary lessons and your eventual awakening.' Quoll supports us as we learn to stand in our power, radiate pride and self-love and to speak up and champion our values and personal beliefs, instead of restricting them to the privacy of our home or inner self. Quoll provides the forum to proudly (and openly) integrate our spiritual life with our everyday life, so that the two may coexist side by side, in complete harmony with each other and the world around us.

Rat Kangaroo
Ingenuity

Potoroids are small macropods (members of the Kangaroo family) often affectionately referred to as 'Rat Kangaroos'. Their family includes the Bettong and the Potoroo. The Musky Rat Kangaroo is no bigger than a common Rat and feeds on mushrooms, roots and insects. Many live in dense undergrowth and make nests from material carried in their curled up tails. The Desert Rat Kangaroo (now very rare), however, inhabits the driest, most exposed regions of Central Australia. Of the nine species currently recorded, two have fallen prey to extinction due to habitat loss (as a result of farming) and introduced predators such as Foxes, Dogs and Cats.

With natural ingenuity bred into the little animal's soul, the Rat Kangaroo is the totem of the creatively minded and the unconventional dreamers among us. Rat Kangaroo walks with those who know it is their destiny to make a difference, to inspire the rest of humanity to think outside the box and to let their eccentricities shine. Rat Kangaroo people are independent thinkers. They push forward against the odds and achieve by willpower alone, venturing to prove wrong claims that they are too radical or alternative to ever amount to anything. Ordinary people with extraordinary ideas, Rat Kangaroo people see the world through innovative eyes, perceiving typical things from atypical perspectives. They can see clearly the flaws that hinder progress and stifle creativity, thus doing easily what others may take years to achieve. They know how to make mundane jobs easier and time consuming tasks more productive, with minimal effort and cost. Problem solvers and networkers, Rat Kangaroo people simplify, modernise and enhance all that they touch. If there is a better way to do something, you can generally rely on a Rat Kangaroo person to discover it. When resourcefulness is invoked with true intent and selfless integrity, Rat Kangaroo people manifest awe-inspiring levels of creativity and personal wealth with glory, ease and joy. Proudly marching to the beat of its own drum, the free-thinking Rat Kangaroo encourages us to follow our dreams and welcome a life of discovery and invention so that we may live meaningful, productive lives richly imbued with promise, purpose and pleasure. Their motto: 'What else is possible?'.

Rock Wallaby
Foothold

With shorter, broader hind feet than regular Wallabies, the Rock Wallaby has coarse, thickly padded soles that afford a greater degree of traction on slippery surfaces and gravelled terrain. Rock Wallabies inhabit the rocky outcrops, hazardous edges and precipitous faces of cliffs and gaping ravines. They venture down to the flat grasslands to graze in the mornings and early evenings. Feral Goats have negatively affected the numbers of Rock Wallabies as they compete for habitat and food, as have introduced predators such as Foxes, feral Cats and wild Dogs.

An inherently surefooted animal, the Rock Wallaby affords balance and stability to those feeling insecure, confused and overwhelmed. It guides those who find themselves emotionally lost, leading them back to a place of certainty and precision. It bolsters those teetering on the edge and those dangerously close to losing their foothold on life. It slows the gradual decline into depression by offering windows of clarity and redirection. It offers choice and support to those sliding into despondency, while providing an encouraging leg up or a sympathetic hand to reach out to. Rock Wallaby provides reinforcement by instilling its family's 'Onwards and Upwards' attitude into the hearts of those who seek its counsel. It reminds us never to glance back with regret, fear or grief, and to seek professional help when necessary. Rock Wallaby champions the belief that everything happens for a reason and that neither accidents nor mistakes actually exist. It primes us for growth by authenticating our resolve, endurance and readiness to embrace change. It tests our courage by shaking our foundations and checking our courage to surrender the past and welcome the future. It dares us to reject insecurity, uncertainty and apprehension, and to do whatever it takes to instil a sense of sanctuary, conviction and self-assurance, even if it means taking quality time-out, initiating permanent changes or seeking the professional support of a counsellor or therapist.

Seal
Inner Voice

Seals belong to the 'pinniped' family, which is Latin for *feather foot* or *fin foot* in reference to their fin-like flippers. Seals are aquatic mammals that come ashore to breed, give birth and raise their young. The pinniped family is split into three groups: 'Earless' Seals or 'true' Seals, 'Eared' or Fur Seals and Sea Lions, and Walruses. Earless Seals (seals that lack external ear flaps) have rear flippers that point backwards, making movement on land difficult. They also have a layer of blubber that offers insulation. Fur Seals and Sea Lions, however, have external ear flaps and are able to rotate their hind feet forward enabling them to move with considerable speed on land. Instead of blubber, Eared Seals have dense fur that traps air bubbles and offers insulation.

Selkies are gentle faerie-folk that inhabit the waters of Orkney and Shetland. The term 'Selkie' is a local word meaning 'Seal'. Also known as Silkies, Selchies or Roanes, they appear in the form of Seals, but assume human form by casting off their Seal skins. They require the Seal skin to return to the sea, however, so if their skin is stolen or lost they become trapped in human form until the skin is retrieved. Whilst in human form, they are incredibly beautiful; almost irresistible to humans. Occasionally a human male will find a discarded Seal skin, thus trapping the Selkie in human form. Legend has it that the beautiful maiden must marry her captor and bear him children. The Selkie inevitably finds the hidden skin, however, allowing her to return to the sea. Seal Dreaming invokes a sense of playfulness, magick and romance in human relationships, especially those forged between lovers and dreamers. Seal Dreaming emphasises the supremacy of the inner voice, reminding us of the power found within our personal rhythms, emotions and intuition. Seal Dreaming helps us 'sing' from the heart for our soul mate, while simultaneously helping us find a healthy balance between love and lust, and sensitivity and sensuality within ourself and all our other relationships. It explains that how we perceive ourselves will ultimately influence the type of energy we will attract. The self-image we carry usually determines the integrity of the people we draw to us. To exude unconditional love will, eventually, attract the same. Seal Dreaming supports us as we bask in the glow of our inner knowing. It shuns superficiality and compromise, drawing to us the partner (and the other rewards we feel we deserve) best suited to fulfil our heartfelt requirements. Seal Dreaming augurs a time of peace and balance. It rejects force, assumed lot in life and the wandering eye. It calls for us to be clear in our expectations and to surrender jealousy, resentment and discontent. Seal Dreaming encourages us to acknowledge and listen to our inner voice, the only counsel we need in our search for unconditional love, acceptance and loyalty.

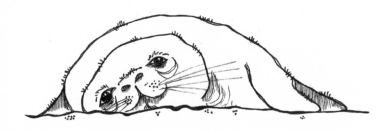

Tasmanian Devil
Purification

Although the Tasmanian Devil will occasionally kill and eat small mammals and reptiles, it prefers to feed on carrion usually in the form of road kill. The Tasmanian Devil is Australia's only true indigenous carnivorous mammal. The Dingo, assumed by many to be Australia's largest native mammalian predator, was introduced from Asia some 40,000 years ago. Tasmanian Devils once inhabited the southern mainland in healthy numbers, but due to habitat loss and hunting, they now only exist in their wild state in Tasmania (although occasional sightings are still reported in Victoria).

The generic name of the Tasmanian Devil, *Sarcophilus*, means 'flesh-lover', indicating its carnivorous dietary preference. Meat is what nourishes the Tasmanian Devil. It instinctively knows that meat is the only fare that will supply it with the strength and endurance to fulfil its duties to Mother Earth. Choosing the life of the humble yet cantankerous recluse, however, the Tasmanian Devil is a shy creature that prefers to feed on carrion and road kill rather than relying on its skills as a capable hunter. Thus, the Tasmanian Devil is seen as the cleaner, the one whose responsibility it is to ensure that the deceased are returned to Mother Earth as efficiently as possible, minimising the risk of putrefaction and contamination of the land and water ways. Tasmanian Devil teaches us to purify our lives, to honour our bodies and to exorcise all that is corrupted from our systems. Eating all that is wholesome, drinking all that is pure and honouring our bodies by regularly exercising and getting adequate rest are lessons afforded by Tasmanian Devil, as is only ever doing what is right for us while avoiding the propensity to base our decisions on what others may do, prefer or expect. Tasmanian Devils are famous for their powerful jaws and crushing bite. Tasmanian Devil teaches us to honour ourselves on a communication level, therefore, by using the vice-like power of its jaws to speak with vice-like force or, when appropriate, with gentle humility. He validates the art of cutting through pretence to get directly to the heart of things when required, thus purifying our relationships of dishonesty and misunderstanding. Tasmanian Devil prompts us to purify some aspect of our life. The cleansing process personified by the appearance of the Tasmanian Devil can be as tender and healing as you like, or equally, as gruesome and devastating. It all depends on how it is approached and whether or not it is handled in a sacred manner. To remove all that is stagnant from one's life is to realise the fertility that comes with release, liberation and freedom. It is to strengthen one's foundations and to nourish one's desire to expand.

Thylacine
Wisdom

The Thylacine, also affectionately known as the Tasmanian Tiger or the Tasmanian Wolf, is an enigmatic creature of great wisdom. The last-known surviving Thylacine, once common throughout Tasmania, died in captivity on September 7, 1936. Dog-like in appearance and classified as the largest of all carnivorous marsupials, the Thylacine has a slender body, large head, powerful jaws, a long whip-like tail and thick stripes on its back. A large percentage of Tasmania's wilderness still exists in its virgin state, completely unspoiled by development or land clearing. Many believe, therefore, that the Thylacine still endures in secrecy deep within the heart of the Tasmanian forest, protected by both the inaccessibility of its habitat and its elusive nature.

Carrying folklore status on par with the Loch Ness Monster and Yeti, reports of sightings are common, but never substantiated by photographic or videotaped evidence. If the myths are true, and the Thylacine does indeed still subsist, its acumen alone has kept it safe and hidden for almost 70 years. When life becomes overwhelming, excessively busy or too fast, Thylacine advocates having the good judgment to withdraw from the mob and walk alone for a spell, perhaps spending time exploring the truths buried deep within the inner landscape. Thylacine offers a time of calm; the chance to contemplate our purpose and reasoning rather than seeking the counsel of others. She espouses quality time spent in solitude. She prompts us to stop and ask, 'What is the purpose of my life? Why have I experienced all that I have? Why am I here?'.

Thylacine represents our desire to seek a deeper reality and a more defined truth. She supports this quest by encouraging us to journey inward to form a relationship with our own thoughts and the natural impulses that instigate our actions. If Thylacine is speaking to you today, you are being encouraged to seek out a silent place of solitude. Use this sacred space as a vehicle to better know yourself. Use the sacred silence as a means of deepening your own knowledge and your innate sense of wisdom. Wait until your instincts tell you that the time has come to return to the people, to share your knowledge and hopefully widen the perception of those around you. Thylacine teaches us to deepen our inherent wisdom, to study it, to become one with it and to share it with others when the time is right. Gathered over a lifetime of experience, our wisdom is what marks us as unique. It represents the inherent skills we hold that someday may be presented to the world as instruments of healing and learning.

Tree Kangaroo
Realisation

The Tree Kangaroo is a thickset, arboreal member of the macropod family, scaling the rainforest trees with its powerful hind claws and its forepaw's opposable first and second fingers. Able to leap distances of up to 9 metres from one tree to the next, the Tree Kangaroo is equally as competent on the ground, bounding along at high speeds using its arched tail as a kind of 'rudder'.

While honouring the wisdom of its ground dwelling cousins, the Tree Kangaroo has symbolically enhanced their Dreaming by literally taking their teachings to new heights. Like the Kangaroo and Wallaby, Tree Kangaroo reminds us never to look back with regret and to do what we can to ensure our movement forward is tackled with confidence. It also encourages us to employ the laws of attraction to bring to us all that we deserve, to take responsibility for our life and that of our family and to strive for new heights with every step we take. In doing so, the quality of our life will be enhanced and our potential realised with greater ease. Just as Tree Kangaroo has discovered the security and opportunity afforded by the forest branches, we too can explore the higher realms of our existence by likening them to the world's varying perceptions of Spirit and the potential held in store by the Universe. The branches of the Tree Kangaroo's 'Life Tree' can be viewed as different paths of Spirit, alternative religions or spiritual beliefs or other channels imbued with knowledge, sacred acumen and potentially life-affirming perspectives. Thus, life can be viewed as a mighty, aged Tree, with each branch representing choice and opportunity and an invitation to explore, grow and heal. The twigs that extend from its blessed branches symbolise the gifts, opportunities and lessons Spirit intends us to explore as we journey inward and out. Tree Kangaroo urges us to see our life as the foundation on which great things can be built, while offering its powerful tail as a directional rudder, steering us to wholeness. It asks that we never stop striving for greater heights or daring to explore and try new things. The lesson is to dream and see yourself as worthy of greatness, to acknowledge your potential and to do what is necessary to realise it and bring it to fruition.

Water Rat
Habit

Hunted relentlessly by Australia's early settlers, the Water Rat's waterproof coat was sought after for its beautiful, sumptuous, silky texture. It is now completely protected by law. Eating freshwater crustaceans, fish and carrion found along the banks of rivers and waterways, the Otter-like Water Rat feeds ritually in one spot – a 'table' usually in the form of a flat rock or a half-submerged log. Food scraps are commonly found scattered about this table betraying its presence.

According to an Aboriginal Dreamtime legend, the Platypus was birthed from the illicit union of star-crossed lovers from rival tribes. The two apparently eloped, but later returned to seek the blessing of their elders and to express regret for dishonouring their families. Unfortunately, their reception was hostile. Bewitched and banished forever, he was transformed into a Water Rat and she, a Black Duck. If only the two had stayed away, trusting their hearts, instead of feeling the need to appease their clans – surely then they would have lived a good life together, free from indignity and consequence. Returning habitually to its favourite feeding station to devour its prey, the Water Rat demonstrates the tendency many of us display whenever life becomes emotionally taxing. It is human nature to seek the nurturing comfort and emotional support theoretically found in a familiar place like home. We routinely return to what we know when alternatives prove unrewarding. It's not always the case that what we have grown to know is right for us, but often a lack of self-worth and fear of success draws us back, blinding us to the different choices available and the prospect of autonomy. Instead of following recognizable patterns, Water Rat encourages us to seek alternatives that provide for us and enhance our sense of self-worth and inner-beauty. It primes us to broaden our horizons when seeking sustenance and to learn from our mistakes and past experiences. Not meaning to gratuitously dishonour or undervalue the love and support ideally found in family and friends, Water Rat simply asks, 'Why would you repeatedly seek such support when it has never been there before? How can you expect to grow to your greatest potential if you insist on returning, by habit alone, to comfort zones that no longer provide for you?' The 'devil we know' may not always be 'better' than the choices and opportunities yet to be taken. Water Rat Dreaming calls for us to test life's waters and to trust our sense of personal power, judgment and intuition. Only then can we hope to break with tradition and establish ourselves as self-governing masters of destiny.

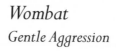

Wombat
Gentle Aggression

Closely related to the Koala, the Wombat has a large head, wide snout, thick whiskers, short stumpy legs and powerful claws. Despite their size (adults can weigh up to 40kg) and clumsy appearance, Wombats can sustain bursts of speed of up to 40kph over short distances. They are also adept swimmers. The Southern Hairy Nosed Wombat, the critically endangered Northern Hairy Nosed Wombat and the Common (or Naked Nosed or Forest) Wombat all live in underground burrows up to 20m long, excavated by lying on their side, digging with their front legs and pushing the dirt out with their hind feet. And so they don't fill up with dirt as the animal digs, all three species of Wombat have backward facing pouches to carry their young.

Equipped with cartilage plating in her rump, a female Wombat will block her burrow by sitting face first just inside the opening of her den when a predator threatens entry. A hungry Dingo, for example, may attempt to force access by chewing on the rump of the Wombat, but with no feeling to weaken its stance the Wombat proves a fearless adversary. Determined to protect her young, she will wait, expecting the Dingo to see the futility in its actions and to wander off. Driven by hunger, the Dingo often persists. In this scenario, the Wombat will crouch down, apparently allowing access to the Dingo. Eager to get to the young, the Dingo crawls over the Wombat, wedging itself between the roof of the den and her strong backbone. With the Dingo helplessly stuck, the Wombat stands up, crushing its victim against the roof of the tunnel. Wombat chooses to express herself assertively first, reverting to aggressive confrontation only when necessary. She relies on the virtue of her rivals, hoping they will see her point. She never wages war as her first plan of attack. She prefers to negotiate initially, expressing herself plainly, regressing to force only when all else fails. Wombat walks her talk, expressing things exactly as she sees them. She will not be put down or belittled by anyone. She views her opinions, beliefs and values as sacred and definitely worthy of recognition. She insists that others take heed of her opinions and is self-assured enough to outwardly express her demands. If she has to, she will enforce her expectations vehemently, even physically, but until the need arises she expresses herself with influence and tenacity. Wombat empowers you to speak with assertiveness instead of irrationally 'hitting the roof' whenever you feel threatened. Wombat allows you to speak up, confronting perceived wrongs with innate confidence and assuredness without being excessively violent or rude. To treat others as you would like to be treated is the golden rule of the Wombat. She understands how easy it is to feel intolerant toward those who choose to ignore your advice, however, especially when you know it to be wisdom gleaned over a lifetime of experience.

introduced / 'feral' mammals

Camel
Replenishment

Australia is the only place in the world that boasts pure, wild Dromedary (or Arabian) Camels. We have, on occasion, exported them back to the Middle East from where they were originally introduced to carry inland explorers and cargo over vast arid terrain. The advent of the car, however, and the development of the railroad, saw the Camel become redundant as a means of transport with many set free. The descendants of these Camels now roam the Outback in large numbers. Dromedary Camels have a single hump in which fat is stored. This fat offers nourishment when food is scarce. Herbivores, Camels are capable of drinking water too brackish for other mammals and can survive several days without having to drink. When given the opportunity, though, Camels will drink up to 250 litres of water, storing it in their body tissue. As they breathe, the oxygen mixes with hydrogen atoms stored in the hump, creating water, which the body absorbs as if taking a drink. Dromedary Camels have a double row of eyelashes and thick eyebrows that help to protect their eyes from sand, sun and strong winds. They can also completely close their nostrils for protection.

According to tradition, Camels are said to epitomise obedience and humbleness, royalty, sombreness, fortitude and restraint. The truth is though, Camels only sanction obedience and humbleness when their loyalty and compliance is acknowledged respectably and returned in kind when need be. It must be a two way street when working with Camel Dreaming. Camel is more than happy to offer its strength and endurance, but not at the expense of its own wellbeing. If, when supporting another, it turns out your best interests are being compromised beyond tolerable levels for example, Camel can be invoked to help you soberly take the reigns and steer your life back into a more fruitful, personally rewarding direction. Although self-control is a keynote of the Camel, encouraging level-headed yet candid interaction with those around you, it rejects negotiation that doesn't allow for a middle ground to be met and it will rancorously spit at anyone who abuses or ignores such a fair-minded stance. With long eyelashes and pad-like feet, the Camel is perfectly equipped for arid conditions, sand storms and strong desert winds. Similarly, it buffers us against emotional barrenness and inspires us to step out on our own and quest for purpose, self-worth and unconditional love when life becomes uncaringly arid and devoid of enthusiasm and equality. Camel Dreaming offers fortitude to those embarking (or preparing to embark) on a journey, for example, that promises little if any emotional or financial assistance and no conscious destination. It walks with people about to strike out on their own after divorce or separation, a death, eviction or termination of employment. Camel offers sound navigation and a healthier chance of survival to those prepared to take risks, trust absolutely, and go without for a while in order to better their life. Camel Dreaming affords replenishment and the strength to adapt and take opportunity by the horns, while providing endurance during difficult times, particularly when we feel emotionally, spiritually and physically parched. Although Camel may warn that the path ahead is set to be difficult, possibly devoid of emotional support, love and incentive, it swears that we can traverse it with ease and success if we acknowledge that we have all we need within us and trust that, by journey's end, we will be replenished. When we invoke the spirit of the Camel, we emerge emotionally stronger and more self-reliant for it.

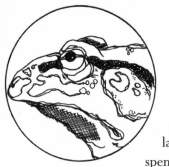

Cane Toad
Hidden Beauty

Cane Toads are amphibious creatures that start life in water as Tadpoles, but spend the majority of their adult life on land. Nocturnal by nature, Cane Toads spend the daylight hours hiding in a cool, damp spot. Cane Toads have stocky bodies, short, powerful legs and 'warty' looking skin. They carry venom in glands above their shoulders, lethal to any animal that would naturally feed on native Frogs. Cane Toads were introduced into the Australian sugar cane fields in 1935 to supposedly protect them from the Cane Beetle, but the experiment failed. With no natural enemies and a life span of approximately twenty years, a single female Cane Toad can lay up to 40,000 eggs annually. The Tadpoles initially breathe through gills but, as they grow, their tails diminish in size and they develop lungs for life on land. Cane Toads eat insects, other amphibians and even small mammals.

Toads have been associated with both positive and negative forms of mysticism since the beginning of time. To the Chinese, for example, the Toad is an emissary of good fortune and long life, while in Mexico it is a symbol of illumination and enlightenment. Typically viewed as a symbol of darkness and deceit, muddy pools and quagmires, however, the Toad has long been considered a favourite witch's familiar and a fabled ingredient in charm work. In Celtic legend, the Toad is said to appreciate its lack of appeal, its ugliness and the horror felt by those who stumble across it by chance. It is said to carry a precious stone in its forehead, however, which holds the power to reverse the effects of any poison and the ill-affects of criticism, judgement and ridicule. Despite its external ugliness, on a spiritual level the Toad holds within itself the antidote to its own toxin and a release from its self-loathing. Cane Toad, with its superficial stare and hollow eyes, calls to us to look beyond the physical body and all perceived limitations so that we may unearth our true inner-beauty and self-worth. When we view ourselves as ugly, worthless or stupid, we emanate an equally toxic aura or personality. People fail to see us for what we are inside, instead they base their decisions on what they superficially see and feel. Cane Toad Dreaming suggests that we reach deep down inside ourselves in order to find and retrieve our hidden potential, because once discovered and nurtured, dormant beauty can transform our lives and ultimately set us free. To embrace Cane Toad Dreaming in a productive way, therefore, may see us retrieve our 'sacred stone' and shed our 'warty' exterior to reveal true beauty that honours our emotions and creates a foundation for a happy, fertile new beginning.

Deer
Gentleness

The Deer was originally introduced into Australia as an alternative farming option. When the demand for venison suddenly waned, however, thousands of Deer were released. Feral Fallow, Samba and Red Deer now populate many rural areas of Australia.

Deer teaches unconditional love and the knowledge that to walk gently upon the Earth means to walk in balance, in beauty and in honour of everything and everyone who shares this planet with us. To walk gently requires us to show respect for the Earth as our Mother and all living things as our brothers and sisters. Deer asks that we respect the right of all things of nature to enjoy abundant, interrelated lives and to realise that the impact we have on our environment now will determine the quality of our lives in the future – be it in our lifetime or that of future generations. Deer urges us to treat everyone and everything as our equal; to treat others the way we would like to be treated. It encourages us to demonstrate respect, trust and honesty in all that we do and to those whose paths we may cross. Deer does not insist that those who embrace its wisdom live a life of piety, but it does ask that we remain mindful of our actions and the affect they have on others. Everyone is inherently imbued with the qualities of Deer. It represents our collective potential and unity as a people. Sadly, many are unaware of its spirit and remain disconnected from the world around them, lost in a quagmire of confusion. Only the expression of unconditional love for both ourselves and for everything of Creation has the capability of dissolving the barriers that prevent unity. Random yet sincere displays of compassion and empathy are the strengths found in those who carry Deer Dreaming. Deer embodies the future vision of humanity walking as one, hand-in-hand and united as a people. It offers a simple exercise intended to support this vision and to help bring it to reality. The next time you are feeling alone, overwhelmed or downhearted, put out your hand and whisper to Spirit, 'I do not wish to be alone right now' and wait for someone to take it, energetically. The humbling thing is, with practice and pure intent, you will actually feel someone holding your hand; perhaps the energy of an ancestor spirit, your angel or guardian spirit. Either way, you will know you are no longer alone, for the love of the Deer will be harnessed and integrated on a soul level.

Fox
Shadows

The Fox is indeed a handsome creature. Foxes have predominantly ginger-red fur, with white under the chin and down the chest. Their brushy tail is also tipped with white, unlike their ears and legs, which are stained black. They are found throughout Australia. Skilful and adaptable, inhabiting rural, suburban and inner city areas alike, many are known to establish their dens in close proximity to human dwellings, raiding compost heaps, orchards and poultry sheds for Chickens and eggs. Omnivorous by nature, Foxes eat fruit, berries and grain. They also eat birds, insects and small mammals like Rabbits, Hares, Mice and Rats, as well as a wide range of native wildlife. A baby

Fox is called a 'Kit'; a male is called a 'Dog', while a female is called a 'Vixen'.

The Fox lives in the shadows. It is an animal of the night: a creature of mystery and kenning. Twilight is the power time of the Fox; that time between late afternoon and evening, too late to be called day but too early to be classified as night. Fox is a fringe-dweller. It is an animal that lives between the worlds. Known to share territory with humans while keeping its distance, it represents those who live on the outskirts of society, but who yearn to be included, involved and welcomed. Foxes often build their dens along fencerows, indicating a desire to stay within their comfort zone while safely contemplating the wider world from a familiar point of view. Fox Dreaming nurtures those among us who are too shy to show our true selves. It represents those of us who are too afraid or self-conscious to offer opinions, socialise or try new things. Afraid to draw attention to them selves, Fox people long to be like everyone else, but lack the confidence to integrate fully. A creature known to lurk in the shadows as a way of ensuring its survival, Fox Dreaming is demonstrated by those who desire to step 'out of hiding' and introduce, perhaps for the first time their true selves and share their potentials and gifts of knowledge and experience. Secluded by uncertainty, the Fox covers its tracks and hides its presence behind a veil of kenning and suspicion. It inspires us to leave the shadows, therefore, to break through insecurities and say to the world, 'Here I am, now deal with it'. It affords the self-confidence and inner strength to put us 'out there', no matter how insignificant the initial steps may seem. Fox Dreaming allows us to stand in our power by instilling the belief that we can master any situation and overcome any limitation by reminding us that we are just as important, worthy and sacred as the next person.

Hare
Lunar Energy

Hares occur as an introduced species throughout Australia and New Zealand. They are larger than Rabbits and adapt quickly to new environments, surviving in habitats known to offer little or no protection against the elements and predators. Hares are solitary by nature and do not dig burrows. Instead, they sleep in shallow indentations, or forms, dug into the ground usually under a shrub or a hedge or among blackberries or tall grass. They crouch low, with their ears laid flat against their back. In this position, they are almost undetectable. When disturbed, however, they will bolt with their tail tucked low and their body carried high on their long, powerful legs. Most active during the early hours of the morning, or at dusk, Hares reproduce throughout the year. The males are referred to as 'Jacks' and the females, 'Jills'. Young Hares are called 'Leverets' and are born into grass-lined nests built above ground, fully furred with their eyes wide open. Foxes, Cats, Hawks, Eagles and Owls predate Hares. If lucky enough to reach maturity, though, they are known live up to 10 years.

Easter is a sacred Christian holiday that combines traditional belief with untypical Christian practice. The term 'Easter' sprang from the Scandinavian goddess *Oestra*; a moon goddess of spring and fecundity who was sometimes depicted as having the head of a Hare. The 'Easter Bunny' was inspired by the legend of Oestra's Hare; a symbol of fertility, renewal, and the return of spring said to lay the egg of new life in a hollow in the ground, thus announcing the rebirth of the New Year. So potent was Oestra's fertility, the derivative 'Oestrus' became the indicator of when an animal was in 'season', heat or rut. Spring, after all, is the season that most inspires all animals to mate, ensuring the longevity and fertility of their species. The menstrual cycle in women was once referred to as the 'Moon Flow', indicating the flow of blood released by the uterus after it has prepared for the implantation of an egg. It was observed that this fertile time often fell concurrently with the expanding full moon. Hindus believe the spots on the moon clearly form the shape of a Hare, which explains why Sanskrit describes the moon as being *cacin*, or 'marked with the Hare'. Superstition once ruled that women should not bother praying to God because God was deemed the 'God of Men'. Instead, it was considered fitting for women to pray to their own heavenly body: the moon. Consequently, Hare Dreaming has come to suggest the art of 'drawing down the moon', a ritual used during the different phases of the moon to empower and unite one's feminine essence with the Goddess. Although the moon goes through several phases as it traverses the lunar sky, only the three 'main' phases are celebrated: the new or waxing moon, the full moon and the waning moon. The waxing moon is said to embody the qualities of the 'maiden', or the young girl who has not yet experienced her first moon flow. The full moon is said to represent the 'mother' with a full, round belly; the woman as she prepares to give birth to new life and potential. The waning moon describes the 'crone', or the time later in life when our experience is sought as wisdom or when we are preparing for our soul to pass to the Underworld. During the new moon, prayers should focus on issues associated with inspiration, bravery, change, improving health, career and job prospects, patience, love and romance. The full moon should be celebrated as a time to focus on our children's potential, decision-making, self-empowerment, healing and dreams. It is a powerful cleansing time and a time to welcome new beginnings. The waning moon is a time of ritualistic 'death', surrender and release. As the moon decreases in size and power, so too do our addictions, stresses, weaknesses and level of victim mentality. The waning moon is an ideal time to address and resolve issues related to divorce, poor health, change, perceived obstacles and limitation, fights and arguments, legal issues, separation and the residual effects of theft and abuse. It is a powerful time best suited to deliberation, meditation and introspection in an attempt to regain clarity and understanding. Hare governs the feminine aspects of intuition, esoteric knowledge, wisdom, higher learning, especially if its power is harnessed and channelled productively. Hare Dreaming represents the greater balancing force that cradles and nurtures the perceived world. It personifies the mysterious or unconscious energy that provides the fertile basis on which creative events occur. It also represents the dormant potential just waiting for the active (physical or masculine) principle to bring things to fruition.

Mouse
Scrutiny

'Mouse' is the common name for any small member of the rodent family although it has no exact meaning in classification terms. Mice are prolific the world over, usually found inhabiting fields, barns, granaries and human dwellings. Nocturnal by nature, Mice run swiftly, are good climbers and jumpers and are adept swimmers. They have excellent vision and hearing and a keen sense of smell. They also use their whiskers to feel air movements, thus detecting predators long before they are physically present. Australia has several native species of Mouse, although none are considered pests or vermin like the European House Mouse. Australia's native species include the Spinifex Hopping Mouse, Mitchell's Hopping Mouse, Western Chestnut Mouse, the Fawn and Dusky Hopping Mouse, Silky Mouse, Kakadu Pebble-Mound Mouse, Sandy Inland Mouse, Kimberley Mouse and the New Holland Mouse.

The people of medieval Europe believed that when someone died, their souls took the form of a Mouse. It was assumed that the soul, as a Mouse, exited the body via the mouth and that white Mice personified the souls of children. They also believed that Mice could plant reincarnated souls back into the bellies of women, placing them in the womb to await re-conception and eventual rebirth.

Mouse Dreaming not only promises new beginnings and rebirth, it can also be invoked to help tie up loose ends and initiate fruitful progression on all levels. A legend once told of a Mouse that offered to free an ensnared Lion that was hopelessly fastened with rope bindings. The Lion initially scoffed at the Mouse's timid offer of assistance, suggesting that if a mighty and brave Lion could not break the bindings, then how could a Mouse expect to do any better? The Mouse insisted and, little by little, gnawed through the bindings and eventually set the Lion free. The story reminds us that we can achieve great things if we look at all situations from varying vantage points, taking one step at a time and checking our progress regularly. With Mouse as a mentor, even those who seemingly wield minimal influence in the world, therefore, can achieve some degree of prominence if they believe and hold greater expectations for themselves. It demonstrates that sometimes strength of mind prevails over strength of body, with most of the answers we seek hidden in how we perceive the problem. Mouse also speaks of vigilance and scrutiny. Mouse is always careful not to overlook any small detail that may eventually come back to haunt him. He remains ever aware that he may, should he ever let his guard down, someday feel the searing pain of Owl's talons in his back. Mouse relies on his keen sense of smell to test the air for danger. Mouse Dreaming encourages us to check our options, and then to check them again, before assuming that all is safe and sound, particularly when signing agreements or contracts or when considering new projects, proposals or ventures involving other parties. Although it is admirable to have the ability to look at the world through the eyes of the Hawk, so as to see the bigger picture in all that we do, Mouse Dreaming reminds us to always be vigilant with the smaller or subtler aspects first and to check for pitfalls or hidden opportunities before rushing into anything. Mouse promises that when we embrace scrutiny as a quality, we will never again overlook the obvious.

Rabbit
Fertility

Endearing mammals with fluffy tails, large hind legs, long, erect ears and big, dark eyes, European Rabbits were introduced into Australia in 1788 as a familiar source of meat for the early settlers. They reproduced quickly and today over 200 million Rabbits run wild, aggressively competing for food and environments traditionally reserved for native species. Nature compensates the Rabbit for being one of the most popular prey animals among all carnivores (including Dingos, Cats, Owls, Hawks and Eagles) by gifting it with rampant fertility: a single female can produce as many as thirty offspring a year, for example, with each of them reaching sexual maturity at barely ten months of age.

Rabbit embodies nature's ever-changing cycles of growth; life, death and rebirth. Championing the cyclic journey that is new life in the Spring, energy and vitality in Summer; the inward contemplation of Autumn and the wisdom and maturity of Winter, Rabbit Dreaming echoes the splendour and awe of seasonal change. It keeps us in touch with the great circle of life and the natural harmony that exists in all things of nature. It is an ancient understanding that rings true for many that when we acknowledge our relationship to all things, the Web of Life is honoured and balance is re-established. As the children of the Earth Mother, when we honour the ebbs and flows of nature, we find that we are often rewarded with her fertility and her desire to see us live abundant, loving lives. To give to the Earth Mother by walking with her (instead of simply on her), the quality of our lives deepens, with all ventures embarked on prospering beyond our wildest dreams. To walk gently on the Earth, with reverence in our heart and with respect for all other things, will see our wants and needs nurtured by Spirit and our life become more fertile, abundant and free of obstacles. When we choose to consciously walk in harmony with the world around us, we become one with it. Rabbit Dreaming helps us notice nature's portents and the cycles of change within ourselves, on a physical, spiritual and emotional level. It helps us notice the subtle internal changes that take place when we start to view our body as a sacred thing; a temple, a representation of Spirit and a way of acknowledging the miracle of life. Taken to heart, Rabbit Dreaming ensures that our lives become more aware, fertile and abundant with ease, joy and glory. All that is required from us is dedication, empathy, passion and a willingness to embrace the sacred in all things.

Rat

Restlessness

Rats are both feared and loathed the world over as bringers of disease, death, filth and decay. The Brown Rat, or House Rat, is found in most human populated areas. They breed rapidly, producing up to a dozen offspring four or five times a year. At the age of 11 weeks, the offspring is sexually mature. Black Rats, also known as Ship Rats, can produce as many litters as the Brown Rat, but their offspring don't reach sexual maturity until the age of four months. Rats have soft, smooth fur, sharp snouts, beady black eyes, large round ears and long, scaly tails. They often nest in trees and in burrows, basements and sewers. Nocturnal by nature, Rats are opportunist feeders – they eat almost anything. They are adept at running, climbing, jumping and swimming. Rats first came to Australia as stowaways on the European convict ships, exiting via the ropes that secured the ships in port. It is said that when a ship is about to sink, any Rats that may have stowed away onboard prior to departure by running up the ropes securing it in port, will make their way to the highest point before leaping overboard long before the ship shows obvious signs of going down.

Rats seem to have an instinctive ability to know when things are going wrong and, as demonstrated in the movie 'Titanic', for example, will quickly evacuate a threatened area long before their suspicions are realised. Symbollically, the Titanic could be deemed a metaphor of our need for security; the iceberg as unexpressed, cold, resentful, hurtful emotion; the ocean itself the emotional pool of life that torments and tests us each and every day, while the Rats, shown running up the halls en-route to the main deck, were the subtle omens of change, forewarning impending fate. Rats are survivors and will do what it takes to ensure their endurance. When consulted as guides, they provide powerful strategies for us to do the same. In times of upheaval, confusion or breakdown, Rats offer suggestion of what evasive action could be taken, when and how. In regards to relationships, for example, Rat Dreaming suggests we act upon ill feelings and difficulty the moment we suspect something is wrong. It calls for us to air our concerns and make decisions that serve and protect our wellbeing. Instead of suppressing our feelings or freezing up emotionally in the hope that things will miraculously sort themselves out, Rat helps us decide if our interests would be better served by staying 'aboard' in an attempt to work things out, or by devising an escape route, packing our stuff and 'jumping ship' before the waters become even more turbulent. The decision is always ours of course, to either allow the ship to sink by leaving the relationship for good, or doing what we can to formulate positive, lasting change within the relationship by sending out help signals and offering a reconciling life raft to our other half. It may be of interest to learn that the Native Rat is an animal and totem of great importance to some Indigenous People of Australia. According to the ways of a small number of tribes, a 'Rat' person must only marry an individual from an 'Emu' tribe. With this in mind, if Rat is calling to you at this time, it may be useful to investigate the Dreaming of the Emu after reading about what Rat has to say.

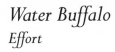

Water Buffalo
Effort

Broad hooves and short legs make the Asian Water Buffalo ideally suited to muddy and swampy habitats. Having insufficient sweat glands, it is necessary for them to wallow in pools of water or mud in order to keep cool. When they wallow, Water Buffalo submerge their entire bodies, leaving only their nostrils exposed. Such a habit also helps rid them of parasites. The Water Buffalo was brought to Australia from Indonesia in the 1820s as a marketable source of rich meat. The bottom soon dropped out of the market, however, and many Water Buffalo were relinquished to the wild. An environmental disaster for the wetlands of northern Australia, their wallowing habits have proven so detrimental to native flora that a major culling program was implemented. Populations have since been reduced to manageable levels thanks to licensed feral trackers.

The village farmers of southern Asia have long employed the docile Water Buffalo as a beast of burden. Easily domesticated, Water Buffalo are frequently seen being worked by children as young as six years old in the cultivation of rice paddies. Thought to have first been yoked around 4000 BC by the people of China, the Water Buffalo has grown to understand its sacred role and, as a result, honours servitude as its Dreaming. A tale from Rudyard Kipling's collection of 'Just So Stories' speaks of a time when the world was new and the animals had just started working for humans. According to the fable, there were four animals that took the role of 'servant' to man: the Dog, Horse, Camel and Buffalo. Each knew its job and each fulfilled its function without question. The Buffalo was yoked and fitted with a plough that it pulled back and forth all day long, harrowing the paddocks and tilling the fields without question. The Camel, however, balked at such hard labour and resisted domestication. With the help of the others, it was the Buffalo who showed the Camel the error of its ways ... and it has continued to honour this responsibility ever since. Its efforts have not gone unnoticed, either, with people from many cultures realising that without the Buffalo they would not be able to sustain the lifestyle required to productively support their communities. In many traditions, the Buffalo has been rewarded with protection and varying degrees of sacredness in honour and respect for its stamina and endeavour. Buffalo demonstrates that embracing demanding employ will eventually lead to reward – for the self and others. Through its Dreaming, the Buffalo offers strength of resolve to better understand the sacredness of hard work and reminds us that without dedication and effort, we cannot expect to advance on any level.

introduced / domesticated mammals

Alpaca and Llama
Offerings

The Alpaca is one of two domesticated animals of South America derived from the wild Guanaco. The other is the Llama. Alpacas and Llamas are herded in large flocks: the Alpaca for its fleece, from which blankets and ponchos are woven, and the Llama as a beast of burden. First domesticated over 5000 years ago, Alpaca fleece was once considered so fine that it was reserved solely for Incan royalty. Alpaca is native to the central Peruvian and Bolivian Andes. A close relative of the Camel, Guanaco and Vicuña, Alpacas and Llamas resemble large sheep, but have long necks, handsome heads and relatively long legs. Like all members of their family, Alpacas and Llamas spit when they are annoyed or feel threatened. Alpacas were first introduced to Australia (New South Wales) in 1858 aboard the 'Salvadora' under the care of Charles Ledger. The 250-strong flock also included Llamas and Vicuñas. Today, there are over 40,000 Alpacas in Australia, with the economic outlook for fibre sales improving each year.

The offerings made by these animals to the people are many. Physically, the Llama provides its endurance and strength while the Alpaca gives of its fleece and protection. The outwardly gentle and servile Alpaca has an inbuilt hatred and 'no fear' attitude toward Dogs and Foxes. Alpaca are known to run down, trample and kill predatory animals that trespass, making it a powerful guardian of other domestic animals such as Goats and Sheep especially during birthing time. There is an ancient belief that says the souls of the dead often enter and reside within Alpacas and Llamas, especially white Llamas which are considered the most sacred. But even this is not their most sacred gift. To this day, Alpacas and Llamas relinquish their unborn young to the people of their homeland so that they may, in turn, be surrendered as soothing gifts to the gods. Their foetuses are gathered, dried and sold in markets, to be buried under the foundations of new buildings to ensure their stability and longevity. It is indeed a powerful Dreaming that provides compassion and understanding enough for one to, on one hand, yield something as sacred as her own progeny for the higher good, while, on the other, vow selflessly to protect the brood of others. Through experience, the Alpaca has come to realise that in offering something of great personal worth, of a sacredness that cannot be compared, the rewards are usually great and equally as inconceivable. Because of the sacrifices the Alpaca readily makes with its fleece and its young, it has been rewarded with the role of protector, guardian and mentor to others, the provider of nourishment to many and the bringer of warmth to even more. To give selflessly with little or no thought of recompense is the message of these beautiful animals. To provide and share; to protect and shelter; to surrender and sacrifice; these are the lessons of the Alpaca and Llama, the totems of people who have experienced or witnessed the effects of extreme personal loss, but make it their mission to enrich or improve the lives of others nonetheless. Those who foster children, care for the sick and dying or who provide shelter and food for the homeless and abandoned (while often exacerbating their own disadvantage) carry the Dreaming of the Alpaca in their hearts and honour its essence by simply rising from bed each morning.

Cat
Sexual Healing and Protection

The Domestic Cat is a direct ancestor of the African Wild Cat, an animal first domesticated over 3,500 years ago by the Ancient Egyptians. Cats are skilled predators, indiscriminately stalking a very wide range of prey including small mammals, birds, eggs, insects and reptiles. They have retractable claws and sharp teeth, used for grabbing, holding and tearing the flesh of their prey. Cats have been in Australia ever since European settlement, although there is speculation that they may have arrived with the Dutch (after being shipwrecked) in the 17th Century.

Cat Dreaming encourages us to honour our sense of sensuality, self-worth and inherent self-love, and to see ourselves worthy of new beginnings, creation and rebirth. Powerfully sensual, self-confident and aloof, Cat Dreaming can be invoked as a powerful form of sexual healing and protection. As the designated guardian of the female sexual region and the root or base chakra, the Cat is often referred to as the 'Pussy' Cat, a slang term, often considered vulgar, that figuratively links the animal to the archaic 'yoni' symbol, the vulva, the place of origins and the ultimate representation of primed fertility. Cat Dreaming (particularly Black Cat Dreaming) dares us to question if we have a sexual issue that requires attention. Are you tempting fate by participating in unprotected sex? Have you had a miscarriage that has not been fully dealt with emotionally, or is it fast approaching the anniversary of a termination that has not been honoured with suitable grieving or counselling? Is there a sexual issue, trauma or interference left unaddressed or not yet fully integrated? Black Cat Dreaming affords the strength and self-empowerment to confront sexual issues face on and to do what needs to be done to reclaim a sense of peace and self-worth. Cat Dreaming provides a voice that is guaranteed to be heard; a voice that will both attract the attention of qualified support and ward off and expose the unwanted advances of 'Stray Toms' who harass, taunt and abuse their position and sexual power. The spirit of domestic Cats of other hues can be invoked for their equally as powerful protective qualities, too. The Ginger Cat, for example, is the totem of those (usually male) who have known trouble with authority figures as youths, but who are now destined for law-based, social work or counselling careers. White Cats protect the usually female, and generally only temporary 'home angel, street devil' types; those who are perfect angels around the home, but seem to 'shape shift' after dark; the type who help around the home with mundane chores, care of siblings and organisational responsibilities, but who yearn to experience life outside the confines of home and the restrictions of expectation. A quick change of clothes and a silent exit through the bedroom window, for example, will often see the White Cat transform from an 'angel' into a street-wise wild child who knows no boundaries. Tabby Cat helps us strip away our exterior persona — that veneered part of ourselves that has been practised and rehearsed for years with the intention of hiding who we truly are. She calls for us to speak from the heart and to expose the forces and influences that would prefer we remain compliant and pliable. Toppling a façade of sorts, Tabby Cat dares us to reveal our true face and our core essence, to return to our authentic selves and let our 'wild nature' show. As long as the Cat walks with us, protection, maturity and rebirth is assured. The path ahead remains full of fertile promise and potent opportunity as Cat Dreaming offers support enough to fulfil any goal, heal any issue and bring any dream to fruition.

Cattle
Nourishment

The term 'cattle' describes any domesticated herbivorous even-toed, hoofed mammal of the family Bovidae. Cattle were first domesticated around 6000 BC. Most contemporary breeds of beef and dairy cattle, particularly the more 'ancient' kinds (those characterized by shoulder humps or low-hanging dewlaps) originated in India. Australia's export-quality beef was originally birthed from Britain's strongest breeds of cattle, introduced by the first settlers. Today, the beef industry is dominated by breeds such as the Devon and South Devon, the Simmental, the Charolais, Galloway, Murray Grey, Tasmanian Grey and the Chianina; the Hereford and Poll Hereford, the Angus and Red Angus, the Red Poll, Brahman, Santa Gertrudis and the mighty Droughtmaster. Cattle have four chambered stomachs, a decreased number of teeth (compared with other herbivorous mammals), with no upper incisors. Most breeds also have horns that are not shed after the breeding season. Cattle are distributed throughout the world.

Bull - *Potency*

In Celtic history, the number of Cattle an individual owned indicated his family's level of wealth. The Bull, in particular, was venerated as a symbol of wealth, authority, success and productiveness. A symbol of prosperity, the Bull featured prominently on early Celtic coins. To this day, the phrase 'a Bull Market' describes a compelling and quickly rising stock market. Celtic Warriors, to be considered brave and strong, needed to personify the strength and endurance of the Bull, especially the White Bull that, as the most sacred, was ritually sacrificed to emphasise the point. When the time approached for a new King to be inaugurated, for example, a White Bull would be slaughtered to determine who would win the crown and when. To divine the man to be inducted, a High Druid Priest would perform a sacred ritual that involved drinking the blood of the butchered animal, eating its raw flesh and then retiring for the night swathed in its blood-soaked hide. The future King was said to appear in the Druid Priest's dreams, thus confirming who was to be crowned. The White Bull represented the Sun and was held sacred as a symbol of new life. The Cow, meanwhile, was said to embody the nurturing qualities of the Goddess and the Earth Mother herself. Over the millennia, the Bull has continued to grow as a powerful symbol of wealth and influence. Bull Dreaming calls for hard work, dedication and endurance: qualities that promise achievement, success and a long, fruitful life. Bull Dreaming espouses taking our time and not rushing at things like a 'Bull at a gate', or bustling through life like a 'Bull in a china shop', because when progress is ill-managed, the results often prove disastrous. It instead favours the quieter, more exacting 'one step at a time' approach to cement true advantage. Bull Dreaming instils steadfast determination to achieve any goal. Often perceived as being stubborn and inflexible, Bull inspires us to live life to the fullest, but warns against becoming self-destructive, self-indulgent or driven by desire and greed. Bull people have strong personalities, but grow to become mature, stable and awe-inspiring leaders when their positive qualities are nurtured.

Cow - Motherhood

The Cow, long reputed as a lunar-influenced creature, is a celestial beast that exemplifies the nurturing qualities of both the Moon and Mother Earth. Also carrying deep association with the Mother Goddess in her many guises, the Cow literally acts as 'wet-nurse' to humanity, and has done so for thousands of years. Ancient legend honours the Cow as the personification of the Great Goddess who birthed the Earth or whose milk flowed as the four primordial rivers nourishing ancient man (exemplified by the fact that a Cow's udder has four teats and the notion that the Milky Way constellation was born from the udder of Isis-Hathor). Cow's milk has been portrayed as life-giving by many traditions, with some cultures labelling the Cow itself as sacred, never to be slaughtered while others observe it as giving readily of itself, demanding very little in return. Cow offers the horn of plenty to those who embrace its wisdom, along with the gifts of fertility and sustenance. It embodies what it means to be a mother: the giver of life, caregiver and protector of children. Cow Dreaming prompts you to rate the relationship you currently share with your mother and the influence she has had on your self-image and view of the world. It initiates healing that must take place between you and your mother if you are to grow as a person, its healing best centred on issues from childhood that have perhaps left you feeling confused, abused or forsaken. It offers permission to review the effectiveness of your mother's role and, when relevant, your own role as a mother. Cow, by nurturing us, fosters both our mother and children in chorus. It releases us from the cyclical roller coaster of past and future 'mother issues' and their associated emotional burdens, unproductive parenting patterns and the fruitless maternal programs that hinder our personal growth and development. When we rid ourselves of limiting 'mother issues', we effectively pull them like redundant files from our personal history, thus removing them on a genetic level from our children's personal history, too, freeing them forever.

Dog
Loyalty

The Dog was the first to strike an agreement with man offering its protection, warmth, loyalty and companionship in Asia, around 150000 BC. They are highly social, pack-oriented creatures that, by human standards, are colour blind, because of the flatness of their lenses, which limits the degree of detail they can see – despite the fact that most breeds have a greater field of vision than any human. Apart from having excellent vision, they can also detect very low frequency sounds and can quickly and accurately pinpoint the exact source of any noise. Not only that, but Dogs also excel in detecting scent. They can distinguish two different types of scent: a subtle air scent left wafting by something recently passed by, and a more noticeable ground scent that lingers for a more substantial period of time. Dogs have played a major role in Australian history as companion animals, Sheep and Cattle herders, police and guard Dogs and guides for the blind. They also helped the first settlers as protectors against the understandably curious and angry Aboriginal people of the time.

As a demonstration of loyalty in its purest form, Dog embodies unconditional love, faith and tolerance. Treating a Dog with respect and commitment will see it return that love and devotion ten-fold – if not more. Stories abound of Dogs that have dragged their people from burning houses, Dogs that have located lost skiers buried deep under heavy snow or that have travelled great distances against insurmountable odds to return home to their family. Such is the loyalty of the Dog. It doesn't seem to matter how badly a Dog is treated or neglected, their love remains firm, regardless. Or does it? While Dog strongly believes in loyalty, commitment and hierarchy, she also has faith in maintaining the integrity of our personal values and beliefs. On one hand, for example, she says that before you strive to do anything for yourself, the needs of your pack must first be considered while, on the other, she espouses allegiance to the self first and above all else – particularly when there are young ones involved. Dog nurtures the ability to forgive when appropriate, to accept imperfection and to maintain truth and loyalty toward others – but more importantly, she demands you treat yourself with the same level of respect. Dog will only take abuse for so long, you see, before it turns on its oppressor in order to regain power, protect itself and to retain integrity. Dog is a powerful teacher that inspires trust, love and acceptance – qualities that can only be harnessed in others when first established in and for the self. Dog Dreaming reminds you of the love you have surrounding you at any one given time; love that you may be taking for granted or that you believe is no longer there. Is your loyalty to another a bit one sided or no longer nurturing your needs? Are you sacrificing your true feelings for fear of being rejected? Is the loyalty in your relationship out of balance? Dog Dreaming reminds us to maintain the loyalty we have for ourselves as our prime objective, for without it we cannot expect loyalty or unconditional love to be returned to us in any form.

Donkey
Modesty

First domesticated in Egypt around 4000 BC, Donkeys are best known for their stubbornness. If the truth be told, though, Donkeys are not so much stubborn as they are intelligent. They are animals imbued with a strong sense of self-preservation. If a Donkey feels that something is not in its favour, for example, no amount of coercion will persuade it to do it. Although not as swift or regal looking as a Horse, a Donkey shows great stamina and is more economical to keep. Donkeys make ideal pets. They are demonstrative and gentle and are perfect for teaching children to ride. They were first brought to Australia as pack animals by the early explorers and the first settlers. Due to poor fencing, many escaped or were intentionally released. Donkeys now populate outback Australia in large feral herds.

Christianity deems the Donkey sacred, for the reason that Mary apparently rode one when in child with baby Jesus. Later, the gospels describe Jesus himself riding a White Donkey into Jerusalem (the day now celebrated as Palm Sunday); in recognition, the Donkey's shoulders were stained with the sign of the cross. Chaldean history records the Donkey as a symbol of life, death and rebirth; an animal that embodies acceptance, determination and humility. Supposedly stubborn and difficult to work with, the Donkey graciously accepts its role as a beast of burden and 'servant' to others. It submits to its fate, but fosters an inner yearning for personal achievement and respect. It plods discreetly through life, holding sacred a deep sense of resolution; a knowing that its loyalty and servitude will be compensated some day, if not by its owner, then perhaps by Spirit. It lives with moderate expectation for immediate change, for it knows with patience, faith and dedication, any goal can be reached. Donkey demonstrates that when we keep our goals realistic, and live within our means; when we seek to obtain only what we need and no more, we are often rewarded with more when the time is right. Donkey people are quiet achievers.

They are modest, reticent and avoid attention. They are happy to work under a boss, attracting favourable attention and recognition for their efforts. They know they are meant for greater things, but assume nothing. They remain focused on their employed role, offering it complete allegiance and promise. Donkey Dreaming assists in the creation of a dependable, productive life. It encourages us to listen to our inner voice, to work hard, and to spurn material greed and power lust. When approached with modesty, Donkey Dreaming has the very real potential to take us from the ordinary to the extraordinary.

Ferret (Polecat)
Instinct

Gamekeepers heavily persecuted wild Polecats during the 1800s and early 1900s, so much so they were almost wiped out as a species. Luckily, the hunting only lasted until they were no longer perceived as a threat to game stock. Over the subsequent years, wild Polecat numbers have gradually recovered. Polecats were originally domesticated in Europe (as 'Ferrets') as an effective hunting aide (they are flawlessly shaped to enter and flush rabbits from the most intricate of burrows), and today are kept as pets, despite their offensive odour. The bucks, in particular, release a strong, musky aroma from a scent gland at the base of the tail, especially when threatened, excited or during the mating season. Ferrets have long, willowy bodies, short legs and hirsute tails. Shakespeare was known to use the word 'Polecat' when referring to people of disagreeable nature. The French referred to them as the *poule chat*, which means 'Chicken Cat'. Despite the fact that they are infamous for killing Chickens, however, Polecats are not even vaguely related to Cats.

Naturally inquisitive, Ferret people have an uncontrollable propensity to delve, probe, explore and hunt for information. They love to ask questions, find answers, solve problems and gossip. They have difficulty leaving well alone, instead insisting on 'ferreting' for answers that may or may not be there. Despite the risk of discovering little or nothing in their quest, they push on, believing themselves to be close to unearthing hidden truths. When we 'ferret' for information – search with enthusiasm and blind conviction – we sometimes reveal paltry reward or, worse still, nothing at all. The tendency to push toward something or to strive to achieve a goal prematurely is called '*away-toward*', meaning that which we are working toward is being pushed further away … and out of reach. Ferret asks that we refrain from searching for the truth, resist asking probing questions and avoid seeking the counsel of others when we sense that something is wrong. Ferret teaches us to avoid 'away-towards' by encouraging aloofness, silence and watchfulness as effective alternatives. It espouses sitting still, watching and waiting with patience and clarity, so that all things hidden may be revealed in the most appropriate and beneficial moment. When we do this, the things we seek are usually found earlier (and more easily) than expected.

Goat
Determination

Goats were first domesticated between 6000 and 7000 BC with many of the contemporary breeds believed to have originated from the ancient Bezoar Goat. Goats revert back to their wild state with very little effort. Goats are farmed commercially for their milk, cheese, meat, fleece (namely mohair and cashmere) and leather the world over, and very easily, too, because of their adaptability. Goats thrive in areas unsuitable for most other stock animals. Browsers rather than grazers, Goats feed on bushes, trees, desert scrub and aromatic herbs. As such, they are sometimes kept as a way of combating bush land and weeds that threaten the integrity of pasture. Brought to Australia with the First Fleet in 1788, feral Goats are found in most states.

They are harmful to the environment, affecting the native animals and vegetation.

Although the Wild Goat portrayed in the Old Testament was probably an Ibex (an animal similarly confused with the Gazelle and Antelope), it was considered a dignified creature of good conduct and' moral attitude when leading its own kind. When seen with Sheep, however, it symbolised immorality, freedom and infidelity. Universally, the male, or 'Billy' Goat, has become a symbol of masculine virility and creative potency, while the female 'Nanny' Goat has long embodied feminine fertility and abundance. Pan, the half-man/half-Goat fertility God of Greek mythology (sometimes depicted with an erect penis), personifies the potency of the Goat's fecundity, as do creatures of equally fabulous ilk: satyrs, fawns and pookas. When negatively directing their potential, Goat people are typically followers who inconsequentially indulge themselves in shameless activity. They may drink to excess, for example, partake in illicit drugs, boast about their sexual conquests and forcefully exact their sexual wants and desires. They play harmful practical jokes, amuse themselves with cruel taunts and activities that frighten others (reckless driving, for example) and often adopt irrational or unreasonable attitudes regarding the environment and the world as a whole. When demonstrating their positive traits, however, Goat people are gentle and loving. They have an inherent love of animals, plants, the waterways, mountains and nature. They are demonstrative, funny and sensitive. Goat people are often described as being the 'Salt of the Earth', grounded and sound. As well as its fertile creative potential, Goat Dreaming represents survival instinct, determination and the quest for advanced knowledge. It epitomizes drive and the determination to push to greater heights. It encourages us to set ourselves free of unreasonable expectation and bondage of any sort. This is why Goats are never satisfied to remain on their side of the fence or to eat only that which their tether allows them to reach. Instead, they constantly strive to obtain things seemingly out of reach. It should be remembered that never being satisfied with the things we have can lead to greed and discontent, while demonstrating a balanced sense of ambition leads to productivity and success.

Guinea Pig
Motivation

Known more as a laboratory creature than a wild animal, the Guinea Pig, or *Cavy*, was first domesticated over 6000 years ago as a source of meat and as an animal of offering during ritual and ceremony. With a captive life span of about eight years, the strictly vegetarian Guinea Pig has become a much loved pet in many households the world over (including Australia) due to its unassuming nature, minimal needs and its wide variety of colours and hair lengths. With four toes on the forefeet, three on the rear and no tail to speak of, flaccid ears and a snub nose, the Guinea Pig is an endearing animal. Guinea Pigs are easily housed, rarely jump, bite or scratch and are not known for their burrowing abilities: these traits having been bred out over decades of domestication.

The term 'guinea pig' has come to describe someone whose job it is to trial new ideas, skills or products, or someone unafraid to experiment in order to find answers to a problem. For example, one might say, 'I used my good friend as a guinea pig for a new recipe', or 'He volunteered to act as guinea pig for a groundbreaking new treatment'. As such, Guinea Pig Dreaming offers its wisdom as a guiding light, a beacon that illuminates the road to new discovery. The Guinea Pig is the test pilot that leads the way to the innovation of new forms of healing, medicine and scientific exploration. Guinea Pig people themselves are driven by discovery. They are passionate about helping people and find great joy in helping find *better* ways to help people. Despite unexpected setbacks, obstacles and sceptical criticism from those around them, they push forward in their quest to unearth new discoveries. Few truly understand the motives that drive the Guinea Pig person, but all are amazed and grateful for the fruits of their labour. A guide that lights the way, the Guinea Pig metaphorically channels new information, giving selflessly to benefit the people. Guinea Pig Dreaming primes us for new discovery, a surprise suggestion or new idea, the investigation of an alternative form of healing, medicine or health treatment or an offer to participate in some innovative study that promises to enhance the planet.

Horse
Personal Power

Since the beginning of time, no single animal has afforded mankind the gift of physical freedom as the Horse. As a means of transport, Horses proved to be worth their weight in gold whether pulling a carriage, chariot, Horse-drawn boat, stagecoach, tram or plough. Over time, however, the Horse has gradually been abandoned for the convenience of the automobile. They are still kept for leisure, sports and entertainment. Wild Horses run free in many parts of the world, either as a native species or a 'feral' breed. Australia, for example, is famous for the Brumby, a resilient 'wild' horse of inconsistent size, conformation, color and mixed type. The Brumby is a derivation of the domestic Horse brought to Australia during European settlement. Over time, many of these Horses were intentionally released or escaped due to poor fencing and gathered in wild herds.

When first introduced, Horse strengthened and deepened the people's view of the world. It afforded them greater understanding of the land because it allowed them to explore the horizon on a level never known before. With obvious links to movement and travel, Horse sanctioned the exploration and conquering of the physical setting, the breaking of boundaries and the expansion of territory. In similar fashion, Horse Dreaming embraces the essence of Personal Power and what it means to spiritually journey within in search of inherent wisdom. Personal Power represents the wealth of knowledge one may accumulate over a lifetime of experience which, when honoured, shifts us from the mundane and familiar into a world of unlimited potential. Traditionally a Horse stands at each of the four cardinal points on the great Wheel of Life, with the yellow Palomino protecting the East, the red Chestnut standing in the North, the black Horse guarding the West and the White or Dapple Grey representing the energies of the South. Each of the four directions offers a sacred gift of Power and a wealth of corresponding energetic wisdom. It is up to us to go out and seek this knowledge and, once found, integrate it into our life. Journeying to the East, for example, brings with it the gifts of illumination and introspection, while heading to the North inspires a healthy blend of innocence and passion. In the West we learn to understand the art of introspection and meditation, and in the South we are offered maturity and judgment. Horse prepares us for a journey of great Power. We all subconsciously know where our Personal Power lies, and as long as we instigate its search, we will ultimately find it – resulting in enhancement on all levels. Remember, all journeys start with a simple step forward, with any forward movement nurturing growth, and growth leading to development and enrichment. Promoting a sense of complete freedom, the appearance of Horse suggests travel of all kinds, both inner and outward; emotionally, physically and spiritually.

Pig / Hog
The Underworld

The term 'Boar' traditionally describes a mature male Hog. A 'Sow' is a female that has born young, while 'Gilt' refers to a female that hasn't. The term 'Pig' refers to an unweaned baby; a 'Piglet' is a very young animal, while 'Shoat' refers to the same animal after it has been weaned. Collectively, they are known as 'Hogs' when domesticated, and 'Boars' or 'Razorbacks' when in their wild or 'feral' state respectively. All 23 subspecies of Hog originated from the Eurasian Wild Boar. With ancestry dating back to the Ice Age, Boars were first domesticated about 7000 years ago. Wild Boars are strong and sinewy, with compact bodies, wide, prominent shoulders and long, narrow heads. Boars have prominent, outward jutting blade-sharp tusks capable of fatally slicing open an enemy's stomach. Domestic Hogs were first brought to Australia with European settlement. Often permitted to roam unattended, they were a familiar food source. During the 19th Century, they were taken to other settlements, but due to inferior enclosures and deliberate release, feral populations soon established themselves in the Outback.

According to Celtic myth, the Black Sow is indicative of the Goddess in her Crone phase and the chapter of life that constitutes the wisdom and maturity that comes with old age. An animal said to embody the mystical journey that culminates in the divine death of the familiar sacred self, the Black Sow, as the one that guards the way to the Underworld, represents the unequivocal ending that must be endured before one can experience regeneration of any sort. Put simply, Sow Dreaming indicates the ending of a cycle: the completion of one phase so that another may begin, such as the transition of maiden to mother and mother to crone. Piglets often herald the 'buds' of new growth, or the beginning of a new cycle. Imbued with fertility and the power to cause new beginnings on any level, Piglets can symbolise an unexpected pregnancy or issues centred on children. Just as the Sow represents the cycles of nature and the acumen, power and fecundity of the Goddess, so too can the Boar. To hunt the Boar, for example, was a sign of courage and honour, for only a warrior of brave and noble heart would dare confront such a ferocious creature (imagine shoulder bristles raised in rage; nostrils flared and tusks coated in foaming spittle), and expect to come away in one piece. The Boar epitomises the Warrior, Leader and Chief; the uncultivated, raw power that lies within each of us; energy that can be awakened in times of need. The Boar represents the hero archetype; hence the Boar-bristle crests that adorned the battle helmets of many a warrior. Twrch Trwyth was a Boar-King, for example, who wore a comb and scissors from his ears: Ogham symbols of knowledge and transformation, while the Goddess Freyja was said to ride the Golden-bristled Boar whose mane embodied the golden rays of the sun. The Boar was a symbol of Freyja's protection, too, proudly adorning the shields and weaponry of her soldiers. Hog affords strength of character, endurance and power to move forward in life. It tenders integrity and truth to our words, inspiring others to heed our advice and point of view. Its energy can be volatile, though, and wildly unpredictable. When invoking Hog energy, we must remember to keep a lid on our emotions and not let feelings of frustration or anger boil over. If we do, we may become very destructive, very quickly: our words and actions proving both detrimental and hurtful. To follow the Hog is symbolic of the journey we eventually take to the Underworld; to stalk our limitations and to overcome our obstacles and inherent fears. Hog Dreaming offers knowledge and transformation to those brave enough to face their inner demons and slay them with the determination befitting a true warrior.

Sheep
Conformity

Contemporary domestic Sheep are descendants of the earliest Moufflon, an ancient breed indigenous to Turkey and Iran. Sheep are grazing mammals bred commercially for their fleece and meat and are today found in nearly every country of the world. Australia, for example, is famous for its Merino Sheep, a breed created through selective crossbreeding. Sheep are famous for following the others in their flock without question. Birds will fly in formation, changing direction as a single entity. Sheep, however, simply follow the most dominant individual who happens to be in front. Their leadership is haphazard at best. Males are referred to as 'Rams', females as 'Ewes', while the young are called 'Lambs'.

Sheep Dreaming, in its positive phase, is reserved for those connected to their purpose; people who are stable, grounded and driven. Sheep people know endurance and steadfastness. Practical, sensible and reliable, they are pioneers imbued with determination enough to make groundbreaking discoveries, overcome obstacles and achieve on the grandest of levels. Sheep Dreaming warns against the danger of blindly following others, however, particularly when the example they set is questionable. It explains that when we follow someone driven by ego, confusion, anger, fear, malice or greed, we will eventually end up demonstrating a similar mindset. Before following in the footsteps of another, it is wise to first seek testimonials or endorsements from people who have experienced their attitude and behaviour or who have witnessed their effectiveness as a leader. Ask around, watch their actions, weigh up their motives; do what needs to be done to ensure they are what they claim to be – and then, based on this assessment, make your decision to either follow or not. Conforming to peer-group pressure, or being fooled by a veritable 'Wolf in Sheep's clothing', generally ends in deception and dishonour. To follow someone of questionable character, or a person deemed negative or wayward, will probably see you tarred with the same brush. Their reputation will become yours, by association alone. Following those who work with an honest, altruistic, team-based spirit, though, will see you succeed, reach ever-greater heights and surpass your previous best. Of course, to grow and prosper in life means we all, at times, must bow to some degree of conformity and expectation. So long as you don't compromise your values and beliefs, falling into line has its advantages – especially when tackled as 'team work' or perceived as being for the greater good. Sycophants, and those best described as unimaginative and indecisive, are destined always to be followers and never *true* leaders. Sheep Dreaming forewarns of the risks involved in shunning our personal path and of losing our sense of individuality. It offers legitimacy to those beliefs and values deemed untraditional or 'out there' by society and encourages us to march to the beat of our own drum. It validates personal wisdom sacred to our heart of hearts, and empowers us to stand our ground or to step out on our own. It helps us remember our soul essence and our potential. Sheep allows us to embrace a non-judgemental mind-set so that we might acknowledge the truth found in all values and beliefs, even when they differ or conflict with our own. It leads us back to a state of wholeness and stability, clarity and inner peace; the certainty that inherently supports our personal view of the world and our individuality.

THE KINGDOM
OF THE
WINGED ONES

In many cultures Birds are revered as embodiments of the Soul. Due to the simple fact that most species can fly is an indicator of why they are so often associated with the dearly departed, the Higher Realms and Spirit. They encourage us to strive for greater things and higher levels of awareness, while supporting us as we transcend all mundane obstacles.

native / indigenous / migratory birds

Albatross
Encumbrance

The word 'Albatross' comes from the Arabic *al-câdous* (meaning Gannet) which made its way into the English language via the Portuguese alcatraz. The Albatross is a large seabird with aerodynamically capable wings. The wingspan of the largest species of Albatross is the largest of any bird (exceeding 3.5 metres). Albatrosses travel great distances without needing to rest, maintaining endurance by riding the updrafts. They sustain energy and soar for extended periods with the help of a tendon that locks their wings when fully extended, minimising muscle expenditure. Depending on the species, Albatrosses feed by diving to depths of up to 12.5 metres, taking Crustaceans, Squid and Fish.

The Albatross has long been the subject of superstition, particularly among sea-faring folks. Many believe, for example, that if an Albatross is killed, its death will bring bad luck to the ship and all who sail upon her, while to have 'an Albatross around your neck' means to be plagued by constant bad luck. It is interesting to note, too, that from 1930 until the mid 1960s, America's foremost maximum-security prison was established on a rocky island known as Alcatraz. Alcatraz (named after the Albatross), became home to some of America's most irredeemable and feared prisoners. Today, though, Alcatraz is one of San Francisco's leading tourist attractions. Albatross Dreaming offers clarity, peace and a deeper appreciation of the issues that seem to hamper physical, spiritual and mental freedom. It allows those who embrace its wisdom to see life from a 'bigger picture' perspective by providing the endurance needed to soar with ease through even the most tumultuous periods in life, while affording forewarning of obstacles that further threaten to burden their load and impede progress. Albatross is quick to reward those determined to overcome their encumbrances with emotional and spiritual resilience and sacred understanding capable of lifting them to ever greater heights. Issues that cause deep concern, personal difficulty or impede our movements are dissuaded with the assistance of Albatross Dreaming. Albatross carries the burdensome and troublesome loads that tie us down and lock us in a continual state of lack. It helps build understanding of the karmic implications of being physically or mentally struck down by impediments of any kind. Albatross helps us appreciate and seek freedom; freedom from grief, pain and lack perceived as being caused by poor circumstance or 'bad luck'. It enables us to work constructively through all blockages by teaching us how to take responsibility for them. It helps us find reason for being, instead of denying our existence, blaming others and living a life as a prisoner locked in a self-induced cage. Denying the chance to be free of encumbrance is like willingly going through life with an 'Albatross strung about your neck'. As though providing the antidote to its own venom, Albatross Dreaming dissolves the illusion of 'bad luck' forever, while helping us better understand the Universal Law of Attraction; that you get what you think about because your thoughts literally shape your destiny. Albatross explains, however, that your emotions affect the speed and likelihood of attraction, because it really comes down to how you feel about the subject you are attempting to attract, and whether you regard yourself as worthy of receiving. So, Albatross asks, 'Unless you have healed your feelings of inadequacy and unworthiness, will you ever have the self-esteem to see yourself as worthy of receiving what the Universe has in store for you? Will you ever be truly ready to receive?' Interesting questions, aren't they?

Apostlebird
Sponsorship

Breathtaking landmarks sought out by those travelling the Great Ocean Road in Victoria, Australia's 'Twelve Apostles' are essentially giant rock stacks that rise majestically from the churning waters of the southern Ocean. Named after the Twelve Disciples of Jesus, who stood 'stone supportive' of the tidings preached by Him, the 'Twelve Apostles' strike an imposing sight as they proudly guard the coastline's limestone cliffs, which create a magnificent backdrop. There are about eighty references to the Greek word 'apostolos' in the New Testament, a word derived from the Greek verb 'apostello'. This verb means, 'to send with a particular purpose' and the noun, 'apostolos' means 'one who is sent with a particular purpose', or 'one commissioned'. Once erroneously thought to gather only in flocks of twelve (hence its name), the Apostlebird is a noisy, gregarious bird that partakes in dust baths to rid its body of parasitic mites. It is friendly toward the Chough, a bird that often shares its territory.

Apostle Birds are mud-nesters. Mud – a liquid or semi-liquid mixture of water and some combination of soil, silt and clay – carries archaic symbolic association with the nurturing, life-giving blood of Mother Earth. Tolerant of other birds, Apostlebirds are also named after the twelve alleged followers of Jesus. The apostles were sent to preach the Gospel, to inspire the people as leaders of revolutionary change, nurturing within them the story of Jesus who gave His blood so that humanity may know eternal life. Legitimised by its predilection for mud, therefore, Apostlebirds are said to demonstrate a powerful, caring character – archetypal of an apostle. Their Dreaming is both inspiring and supportive. It offers direction and a path to follow. Apostlebird heralds a fated dedication to a particular belief, charity or movement. It comes as a realisation – a bolt of illuminating light, a chorus of angels or a life-changing flash of knowing. Dedicating your life to a cause, belief or institution, either through spiritual devotion, personal involvement or financial sponsorship is to honour the message of the Apostlebird. Its ambition is to see us come together and walk as one, free of racism, sexism, terrorism and all the other 'isms' that divide, persecute and oppress. It calls for us to not only pray, but to act in a way that demonstrates responsibility and how to live an interconnected, charitable life.

Bellbird
Self-Esteem

The loud, high pitched, bell-like call of the Bellbird, or Bell Miner, is arguably one of the most beautiful; a sound that has inspired more poetry than that of any other Australian bird. Olive-green honeyeaters, Bellbirds live in groups and are often found nesting in the forks of trees growing along rivers and streams. Often hard to see among the branches, Bellbirds divert predators from their nest by flapping their wings and calling loudly, before dropping to the ground and continuing the act. Bellbirds are territorial and will readily scare other birds out of their territory. One reason is to protect the sugar-producing insects that live on eucalypt leaves. Unfortunately, such behavior tends to prohibit other birds that may feed on other parasitic insects, thus causing stress and dieback to the canopy trees of the area.

'The silver-voiced bell birds, the darlings of daytime!
They sing in September their songs of the May-time;
When shadows wax strong, and the thunder bolts hurtle,
They hide with their fear in the leaves of the myrtle;
When rain and the sunbeams shine mingled together,
They start up like fairies that follow fair weather;
And straightway the hues of their feathers unfolden
Are the green and the purple, the blue and the golden.'

- An extract from 'BELL-BIRDS' by Henry Kendall (1839 - 1882)

Bellbird requires us to take a long hard look at ourselves and see if we can't find something to be proud of. Those drawn to investigate Bellbird Dreaming often don't realise they have unique abilities or sacred gifts to share, let alone inherent beauty. Instead, they tend to view others with envy, while protecting themselves behind a veil of resentful indifference. The Bellbird celebrates self-love by reminding us that being ashamed of ourselves is destructive, limiting and completely unnecessary. The Bellbird may look plain, for example, but it has a beautiful voice. In fact, its song is renowned across the land. Beauty is available to all of us: it simply presents itself in unique ways to everyone. Some people radiate physical magnetism and charm, while others demonstrate their beauty in the form of song, dance or artistic ability. How we view ourselves is usually vastly different to the way others perceive us. Although viewed by some as being only skin deep, true beauty actually goes much deeper. True beauty resides at our core, and resonates from every pore when embraced in its most pure form. Bellbird encourages us to identify the things we are proud of; our talents, sense of inner-beauty, community spirit, and so on, and to radiate them from the heart. Make a list of your most positive traits, abilities and characteristics, and then ask others to list their perceptions of you in similar fashion … and share your findings. You may be pleasantly surprised to find they see you as being profoundly talented, physically beautiful or a devoted friend. How you perceive yourself and how you choose to radiate these feelings is simply a matter of self-esteem: a gift of knowledge embodied by the Dreaming of the Bellbird.

Bird of Paradise
Temptation

The Bird of Paradise, or Riflebird, inhabits the rainforests and woodlands of New Guinea and the wet eucalypt forests of Australia. They are famous for their exquisite plumage and flamboyant mating rituals. Weaving their nests from vine tendrils, rootlets and fine twigs, the female Riflebird has also been known, on occasion, to incorporate the discarded skins of Snakes into its nest design. Plucking ripe fruit from the plentiful rainforest vegetation, Riflebirds also stalk insects by probing the bark of the trees with their pointed beaks.

As if personifying the biblical story of Adam and Eve, including the infiltration of paradise by Persuasion in the guise of a Snake and the picking of enticing fruit, the Riflebird warns against making 'shot-gun' decisions, especially those triggered by temptation. Half-baked plans and ill-considered decisions generally end in disaster, with innocence nullified as a poor excuse. So many people find themselves in dire trouble when they arrogantly believe themselves above reproach or unlikely to have their questionable motives or actions exposed for what they are. It is a Universal fact that mistakes and accidents do not exist. Whenever we have an 'accident' for example, or make a 'mistake', we often mutter to ourselves directly afterward, 'I knew that would happen'. Without consciously realising it, we make the decision (moments before the event) to experience the accident or mistake. We literally agree to it. So, the next time you are persuaded by greed, envy or desire to do wrong or act against your inherent nature – don't. You will be found out. You will be caught. When you have to be tempted to do something you know you shouldn't, the warning bells are ringing. Paradise can be found by simply following your intended destiny. To want more than you have is natural, but make sure your intentions and deeds are wholesome when it comes to realising your wants, dreams and desires. Enticement is empowering and attraction is healthy, both afford the strength and self-belief to attain any goal. Creating your own personal nirvana by celebrating the dance of life and harnessing opportunity when it presents is what living a good, healthy life is all about – so long as you don't have to dance with the devil to accomplish it.

Black Swan
Grace

The Black Swan resembles the White Swan in shape, but is almost completely black, save for a splash of white on its wings, a red bill and striking red legs. They are relatively large waterfowl, weighing up to 6 kg (the males are generally larger than the females), with a wingspan of almost 2 metres. Black Swans have long necks, enabling them to reach deeper into the water than most other water birds in order to feed on aquatic vegetation. Unlike mammals that have only seven vertebrae in their neck, Swans have up to twenty, depending on the species. The Black Swan is the faunal state emblem of Western Australia.

Everyone knows the tale of The Ugly Duckling: a child's fable about an abandoned hatchling forced to endure ridicule and rejection, but who ultimately overcame adversity to become a beautiful Swan. The parable demonstrates that until you can look inside and find the innate beauty that resides there, you cannot expect anybody else to. When you look in the mirror and see infinite beauty looking back, however, others will also recognise true beauty (on all levels) when they look at you. Black Swan helps us realise inner beauty by returning us to a state of grace. Grace cannot be learned. It cannot be bought or given – it can only be found within. It must be remembered. Children inherently walk with grace. Grace is innocence and impeccability, doubled with a deep knowing and an unwavering sense of belonging; the knowledge of what true beauty is without having to advertise it. It represents what it means to feel comfortable in your own skin. Without inner beauty, peace and confidence, there is no grace. People who have looked deep within themselves, who have healed their past and reclaimed their inner child, know grace. Grace is the ability to walk through life, head held high with humility, pride and a balanced ego. Grace allows us to be strong, abundant and proud without being aloof, pompous or rude. Grace keeps us grounded and in touch with those less fortunate and those who have not yet reclaimed the knowledge. Black Swan prepares us to recognise our true essence and to trust the grace of our own being. Be prepared to see the golden potential in those around you as you relearn to unconditionally love yourself and radiate the inner beauty that is yearning to be heard. Prepare to awaken the grace that lays dormant. Allow yourself to access Spirit's gifts of self-empowerment so that you may finally learn to believe in yourself on all levels. Ready yourself to transform your sense of abandonment into Mystery so that others may be drawn to you in awe and wonderment instead of being turned away by fear and confusion. Allow your inner beauty to emerge and the world will applaud and shower you with reward. That is Black Swan's promise to you.

Bowerbird
Dowry

Found only in New Guinea and Australia, the male Bowerbird is famous for its bower – an arbour-like mating nest constructed from interwoven grasses, twigs, bark and rootlets. Looking more like a garden arch than a nest when complete, the bower is decorated with found objects of beauty; odds and ends gathered with passionate intent as decoys to attract and inspire a suitable mate. Satin Bowerbirds, for example, have a particular weakness for things coloured blue: blue pen lids, blue drinking straws, pieces of blue paper, blue clothes pegs and blue bottle tops. Essentially, any discarded or lost item can make its way into the Satin Bowerbird's nest, so long as it is coloured predominantly in an attractive shade of blue.

Expert pilferers, the Bowerbird raids outhouses and potting sheds, searching for its favoured plunder to take back to its bower. Identifying acquisitiveness as its main weakness, the Bowerbird validates its behaviour by proclaiming it a necessary facet of its Dreaming. It cleverly translates an obviously infatuated mind-set into sensible and realistic preparations for the future. If it were to ignore its innate desire to gather and collect, the male Bowerbird would have nothing to present to its prospective mate as a dowry. From the female Bowerbird's perspective, the male who collects the greatest amount of objects will ultimately prove to be the most suitable mate; the beauty of his bower signifying a superior level of determination, dedication and effort. As with all animals, potential mates are chosen depending on their deservedness and worthiness, with a belief that affirms, 'the stronger the mate, the stronger the offspring', ruling their final decision. Accumulation and contribution are Bowerbird's gifts to the people. Prudent observation of what is required while employing appropriate and constructive follow-up action is the message of the Bowerbird. It indicates that when you are readying for change of any sort, the trappings, information and resources required to ensure a successful and abundant future will be available. Bowerbird is making preparations for the next phase of your life; encouraging you to begin gathering together all that you need to nurture the transition and to honour the process with a sense of sacredness by rejecting avarice, self-indulgence and fear.

Brolga
Dance

Also known as the Crestless Australian Crane, the Brolga is a bird of the open country: marshland, paddocks, grasslands, swamps and the Australian 'billabong'. Laying two eggs but only ever hatching one, the Brolga builds a rough mound-like nest in shallow water or just at the water's edge. Brolgas are known for their complicated courtship rituals. The pair dance forming a bond that lasts a lifetime.

Spontaneous movement, inspired by a steady rhythmic sound and a receptive atmosphere, is an ancient yet simple way of opening oneself up to the productive cycles of Mother Earth and the nurturing energies of the Universe. The Brolga, as a solar influenced creature, was traditionally viewed as a symbol of power and righteousness and the bringer of sacred dance. Wild Brolgas incorporate movement and dance into their mating rituals, with the belief that if they dedicate themselves to Spirit and express who they are through dance, their mate will not only see their physical form, but also their heart of hearts and their worthiness as a mate and life partner. Many of us are told at an early age that we cannot dance and that we have no rhythm. As we grow we become afraid to express our true selves and we only dance in the privacy of our own homes for fear of being ridiculed. This is a typical way in which we as individuals become fragmented from who we truly are. If Brolga has danced into your life today, you are being shown that dance can be your bridge into other worlds. You are being reminded that sacred dance holds the potential to reconnect you to the Source being nurtured within your consciousness. Through dance, you can experience the unity of the Universe. When you feel pressured, no matter where you are, close your eyes and breathe, allowing your body to reconnect to the rhythm of the Earth Mother's heartbeat and the music orchestrated by the sounds of nature. Find the stillness and participate in the sacred dance of Creation on a level that does not interfere with your daily routine. Simply still your mind and celebrate the inner dance – the freedom of movement that comes with 'just being'. Feel the presence of Spirit. Feel the peace that comes with the wisdom and the ancient knowledge found within the internal dance as it permeates your body. This is your dance that connects you to the Ancients and the Ancestor Spirits of the land. Let Brolga show you how to tap into its power and allow it to shift you from the mundane to the extraordinary within your own life.

Brush Turkey
The People

The Brush Turkey inhabits dry scrub and open woodland, building a nest mound of sand and ground litter. Leaves and branches, twigs and bark are collected and scraped into a heap and, as the ground litter decomposes under the warmth from the sun, heat generated within the mound incubates the eggs. With a naked red head, fleshy yellow collar, yellow legs and black plumage, the Brush Turkey, (or the Scrub, Native or Bush Turkey) strikes an imposing sight as it wanders through the Australian bush. Ground-dwelling during the day, the Brush Turkey roosts in trees at night to avoid predators, such as feral Cats, Foxes, Dogs and Dingos.

Aboriginal artist, Harold Thomas, designed the Aboriginal Flag in 1971 as a striking, uniting emblem for the Aboriginal People and an insignia of their race and identity. The black panel represents unity of the Aboriginal People; the red honours the Earth Mother and the people's spiritual relationship to the land, while the yellow radiates the energy of the sun, as the giver of life. Aboriginals and Torres Strait Islanders adopted it as a national symbol of the people in 1972 after it had been raised outside the old Parliament House in Canberra. In 1994, the Australian Government initiated steps to give the flag legal recognition, and after public consultation, it was decreed as a 'Flag of Australia' under Section 5 of the Flags Act, 1953 and was so proclaimed by William Hayden on July 14, 1995. Similarly, with the way its dark plumage stands out so noticeably against the colour of its legs, collar and head, the Brush Turkey could easily be adopted nationally as the totemic symbol of the Aboriginal culture and their united spiritual self. As such, Brush Turkey Dreaming rouses curiosity to investigate ancestry, family tree and heritage. It is a call to return to your roots – the pure, ancient essence that surges through your veins. It is to find out who you truly are, why you are drawn to behave a certain way or inspired to live a particular lifestyle. To know your lineage is to reclaim aspects of your spirit, to remember your connection to the Earth Mother and to understand better your People's culture, customs and traditional values and beliefs. To reunite with your heritage is to feel entire, balanced, protected and part of a whole. It is to understand that we are not 'apart from' the Cosmos, but rather an essential part of it: a sacred thread in the Universal Tapestry. Brush Turkey Dreaming reconnects us with the Ancestors that protect, inspire and guide us, while reawakening our sense of tribal longing and community belonging.

Budgerigar
Experience

The Budgerigar, or the 'Australian Love Bird' (so named because of its habit of 'kissing' its mate or its own reflection in a mirror) is a small parakeet commonly kept as an ornamental cage or aviary bird both here in Australia and overseas because of its bright coloured plumage, cheerful disposition and its uncanny ability to mimic speech. In the wild, Budgerigars gather in flocks of thousands, nesting in tree hollows and rock crevices. Their call is unmistakeable. The easily recognisable seed-eating Budgerigar has, over generations of domestication, evolved from the natural green hue of the wild species to include a rainbow-array of colours including the traditional olive green as well as translucent lime, turquoise, indigo, sky blue, white and yellow.

No matter what the colour, Budgerigars embody the pure essence of unconditional love, affection, trust and companionship. They radiate acceptance, joy and spontaneity from their charming little hearts (often in excessive amounts), while merrily encouraging us to follow suit. From the moment they were first dreamed into being by the Ancestor Spirits, the green and gold plumage of the wild Budgerigar has come to reflect the vibrational properties of the heart and solar plexus chakras, as well as the colours that have come to represent the Australian Spirit. Pronounced 'shack-ra', a Sanskrit word meaning 'wheel' or 'disk', the chakra system embodies the seven main energy centres that maintain health and harmony within the human body. The heart charka, represented in some traditions as a green or pink lotus flower, symbolises the sincerest of human connections, acceptance and unconditional love, while the 'yellow' solar plexus chakra radiates our feelings, gut reactions and innate sense of knowing. Consequently, Budgerigar's Dreaming predicts a heightened sense of integration. It teaches us to embrace life more richly by making us more aware of the 'little things' that provide beauty, peace and harmony. By simply living in the present, Budgerigar effectively broadens our innate wisdom and learned knowledge, clarifies our life experiences, heals our past, grounds our world-view and street-wise eloquence, while deepening our sense of love, self-worth and our gratitude for those who share our life. For such a small, seemingly insignificant little bird, it is indeed a wise teacher.

Bush-Hen
Identity

The Bush-Hen (also known as the Moorhen, Crake or Rail) has dull muddy olive-brown plumage. Its bill, normally grey in colour, changes to green and develops an orange lobe during the mating season. With an expansive habitat that encompasses swamps, lagoons, creeks and dams, the Bush-Hen is also a familiar rainforest bird often seen patrolling the boundaries rather than the denser inner-regions.

The Bush-Hen is the totem of those who have known more than one identity, or have experienced many changes in residence, parent figures and friends. Its nurturing energy supports the gypsies, fringe dwellers and nomads among us, particularly those who don't fit in or feel as if they don't belong anywhere. Bush-Hen people yearn to assimilate. They yearn to be able to call their house a home, but because of an underdeveloped sense of identity (often forged by a lifetime of abuse, abandonment or neglect), they tend to avoid ever settling down in any one place or with any one person (not for long, anyway). Not really sure of who they are themselves, they have trouble opening up to people. They rarely initiate or foster new friendships or relationships for fear of becoming too emotionally involved – and of being hurt. Usually 'jacks of all trades, but masters of none', Bush-Hen people prefer to move freely from one job to the next. Shunning commitment and loyalty, they can be found backpacking across the country, seasonally picking fruit, sheering sheep and cutting hay. They are very adaptable, very chameleon-like in their approach to life, slipping easily and confidently into new towns and communities as if they have always been there. They are outwardly warm and welcoming, fun-loving and jovial but, the moment they get bored or close to someone new, they pack up and leave, often without warning. Bush-Hen People need to feel as if they are in control. They need to know they are in 'the driver's seat'. Although it usually takes a lot to make a Bush-Hen person feel welcome, needed and loved, it isn't impossible. They simply need to believe they are truly valued for who and what they are (despite their past) – an expectation that can take time and dedication to realise. Alternatively, Bush-Hen can indicate that a non-threatening, patient approach needs to be adopted when considering a new person, place or thing.

Bustard
Confidence

The Bustard (also known as the Plains or Wild Turkey) stands up to one metre tall and must run to gather speed before bursting into flight. It is usually silent, but will 'bark' when alarmed. The Bustard maintains a proud disposition by strolling slowly, regally holding its head high with bill uplifted. During courtship, males attract a mate by fanning their tails and distending their neck-sacs in full ritual display. Hatched directly onto the bare earth, Bustard chicks sit motionless when threatened.

Spirit is all that is. It is the life force found in all things. Spirit resides in the mountains, the trees, the rivers and the clouds, the birds, the insects, the stones, the plants and the four winds. Everything of Creation is a celebration of Spirit – including you and me. To know Spirit is to have unwavering confidence that we will be protected, nurtured and encouraged to live a prosperous life. To walk with Spirit is to know true abundance on all levels: healthy and happy children, meaningful relationships, a balanced life, a healthy body and a sound mind. When we recognise these things as being true abundance, Spirit welcomes more conventionally recognised forms of abundance to flow freely into our lives. The Bustard exhibits a proud faith in the belief that Spirit and Mother Earth will provide all that is needed to live an honest, protected and humble life. It demonstrates how to achieve a modest yet confident air fuelled by trust, stillness and a discreet approach to life. Bustard, does not suggest we strip ourselves of all earthly possessions in order to live a good life, though. It simply warns that to favour material things and the attainment of money is no guarantee of an abundant and happy life. Bustard wonders if you have stopped trusting your relationship with Spirit. Have you lost trust in your connection with the Earth Mother? Have you begun to see the accumulation of material things as being proof of your worthiness rather than the inherent connection you have with all things? Bustard is encouraging you to sit motionless, silent within yourself, and ask whether or not you feel confident that your life is leading you in the direction you had hoped. Are you able to hold your head up, with your face aimed directly at Spirit, and say for sure that your life is all that it was meant to be? Bustard asks that you focus on the wealth and abundance that you already have in your life and give thanks for them. Surrender your fears and limitations and offer gratitude to the Earth Mother and to Spirit for your wonderful life, and feel confident that you will soon know great wealth on all levels.

Butcherbird

Arrogance

Spread widely throughout Australia, there are four variations of Butcherbird: the black, pied, grey and black-backed. Butcherbirds, although blessed with a melodious call, are powerful, aggressive and ruthless predators. They attack small mammals, birds, reptiles or large insects with confidence. They will take hatchlings, too, as the terrified parents try in vain to distract their attention. Depending on the quarry and if not eaten immediately, the Butcherbird may hang its kill in the fork of a tree, reminiscent of the way a butcher will hang a Sheep or Pig carcass in the window of his shop. It proudly displays its handy-work as a mark of its competence, arrogantly returning at its leisure to feed.

The totem of the bully in its conceited phase and the defender of the persecuted in its positive, Butcherbird typically indicates an arrogant soul who gains strength from the violation of others. Petty tyrants and intimidators, people who carry the Butcherbird as their totem sometimes lash out in self-defence. They desperately hide their own lack of self-worth and vulnerability for fear of being exposed and labelled as weak. They typically lack confidence and self-esteem due to their diminutive size, history of abuse and oppression or a distinct lack of positive role modelling as a child. Butcherbird embodies those incapable of showing acceptance, compassion and love, or of offering constructive criticism and useful advice because of an apparent lacking in his or her own life. Be prepared, though, because bullies rarely retain their power for long. Butcherbird can similarly herald a time of retaliation and getting even. It warns that, if you are a bully, you can soon expect to be confronted and deposed. It proclaims a time of uprising during which, if you are the oppressed or tormented, your voice will be heard and justice will be served. Butcherbird Dreaming, when considered with a fair and honest heart, heralds a time of acknowledgement and, though often long overdue, an apology.

Buzzard
Refinement

A stocky raptorial bird of prey, the Buzzard hunts Rabbits, Lizards and smaller birds. Buzzards use small rocks to break open the eggs of larger birds to gain access to the unborn hatchling. Employing tools, although common among primates and Sea Otters, which use rocks to crack open mussels as they float on their back, is an anomaly among raptors, though it is believed that Buzzards inherently carry this skill and that it is not learned by watching others.

An ingenious bird, the Buzzard belongs to an elite band of beasts smart enough to use tools to make life easier. Buzzard encourages you to follow suit, but instead of working harder and longer, it guides you to work easier and smarter, thus gradually improving your current situation. What do you have at your disposal now, for example, that if realised, could improve your quality of life? What skills do you have? What knowledge do you hold? What interests do you enjoy? Consider these questions well...you may inherently carry the expertise required to dramatically change your life with very little effort. Buzzard asks, 'Why would you want to approach life like everyone else when you could draw on your interests and harness those skills to make things easier, varied and more enjoyable? Why would you want to work tirelessly to make your boss rich when, with little effort, you could recognise your own abilities and, in time, line your own pockets – particularly if you are unhappy at work?' Think outside the square when working with Buzzard and you will learn to be more spontaneous and willing to stop and smell the roses. You will stop living to work and start working to live. Buzzard Dreaming supports us as we go about refining our skills in order to simplify and improve our lives. Not sure what your innate skills are, though? Not confident to trust your ability to see the bigger picture just yet? It doesn't matter. So long as you are willing to initiate change and simplify your life, it doesn't matter how you go about accomplishing it. You may want to return to school if you have already left, for example, or continue on to achieve a higher education if you haven't. You could start an apprenticeship, or partake in extra training to broaden the skills you already have. If you enjoy what you are doing and are content to stay where you are, why not strive for advancement or promotion? Buzzard Dreaming helps you realise your strengths while providing the forum to enhance them further. Although it may be true that you are inherently imbued with a special gift, wisdom or skills, however, now may simply not be the right time to embrace them. Take your time and do what you can. At your own pace, explore your skills and, when the time is right, refine them by spreading your wings and taking that sacred leap of faith.

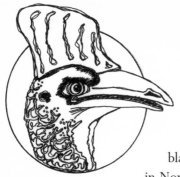

Cassowary
Respect

There are four species of Cassowary found in the world. Solitary and secretive by nature, they are large, black plumaged rainforest birds found in Northern Australia and New Guinea. The Cassowary is a brilliantly coloured, Emu-like flightless bird, heavily armoured with a powerful horn-like casque on its head that resembles a battering ram. On each of its toes, the Cassowary has razor-sharp claws used to defend itself and its chicks. Like the Emu, the male Cassowary raises the young.

One creature or another occupies every square inch of our Earth Mother. The moment we leave our space, we step into that of another. We become their visitor, invited or not. When we drink from a stream or pick fruit from a tree, we are sharing this source of nourishment with other creatures. We share the air we breathe, the warmth of the sun, the refreshing breeze of the four winds and the rain that falls from the sky, with every other living thing on this Earth. We have to view our life as being the only one we will ever have and to honour this chance to the utmost. We have to look at every lesson that is presented as being more important than the last. We only have one Earth and it is up to us to honour the space we inhabit while we are here. Simple. Cassowary asks you to address your sense of Sacred Space and the way in which you treat the Sacred Space of others. If we honour and respect our space, others will learn to respect theirs and if we honour the space of others, they will learn to respect ours. It is okay to refuse the inappropriate or interfering ways of others. Our Sacred Space is our territory and we have the right to feel safe within it. Our home and everything associated with it; our possessions, our body, our feelings, our values and beliefs can all be viewed as Sacred Spaces, and just as a wild animal will only allow other animals who instinctively respect territorial boundaries to enter their Sacred Space, we are encouraged by the Dreaming of the Cassowary to follow suit. It is not important what others think of you. How you view yourself is what counts. You have to live with yourself and to feel proud of how you go about living your life. Cassowary says that in order to attract respect it is vital to radiate self-respect, to show pride in your achievements, to radiate self-worth and to adopt and mirror the favourable qualities of the people that are drawn to you, rather than focusing on their negative traits.

Catbird
Contradiction

Members of the Bowerbird family, Catbirds get their name from the cat-like yowl they make. They also communicate by making clicking and rasping sounds. They have stunning red eyes and green plumage flecked with black on the head and face and white on the chest, neck and wing tips. Catbirds mainly feed on fruit and buds, but will occasionally hunt insects, Frogs and baby birds. They don't build bowers like their cousins. Instead, they simply clear an area and line it with leaves, grasses and fine twigs.

The Catbird is a creature that seems to masquerade as a Cat, expertly mastering a contradictory feline noise as a disguise to confuse its foe. Does it use its cry to create a safe place for other Catbirds when their territory is threatened, for example? Do they want their enemies and rivals to think they are protected by the archenemy of all birds: the Cat? By employing such an illusory sound, their goal would surely be achieved. Incongruity, when employed as a form of protection, stops others in their tracks by forcing them to question what they have just seen or experienced. It confuses sufficiently to provide a window of opportunity for us to either proceed or retreat. To act in a contradictory way to how others expect, is to shift perception of how you are typically observed. It is to harness elusiveness and instil doubt. To master the art of illusion, to make others see what you want them to and for them to believe it to be true, is to bend the rules of reality. Catbird Dreaming coaches us as we generate a veil of healthy confusion in order to protect who and what we are, thus disguising those aspects of self we don't want anyone else to see (just yet). Catbird poses a challenge; a test to see how keen others are to really get to know us. Catbird, by disguising its 'bird-ness' with 'cat-ness', creates a powerful mask of bewilderment that protects, preventing anyone from assuming things about it. It helps us keep people at a distance until we feel comfortable enough to welcome them into our world. It suggests that if people are determined to penetrate the illusion that protects us, then their intent must be true.

Chat

Fraudulence

Members of the Honeyeater family, Chats prefer to walk or run rather than revert to the traditional 'hop' of other birds. Some species are able to survive extremely cold conditions by slipping into a state of lassitude or hibernation. When threatened, Chats will drop to the ground and simulate a broken wing to draw predators away from their nest and hatchlings.

Misleading its predators by feigning illness, while electing a faster mode of escape than other birds, Chats represent fast-talking individuals, con men, impostors and frauds: door-to-door salesmen and telemarketers, for example, and proposals that 'guarantee' quick, sure-fire methods and get-rich-quick schemes. Chats presage empty promises that offer to make life happier, healthier and more abundant; schemes that prove true for the proposer at least ... while they swindle your money and leave. Chats warn of those who promise the world but deliver nothing, an intention hidden by fast talk, feigned effort, false promises and golden-tongued charm.

Chough
Change of Life

Choughs are relatively large birds and are almost completely black, save for a white patch on each wing. They have a curved beak and red eyes. Choughs emit a sombre, sliding shrill. When alarmed, they give a rasping call. Young Choughs are dark grey, and their eyes are brown. As they mature, though, their plumage gets darker and their eyes change from brown, to orange and then to red. At first glance, the Chough could be mistaken for a Crow, Raven or even a Currawong – especially when its white wing patch is seen. Choughs travel in large family flocks, moving from one territory to the next in a strict but cyclic manner, based on the seasons and the availability of food.

As if celebrating the colour correspondences and ancient teachings of the Wheel of Life, Chough Dreaming offers sound advice for those heading into, or currently experiencing the period of life affectionately known as 'Change of Life'. The Chough's black feathers, for example, represent man's introspective nature, and resonate to the energies of the West on the Wheel of Life. The West is where the lessons of contemplation and meditation are developed, while its red eyes are reminiscent of the North (in the southern hemisphere and south in the northern sector), where innocence and trust are learned and natural and emotional perceptions are explored. The Wheel of Life symbolises the developmental stages of growth experienced by each of us as we mature from child to elder. It highlights life's lessons and the gifts of power offered by Spirit. The South is symbolic of our teenage years, for example, when we are filled with power, passion and innocence; when we know everything and nothing at the same time. The West is representational of our adult years, when we, probably as parents, ask ourselves the million-dollar question: 'Is this it?' We find ourselves reflecting on life, invariably tossing around the possibility of a 'midlife crisis'. The West offers the unique chance to return to our teenage years and experience the magick of innocence and spontaneity once again. Chough signals a rare opportunity to revisit the joys of youth, to do the things we have always regretted not doing, and to accomplish what we have let pass. It gives permission to experience the 'midlife crisis', presents the healing opportunities of conscious regression and encourages us to experience the thrill of adventure. Chough Dreaming confirms that life is too short to become stagnant by living a life that no longer serves. It espouses that it is wiser to initiate constructive changes that promote excitement and family accord than to panic and act irrationally in a blind attempt to reclaim lost opportunity. However, before you go making permanent life-changing decisions, consider first those who share your life and include them in your thoughts and decisions. When Chough is prevalent in your life, all the decisions you make are bound to touch every member of your family *and* your circle of friends. So make sure they are part of your new life, or you may grow apart.

Cockatoo

The Cockatoo family includes (among others) the Gang Gang, Sulphur-crested, Black, Major Mitchell, Galah and Corella. Cockatoos live for up to 100 years and are identified by their crest of feathers that stand erect when the bird is excited or angry. Cockatoos travel in huge flocks, sometimes in their hundreds. They are noisy, gregarious, social birds. Commonly kept as pets in Australia, many species of Cockatoo readily mimic human speech. Some species, like the Blacks and Sulphur-crested, have prominent crests, while those of the Galahs and Corellas lack both height and colour.

Black Cockatoo - *The Void*

Some say that in the beginning there was perpetual darkness – a gentle Void; a blanket of nothingness that tenderly swathed the Universal plains. Within this fertile emptiness the Great Mother stirred, as if waking from eternal slumber. As though trying to recall some distant memory she began to unfold, twisting and churning, dreaming herself into fruition. She began to reach out into the darkness as a massive expanse of nurturing energy that seduced everything it encountered, willingly drawing all into her protective womb. Sulphur-crested Cockatoo's dark sister, the Black Cockatoo carries the Genetic Memory of this sacred time and, within her Dreaming, comes the lesson of surrender. Black Cockatoo demonstrates the patience that can only come when we accept that we cannot possibly know everything at the beginning of any journey and that wisdom will present itself at the appropriate time. Black Cockatoo Dreaming helps us to take control of life by insisting that we grow at our own pace and learn what we need to know in our own time. She encourages us to just sit in contemplation and wait for life's mysteries to unfold without consciously seeking answers. At the appropriate time, when our mind is still and our heart is at ease, Black Cockatoo passes the torch of illumination to her sister, the Sulphur-crested Cockatoo. Black Cockatoo allows the Mystery of inevitability to unfold within our lives so that we may finally surrender to change. She teaches us to trust that whatever is meant to happen will, but only in its own time. Black Cockatoo encourages us to confront our fears, to go with the flow and to embrace all new opportunities as they present themselves, thus paving the way for Sulphur-crested Cockatoo's Dreaming to establish itself properly. The Red-Tailed Black Cockatoo is also said to carry the energy of the Grandmothers. It is seen as a lunar-influenced bird as its red feathers represent the blood of the feminine creative force. The Yellow-Tailed Black Cockatoo is said to carry Grandfather energy, with its yellow feathers influenced by the masculine energy of the sun, while the White-Tailed Black Cockatoo offers unlimited potential, and the chance to embrace the wisdom channelled from one's higher-self and the Angelic realms.

Galah - *Joy*

In Australian slang, to be labelled a 'Galah' means you're probably a bit of a hooligan, roustabout, practical joker or someone a bit silly. Predominantly pink and grey in colour, Galahs have a superficial crest, scimitar-shaped beak and powerful claws. They are gregarious, raucous and socially extroverted. The pink chest of the Galah is symbolically linked to the heart chakra. Pronounced 'shack-ra', a Sanskrit word meaning 'wheel' or 'disk', the chakra system embodies the seven main energy centres that maintain health and harmony within the human body. The heart chakra teaches trust, acceptance, self-love and love for others. Galah Dreaming teaches us to love life and to celebrate the joy that it brings. Galah can't help but bring people together, because it draws only the best out of everyone. It represents our fun-loving, social, interactive, outgoing side, while helping us feel happy, safe and content in our own skin. Galah teaches us to not judge others or ourselves. On the other hand, the dominant grey feathers, in relation to the symbology of the colour, can suggest prudence and indecisiveness. Galah helps those cynically labelled as troublemakers and rebels to find the inner strength to ask for help, to seek acceptance and love, and to demand positive attention. Often people act like 'Galahs' to get attention because they do not know how else to attract it. Negative attention is thought to be better than no attention at all. Young people often choose this path because it seems the only option. Galah helps us to honestly assess our actions and assists those close to us to read between the lines.

Sulphur-crested Cockatoo - *Illumination*

Each morning, as it rises in the East, the Sun symbolically heralds new beginnings and a chance to start afresh; its rays stretch out across the horizon, banishing the dark mysteries of the night and initiating golden opportunity. As we wake, our minds are refreshed, our vision is precise and our sense of purpose is renewed. We joyfully realise that the new day offers potential and that our previously unrealised prospects are, once again, there for the picking. Legend has it that when Sulphur-crested Cockatoos eat the seeds of a particular tree, its golden crest magickally appears after dark, illuminating its surrounds.

They metaphorically act as a guiding light for those wandering aimlessly through life. A solar influenced creature that traditionally sits in the East on the Wheel of Life, the Sulphur-crested Cockatoo is a messenger of light; its crest illuminating the end of the dark tunnel for individuals lost in despair. Sulphur-crested Cockatoo primes you for clarity to dawn in relation to one or more aspects of your life, and for stability to once again reign supreme. It offers a time of illumination when truths will be revealed, when energy will flow more freely and obstacles will begin to dissipate. As a guardian of the East Gate and an emissary of the sun, the Sulphur-crested Cockatoo promises a time of mental clarity, clear vision, enhanced intuition and stability.

Cormorant
Support

With webbed feet, slender, hooked bills and long, flexible necks, Cormorants dive deep and swim underwater in pursuit of prey. Although Cormorants spend much of their time in the water, their plumage lacks the essential waterproofing components found in those belonging to other seabirds. As a result, they must spend time on shore with wings outstretched, drying their feathers in the sun. 'Ukai' is the name of a fishing technique practiced in Japan for over 1300 years where the Cormorant is actually used to catch fish for the fisherman. To prevent the Cormorant from escaping, a leash is attached to a small metal ring fastened around the base of its neck. The leash allows the bird to dive and swim freely, but the ring prevents it from swallowing its catch.

Cormorant Dreaming offers relief to those who continually surrender their power or who feel their strength and joy seeping away or being drained by others. Like the ring that prevents the Cormorant from enjoying the fruits of its labour, the joy of helping is often tainted by those we assist when they drain our energy by constantly taking and never giving back. 'Takers' drain their 'victims' of energy just as vampires drain their victims of blood. They make others feel special, strong and needed, and then they feed on these feelings in order to fortify themselves. They feign naivety, ineptness and insecurity in order to lure their prey, effectively placing an emotional noose around their neck. Cormorant reminds us that help is only supportive when it is appreciated and willingly reciprocated. It should only ever be offered, for example, when recompense is on the cards, and only then when what is being offered in exchange is of equal value, and is something that is needed or wanted and not simply a compromise. Cormorant Dreaming offers a sympathetic hand to those who genuinely need help. It supports those who display the humility to seek help and who recognise the sacredness in being offered it. Cormorant provides endurance and opportunity to build self-reliance, so that the need for external help becomes increasingly less frequent. To find the strength to deal with life's obstacles alone without constantly having to look expectantly to others for help is indicative of Cormorant Dreaming.

Crow

Law

There are three species of Crow in Australia – two native and one introduced. The native species are entirely black, though their feathers are white at the base. Crows all have white eyes as adults (the young have brown eyes), except for the House Crow, a drifter from south-east Asia. The brown-eyed House Crow is mostly black, except for a broad smokey brown band around the neck and chest. Although primarily scavengers by nature, Crows may occasionally feed on live prey. They are incredibly intelligent birds. Crows are known, for example, to wait at intersections for the traffic lights to change and for the cars to stop. They then strut out among the cars and place nuts on the road in front of the wheels so that when they move forward, the cars crack them open.

As creatures of the Void (indicated by their black feathers), Crows are believed to exist in the past, present and future simultaneously, to embody darkness within light and light within darkness and to watch over all the worlds and dimensions from all viewpoints in chorus. They make little distinction between right and wrong, but acknowledge the necessity for the existence of both. Without them, we wouldn't learn the lessons afforded by choice. According to legend, when Crow appears, she is challenging our perceptions while daring us to follow her deep into the Void, into our consciousness, to strengthen our principles and our relationship with Spirit. Crow encourages us to seek the wisdom found in the inner silence and to ponder our actions and reactions to life. Apparently we inherently know the difference between right and wrong. Crow asks us, therefore, to trust our judgement and make the most sensible decision when one is required. Her appearance generally heralds a sudden but necessary change, a wakeup call or a lesson in self-discovery. Crow is one of the sacred keepers of Universal Law and the custodian of ancient records. She espouses the law of three: the understanding that whatever we do will be returned to us threefold, that it matters not what we do in this life so long as our actions bring harm to none. She reminds us that all our actions are recorded and, although karma appears patient, it is often ruthless in its delivery. To understand these laws, and to live by them with the purest of intent, will see us exit this life and journey to the next with a clear memory of our previous life and the lessons learned during that time. Crow demands that you listen to your instincts and act upon them in a way that honourably serves your purpose. Treat others as you would like to be treated, never expect others to do what you should do yourself and never act in a way that may cause harm to another. Breaking these simple rules will see the strong arm of spiritual law slam down the karmic hammer. You have all the wisdom and knowledge you need within you to make the right decision. Call upon it now and you cannot make a mistake.

Cuckoo
Freeloading

A parasitic bird that relies on other birds to raise its young, the Cuckoo approaches the nest of a favoured species, kills the hatchlings and destroys the eggs by forcefully removing them from the nest, replacing them with its own. Although preferences may vary depending on the species of Cuckoo (whose eggs are generally an exact match to those of its host), favoured host birds may include Wrens, Wood Swallows, Flycatchers, Honeyeaters, Robins, Crows, Currawongs, Magpies and Sparrowhawks. The Coucal, a subspecies of the Cuckoo, is the only member of the family known to build its own nest and raise its own young.

Cuckoo Dreaming epitomises the user, addict and victim when exhibited in its darker, freeloading phase. Alternatively, when presented as constructive, it provides a protective influence for those vulnerable to predators and negativity as it affords strength, endurance and support. Cuckoo watches over those who lack confidence or aptitude to provide for themselves. It nurtures those who have not yet developed faith in their own capabilities. Cuckoo mirrors those who believe the world owes them a living; people who audaciously take advantage of the benevolence of others without showing gratitude or proffering compensation. What if the host bird was to simply deny access to the Cuckoo, by repeatedly removing the offending bird's eggs and young? The Cuckoo would then be forced to rely on its own skills to provide a nurturing environment for its offspring. The lesson, therefore, for those who have fallen prey to the manipulative pressure of a Cuckoo person, is to simply deny access and support. Cut them off. Make them stand on their own two feet. Stop sacrificing your own wants and needs in order to provide for theirs. Such a step would kick-start their road to growth and responsibility – as well as yours. If they don't surrender to their own self-pity, they will return to thank you some day for forcing them to grow up and be accountable for their actions.

Curlew
Belonging

Slightly resembling an Ibis, the Curlew gets its name from its call – 'car-lee' or 'cur-lee'. A timid seabird, the Curlew is the largest of the migratory waders. It usually feeds in small family groups taking crustaceans, fish and water insects, systematically prodding the sand in search of prey.

Curlew Dreaming is emblematic of man's desire to seek truth and obtain wisdom. It invites us to probe deeply with our questions and to never give up on the sacred quest for knowledge. It also represents the rolling stone; those among us who forever search for a place to call home. Curlew people rarely know what it means to fit in or belong. Although they may know many people, few can be called upon in times of need as friends and allies. Curlew poses the questions: 'What are you looking for and what do you desire?' Curlew Dreaming exposes feelings of confusion, being overwhelmed, melancholic or disheartened, and offers clarity. Curlew is the totem of the 'Black Sheep', the 'odd one out', children who have been fostered but not yet adopted, the 'new kids on the block' and the ones yet to make their mark. The Curlew understands shyness, and so by means of its inquisitive bill, offers tutorage in asking the right questions, so that the most appropriate lessons may be learned and the local language understood, thus affording fruitful direction and purpose. It guides us as we realise new friendships, while offering endurance to deepen existing ones, so that over time our sense of longing can healthily become 'belonging'.

Currawong
Ghost Wisdom

'Currawong' is the general name given to three aggressive Crow-like species of yellow-eyed birds stained with black or dark grey and white markings. There are 3 species in Australia: the Pied, the Black and the Grey Currawong. All three are omnivorous and are savage hunters, killing smaller birds and mammals. They also feed on insects, carrion, food scraps and the eggs and young of other birds. They are also fond of grapes and fruit and are reviled as pests by farmers and wine producers in some areas. It is a notion shared by many that Currawongs appear foolish because they are less responsive than other birds. This apparently overconfident attitude makes them harder to deter. While Crows will immediately flee when shot at, for example, Currawongs will often stay put, even when one of their group has just been killed, a habit which makes them easy targets. Currawongs are social within their own groups, but will strongly defend their personal space and communal territory against intruders.

According to a 2000-year-old legend held sacred by the Lakota people, a beautiful maiden dressed in white buckskin, carrying a bundle containing sacred pipe, descended from the stars and spoke to the people of changes and other things. She was named White Buffalo Calf Woman and she augured a time when darkness and confusion would flood the land; a darkness that would come from the East. During this time it would seem as though all was lost, and all sacred learning would be temporarily forgotten. But, when the darkness passed, heralded by the birth of a rare, pure white Buffalo calf, potent new beginnings would be celebrated by all and the people of the world, the people of all colours, would bond and walk as one. All that was broken would be made whole and the sacred circle of life would be mended and peace would, once again, hold the power. A time would emerge when Spirit would be reborn in the hearts of the people and the animals and crops would become even more plentiful than they were before. The Ghost Dance, a variation of the ancient 'circle dance' performed by Native Americans since antediluvian times, formed the core of a religion that sprung up in the 1890s under the leadership of Paiute prophet of peace, Wovoka (also known by the white American name, Jack Wilson). He prophesied a peaceful end to white American expansion (the predicted 'darkness from the East', perhaps?) while preaching messages espousing clean, honest, co-operative living. He was said to have experienced a vision during a solar eclipse on January 1, 1889, in which God had apparently shown the land rich with plentiful crops and animals. He instructed Jack to return home and tell his people to love one another and not fight and to live in peace with the whites. He did so, and soon began encouraging his people to work and not steal or lie, and to shun war. He asserted that if his people abided by these rules, God promised they would be, in time, reunited with their departed family and friends and that they would never again know sickness, disease or old age. During the vision, God gave Jack Wilson the Ghost Dance. He was told that, if it was performed in a precise five-day cycle, whilst wearing a garment known as a Ghost Shirt, the dancers would ensure their happiness and that of their people, while hastening the assembly of the living and deceased. He became convinced that if everyone danced the Ghost Dance, they would accelerate the chances of all evil in the land being destroyed, leaving a renewed Earth filled with abundant food, love and devotion. Kicking Bear, a Miniconjou elder, on hearing about this new religion, travelled to Nevada to learn more about it. He later returned to his people, however, and together with his collaborator Short Bull, interpreted the religion with a unique slant. Instead of explaining Wovoka's anti-violent teachings, for example, Kicking Bear focused more on the eventual extermination of the white people. Short Bull also told his followers that if surrounded by white soldiers, when singing a specific song, those wearing the ghost shirts would cause the white soldiers to fall down dead. This unfortunate translation is thought to have instigated the Wounded Knee massacre of 1890, which resulted in the deaths of 391 Lakota Sioux. The arrival of white man was considered the beginning of the end for the native people, the land and the animals – not to mention the traditional ways, which were feared lost forever. The white settlers came to be reviled as a scourge; a plague that threatened the very survival of the people, a threat that had to be removed, preferably peacefully but by force if necessary. As if remembering this challenging time, Currawong is one animal that helps us remove negativity from our life; the burdens and baggage, the fear, pain, grief and dishonesty that haunts our heart and threatens our preferred way of life, thus lessening our chances of physical, mental and spiritual growth. Currawong Dreaming helps cut out the dead wood from our life and to exorcise ghosts from our past. It supports us as we endeavour to reclaim our power and expel the weaker, more dependent aspects of our personality. It helps us face our inner demons – and depose them forever, while guiding us to unite our spiritual, mental and physical selves so that they may dance in harmony with one another instead of battling each other for supremacy. Whether offered by the Currawong or not, 'Ghost Wisdom' deals with the more obstructive, damaging aspects of our past, the forces that continue to haunt and ridicule us from the shadows. It does this by shifting our perceptions, modifying our approach and providing a healing foundation on which to re-evaluate our values and beliefs ... and move on. It is to dance the spiral dance of Spirit – the ancient Circle Dance that promises personal endurance, spiritual unity, community strength and global togetherness.

Dove
Peace

The terms 'Dove' and 'Pigeon' are often used interchangeably. Doves are typically plump birds with round heads, short necks and slender beaks. They raise their young in roughly built stick nests, with both sexes contributing to the incubation of the eggs. Doves feed their young 'crop milk', a highly nutritious substance regurgitated directly into the hatchling's throat. Doves are often kept as aviary birds, with some species sporting crests, vibrant colours and iridescent plumage. The call of the Dove is said to inspire feelings of peace, reassurance and homecoming.

Doves have long been revered as universal symbols of peace and devotion, with Noah purportedly releasing one from the side of his Ark (a vessel built at God's command to save a base collection of the world's animals from the Great Flood, accounts of which are contained in the Hebrew Torah, Christian Old Testament's book of Genesis and the Quran) as a messenger. The Dove was said to have returned bearing an olive branch, signifying the emergence of dry land and the waning of the flood. A Dove was also said to have watched over the baptism of the infant Jesus, while in politics, the term 'Dove' has come to describe members who favour a peaceful resolution, while 'Hawk' represents those who don't. Dove Dreaming naturally inspires feelings of peace and harmony because it embodies balance and stability, particularly during periods of emotional upheaval, hardship and pain. It provides vital tools needed to remain grounded and get ourselves back on track. Dove reassures us that, despite what we may believe, we have nothing to fear; we have not been forsaken by God, even though we may, at times, feel stranded, high and dry, or drowning in the depths of despair. Dove settles the heart and re-establishes clarity by encouraging us to surrender our fears and trepidation. By surrendering our fears, we effectively draw to us those things we desire the most. A messenger of possibility, Dove appears as a light at the end of the tunnel, illuminating the way to fertile ground where we may rest, recuperate and start afresh. It symbolises selflessness, replenishment, inner peace, unconditional love and trust.

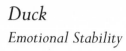

Duck
Emotional Stability

Ducks are easily recognised by their flat shovel-like bills, round heads and webbed feet. Male Ducks are often coloured differently in comparison to the females, with the males generally having brighter plumage and a hooked, upturned tail tip. Only the females make the distinctive 'quack'; the males make a sort of rasping, hollow hiss. Wild Ducks are often hunted for food or sport, either by shooting them while on the wing or by calling them down with living or life-like model decoys. From the use of decoys came the expression Sitting Duck, which means 'an easy target'. Most domestic breeds developed from the wild European Mallard. Australia has many different species of native Duck, including the Black Duck, the Whistling Duck and the Wood Duck or Maned Goose. The Australian Wood Duck is actually the smallest member of the Goose family and not a true Duck at all. It nests in the hollow branches of trees. When its offspring hatch, they leave the nest and drop harmlessly to the ground like little balls of fluff.

Although Ducks appear to glide effortlessly across the surface of the water, beneath the surface their feet are paddling like crazy, with those watching oblivious to the degree of effort being expended by the little bird. Duck Dreaming demonstrates that sometimes it is necessary to hide how we feel in order to maintain an air of confidence and detachment as we navigate our way through difficult periods. Presenting a stoic face and remaining aloof, self-controlled and maintaining a positive attitude even when challenged will see us glide effortlessly through life, bypassing obstacles, confrontations and probing questions. Like Swan Dreaming, Duck helps build an air of grace and tranquillity by sustaining a façade of indifference and calm – despite the temptation to cry, run or freeze. Duck Dreaming helps us balance our emotions, helping us avoid venting them publicly. In the wrong setting, such a display would cost us our credibility and power. We may not always feel comfortable or want to 'advertise' how we are feeling, so Duck coaches us to become masters of apathetic independence. It enables us to appear strong and centred, even when we are experiencing the most emotionally unsettling lessons life can muster. Duck helps us remain focused and dedicated to our responsibilities when it counts; outwardly detached from our worries and concerns so that we may operate effectively and efficiently at work and at home. It helps keep personal things personal, to the point where even our family is unaware of how we truly feel. The danger is, of course, that we can get used to dealing with issues alone, forgetting the network of people who care enough to do anything in their power to help and support us. Duck Dreaming reminds us not to accidentally shut people out, especially those willing to offer an occasional supportive shoulder to cry on or an empathetic ear. Duck suggests that when the emotional pool gets too rough, simply swim ashore and ground yourself. It offers the tools to successfully and gracefully navigate our way through even the most tumultuous periods and to explore and honour our emotions when it matters the most.

Eagle
Spirit

Australia has three species of Eagle: the Little Eagle, the White-bellied Sea Eagle and the Wedge-tailed Eagle – the largest of the three. Wedge-tailed Eagles prefer open woodland, but are known to inhabit arid desert regions, grasslands, mountainous areas and rainforest. The most famous of Australia's Eagles, the Wedge-tailed Eagle has heavily feathered legs and a wingspan of up to two and a half metres. Slow to initially get off the ground, Wedge-tailed Eagles (once airborne) ride on thermal updrafts, spiralling upwards to ever greater heights. With a penchant for carrion, Wedge-tailed Eagles are sometimes struck and killed by passing vehicles as they feed on road kill. With a wingspan sometimes exceeding two metres, Sea Eagles are not true Eagles but are, in fact, giant Kites. Juvenile Sea Eagles resemble those of the Wedge-tailed Eagle, except for their shorter tails and patterned underwings. Sea Eagles take Fish, Eels and Penguins directly from the water's surface and shoreline. They locate their prey while watching from a prominent perch, and then execute the catch by means of a gliding attack.

The number zero rests at the very core of our numerical system – suspended somewhere between the positive and negative. While suspended in the womb, we sit at the heart of our own personal Universe; barren like the number zero with seemingly nothing physical to offer, but innately imbued with a desire to go forth and learn. We sit as if perched on a precipice, waiting for the best opportunity to take the leap of faith that will initiate the rest of our lives. The concept of Spirit is very much like the number zero. Spirit sits between the worlds – it is neither here nor there. Spirit may be intangible but it is not inaccessible. People often say that they cannot believe in something they cannot see. Air is not visible to the naked eye but we trust that it is there. We experience it every time we inhale, each time a child takes its first breath and every time we see a flower swaying in a breeze. We have no tangible proof of its existence, but based on trust and experience we have faith in the fact that it will always be there. The concept of Spirit is exactly the same. We have to trust that it is there and that when we are in need, our calls will be heard. The Eagle is revered as a symbol of the Creator Spirit because of its ability to soar to breath-taking heights. Its piercing eyesight is said to bare witness to the fears we keep locked deep within our consciousness; our vulnerabilities, discomforts and inabilities. And it has the sacred capacity to know our heart of hearts, our sincere and purest intent, and our true essence. Eagle offers comfort in the knowledge that Spirit is guiding and protecting you while you make decisions and grapple with the obstacles you are inevitably going to experience as you journey through life. Eagle comes as a reminder that in order to achieve anything in this life, educated leaps of faith must be taken and trust in your inherent capabilities must be brought to the fore. Without these qualities life is full of possibility but devoid of movement or purpose.

Not until we identify our strengths and the opportunities they afford can we realise the potency and promise within our lives. Not until we find the courage to take the first step and witness the chain of events that lead to the final one can it be realised that all is as it should be.

Emu
Endurance / Responsible Fathering Skills on a Physical Level

Emus live in large family groups, foraging on grassy plains and in open forests, feeding on grass, insects, fruit and seeds. Female Emus make loud 'booming' sounds and rich grunting ones that seem to resonate from deep in their throats. The Emu is the world's second largest flightless bird (the largest being the Ostrich). The incubation of the eggs and the raising of the young are left to the male. From birth, Emus are amazingly fast runners and adept swimmers. Naturally curious, even wild Emus cannot resist investigating any activity that is out of the ordinary.

A solar influenced creature, Emu speaks of the responsibility afforded to fathers who find themselves raising their children single-handedly. Emu Dreaming lends itself to the teaching of effective parenting skills and the endurance that is required to execute the role, especially under difficult conditions. The Emu, being a grounded, flightless bird, offers real and practical relief to the single father. As a 'yang' totem, Emu demonstrates the practical skills needed to guide and raise a child when the nurturing and protective energies of the mother are absent. Emu offers the resilience needed to cope with the day-to-day tasks that tire and exhaust, especially when a job or career is extra-curricular to the responsibilities of the lone parenting role. Alternatively, the Emu can also assist the single mother by offering the masculine support lacking due to the absent father, so that her energies may be preserved and rejuvenated. By invoking the support of the male Emu's Spirit, the children will sense the presence of male energy, pressure will be alleviated for the mother, and stamina sustained. Assuming that the Emu energy is being radiated through the heart of the mother or the residual energy of their absent father, the children will acknowledge the harmony created within the relationship they have with their mother. Emu Dreaming subsequently renders the mother's role more grounded, balanced and less emotional, particularly if the role of single mother is new. Emu supports us physically and emotionally during times of stress. It teaches us to pace ourselves better so that we are able to maintain a manageable level of endurance. Emu promotes a holistic approach to life that incorporates a healthy mind/healthy body philosophy while encouraging you to seize personal quiet time for replenishment whenever you are able. Emu demonstrates how to integrate the positive and supportive aspects of both our 'yin' and 'yang' aspects by drawing their wisdom into everything we do, thus enriching our view of the world and our place (and that of our children) within it.

Fairy Penguin
Willpower

The Fairy Penguin matures at only 40cm in height and approximately 1kg in weight. The smallest Penguins in the world, Fairy Penguins (also known as Little or Blue Penguins) are found along the southern coastline of Australia. They hunt during the day, swimming out to sea in search of food. Fairy Penguins 'flap' their flippers as they dive and swim and are capable of reaching incredible speeds. Hunting small fish and crustaceans, they return to shore at dusk and scamper up the beach in droves, before quickly making their way back to their burrows and their awaiting hungry hatchlings.

All Penguins are celebrated as lucid dreamers; creatures capable of walking with clarity and intent in both the physical realm of ordinary landscape and that of the more obscure, non-ordinary reality. The Fairy Penguin, for example, teaches us to picture in our mind's eye a desired outcome, and coaches us to physically and abundantly bring it to fruition. His strong will and self-belief means he will never be restricted by limitation or inadequacy, and if we follow his lead, neither will we. Having evolved over thousands of years to an aquatic lifestyle, Penguins lack the physical prowess to become airborne like other birds. The strong-willed Fairy Penguin, however, refuses to surrender to jealousy of his sky-roving cousins. Rather than limiting himself, he searches for alternative ways to fulfil his natural impulse to fly. Instead of taking flight like a regular bird and soaring through the clouds, for example, Fairy Penguin takes to the white foam of Grandmother Ocean. An earth-bound bird, Fairy Penguin joyfully circles the water with the subtlety of a Swallow. Dipping and diving through the subterranean valleys, skimming the peaks of submerged mountains and flitting in and out of thick kelp forests, Fairy Penguin 'hawks' for fish in similar fashion to how a Flycatcher seizes insects while on the wing. Fairy Penguin demonstrates that anyone can overcome any limitation by adopting a resolute mindset. Awaken your inherent creativity by listening more intuitively to your dreams and trusting what they show you. Utilise your inner power now and believe in yourself more, because a time approaches that will require you to be a little more independent. Remove the blinkers, because you can achieve anything when you surrender your impediments by drawing on your willpower to find alternative ways of viewing them. Personal limitations cease being a problem when you seek constructive and achievable solutions within yourself. It is time to stop playing the drama queen, to acknowledge the aspects of your life that are hindering your growth and to deal with them appropriately. Penguin is telling you that it is time to harness the willpower needed to fulfil your dreams, no matter what they may be.

Fig-Bird
Conception

Also known as Banana-Birds, Fig-Birds raid crop trees in country gardens and orchards, feasting hungrily on the soft, ripening fruit. Figs and bananas are among their favourites. Fig Birds weave cup-shaped nests from twigs, small vine ringlets and fine hair roots, wedging them firmly into tree forks. They typically lay two to three eggs before sitting.

Although Adam and Eve supposedly wore fig leaves to disguise their sexual characteristics, most esoteric references outlining the symbolic properties of herbs and plants describe the fig as holding a more intimately fruitful association. It is said, for example, that fig tree wood, when fashioned by hand into phallic shapes and carried on the person, can greatly enhance one's level of fertility and chances of conceiving a child. The consumption of figs and bananas has long been encouraged as a remedy to combat impotency in men and infertility in women, due to figs' resemblance to testicles hanging from their braches and the phallic shape of the banana. Fig-Bird is an emissary of conception and birth. Its Dreaming is receptive in nature, carrying a ready, ripe fecund energy. When it appears, Fig-Bird often heralds news of a long-anticipated pregnancy or the birth of a healthy child. Invoke the Dreaming of the Fig-Bird to assist when conception is difficult by visualising flocks of them in and around your home, bedroom and nursery, while imagining your belly ripe and round with child. Similarly, ask the Fig-Bird for assistance in the birthing of ideas when your mind is pregnant with creative thought, or your life is lacking productiveness in other areas.

Finch
Multiplicity

Finches are small seed-eating passerines, or 'perching birds'. Australia is home to several species of Finch, with many others introduced as ornamental aviary birds. Of the 18 species of Australian Finch that can be kept, some only with a permit, others without, the Zebra Finch stands out as a clear favourite among amateur enthusiasts and it is also a common choice for behavioural and laboratory studies. Most Finches weigh less than 30 grams and breed well in captivity. They are kept mainly for their striking plumage and cheerful sound.

Their wide distribution coupled with an even wider variety of species, broad spectrum of colours, array of body sizes and song, Finch Dreaming reminds us that life is a smorgasbord, rich with opportunity, experiences, tastes and styles. It affords the chance to step out of our comfort zone, try new things and experiment with what life has to offer. Finch dares us to dine at restaurants that extend our palate, to seek employment that broadens our range of skills and to mix with people from all walks of life so that our social circle is not limited to just those we feel akin to. Finch Dreaming encourages us to reach out to, and mix with, 'real people' by teaching us that everyone is equal, imbued with wisdom and experience rich enough to improve the quality (and potentially change the direction) of our lives on one level or another. Finch reminds us that, no matter how small or different we believe ourselves to be, we are all born from the same source. It advocates that even though our skin colour, physical appearance, religious belief and place of birth may differ outwardly, inwardly we are all the same. No matter the list of differences that apparently separate us from everyone else, Finch Dreaming teaches that our hearts beat as one. Those who have lost touch with the regular people, or who regard themselves as being superior, more clever, better looking or more talented would benefit from the healing lessons of the wise little Finch.

Flycatcher

Extraction

The term 'Flycatcher' refers to any passeriform or perching bird that flutters about taking insects while on the wing. It is held true that Thrushes, Warblers and Babblers belong to the Flycatcher family. They are common in dense woodlands, rainforests and surrounding areas.

Traditionally associated with demons, dark energy and plague, Flies warn of possible negative forces congregating in areas where their swarms are greatest. Dark vibrations that need to be cleared can easily be uncovered by the presence of Flies, as can negative thoughts inspired by resentment, jealousy, anger and covetousness. Such thoughts and feelings are quickly exposed by the continued presence of Flies, especially those that linger no matter how hard you try to deter them. On a more serious note, Flies sometimes mark individuals unwittingly carrying dark-side 'entities', or those who knowingly incorporate them into their spirit work or belief system. Ancient forms of healing sometimes involved exorcism, or the cleansing or removal of 'bad spirits', demonic energies or dark-side entities. The force or beings needing to be removed were referred to as 'intrusions', with Flies often warning of possible intrusion. Although not necessarily 'bad' or evil, dark-side intrusions are instinctively attracted to those who find themselves spiritually, emotionally or mentally weakened, or who have suffered soul or power loss. They are enticed, just as Flies are drawn to decay and unpleasantness, and by removing these entities, those afflicted are said to regain stamina and life force. Shamans were mystical healers who worked intimately with the spirits, journeying between the worlds, rallying the support and healing help of those inhabiting the other worlds. They were said to consult the spirits in order to learn what intrusions needed to be removed, and what aspects of their 'client' needed to be restored or left alone. When the removal of an intrusion was required, the procedure was executed on the spiritual level only. When the shaman consulted their client, they saw their essence by looking with their inner eyes. In doing so, they were able to identify and remove entities that were both intangible and invisible to the naked eye. The practice of extracting entities was, and still is, a very delicate, complicated and, at times, extremely dangerous procedure, which involved specific subtle tools, skills and knowledge known only to initiated shamans. When we suspect we may be carrying a dark side entity (the actual chances of which are a million to one), or we believe we may know someone who is, Flycatcher suggests we employ someone qualified to confirm our fears and perform the most appropriate extraction procedure. On a gentler level, Flycatcher recommends the cleansing of negative thought by surrendering feelings of anger, resentment, jealousy and fear and tempering them with gratitude, tolerance and love. When negative energy accumulates in or around the home, office or other space, Flycatcher espouses the cleansing of such space via the invocation of 'white light'. The procedure, known as 'white lighting', involves constant and fully maintained concentration, with intent kept pure and focused at all times. White light cleansing involves 'surrounding' the self or another or 'filling' an entire space with visualised white light energy. Like turning on a light in a darkened room, the intention of white lighting must be to transform negative energy into positive energy while visualising it being absorbed by the Universe and neutralised by Spirit.

Friarbird
Prayer

Friars were members of a mendicant religious order that emerged in Medieval Europe who dedicated its followers to a life of poverty, forcing them to rely solely on the charity of others for their survival. Following an apostolic way of life, their sole purpose was to venture out into the world and preach to the people. They begged for food and shelter and, in exchange for the support they were offered, helped the poor and cared for the sick. Living a minimalist life, they sacrificed a life of material possession in favour of spiritual attainment. Friars compromised things that other men worked hard to acquire because they believed such things held them back and distracted them from realising the truth. They lived a life of concession, a balancing act that provided a way to honour their calling and the essentials required to live a simple, yet productive and helpful life. The Friarbird is a large member of the Honeyeater family. It has a heavy, down-curved bill that enables it to create a varying and unique range of calls. Friarbirds are fairly aggressive, especially when defending their territory and favourite source of nectar. Preferring a more tropical environment, Friarbirds are very similar in appearance to the temperate Wattlebirds. Plain brown in colour, they are comparable in size and are both exceedingly noisy.

Not afraid to stand in its power and fight for what it holds dear, the Friarbird celebrates the golden nectar offered to those dedicated to being of service to God or Spirit. It demonstrates that, with effort and devotion, life can be rich with reward on all levels, especially when commitment is given with no thought of recompense. It encourages us to celebrate a spiritual life, and to show gratitude for everything we have ever known, witnessed or experienced. Friarbird preaches that we can live deeper, richer lives free of the burdens that come with materialism, judgement and jealousy by simply opening our hearts to tolerance, trust, peace, joy and compassion. Living a life haunted by negative feelings, beliefs and actions is a waste. Life should be animated, vibrant and dynamic. And by inviting Spirit into our lives, it can be...and so can we. One way is no better or more right than another. Spiritual development is individual, so take heed from whatever tradition inspires you to explore. When you do find a path that rouses you, allow yourself to be touched deeply by its teachings. Open your heart up to love and compassion so that you may never know doubt and fear again. One way of discovering the existence of Spirit is through prayer. Prayer sustains and enriches us. It is a vital step in the uniting of the body, mind and spirit. Our everyday experiences, needs and wishes provide the substance for our prayers, so try to create some simple prayers that can be said daily, or used in meditation. Try following the three steps that I have come to trust:

1. Surrender your fears, wants and needs. Surrender them all to Spirit so that they can take care of them for you.
2. Offer gratitude for all your experiences and the beauty that surrounds you today. Our experiences are what help build wisdom, and it is the beauty that surrounds us (in the form of family and friends) that make our experiences worth while.
3. Make a commitment to do better. By committing to improve your life (whether it be physically, mentally or spiritually), you are not only making a pact with Spirit, you are also forging one with yourself.

Always remember, great change and positive manifestation can be achieved if you invite prayer (no matter how brief or in what form) to become a sacred part of your life.

Frogmouth
Secret Keeper

The Frogmouth is an anomalous member of the Nightjar family and is not a true member of the Owl family, as is often assumed, despite its nocturnal habits and similar hunting techniques. Frogmouths sit stock-still, their faces pointed skyward, like a dead branch. Their grizzled tawny-grey plumage artfully camouflages the Frogmouth among the bark and rotting limbs of old trees.

The Frogmouth's tawny-grey plumage is reminiscent of the silver-grey hair of our Elders, the secrets they hold and the experience they can impart. Elders were once revered as 'wise ones', simply because their wisdom had been accumulated over many years of life experience. They appeared to walk in beauty and in harmony with all things. They were seen as being 'content' and at peace with their lot in life. They were free of the mundane issues that hinder the progress of the everyday man. They had learned from their life experiences, integrating this accumulated wisdom into their future perception of life, thus freeing themselves of the burdens and restrictions that promote anxiety, anger, guilt and resentment. Their knowledge was sought because they were believed to be able to see through the self-created illusions of fear and regret that bind us and prevent us from moving forward. Frogmouth encourages us to seek out the secrets being held in trust by our Elders. Approach them with respect and ask them to share their sacred knowledge. Ask questions about their history, their childhood and the way of their generation. Inquire as to what life was like for them, how they interacted with their peers and kin and the responsibilities expected of them by their seniors. Speak of chores, education and wars, of times spent at school, of love, fashion and economic flow. Most importantly though, ask the Elders of Spirit, God, Creation and the medicine ways of all things. Seek their opinion on things of nature, for example, the cycles of life and the Universe. Ask about the things that make your heart sing, of what saddens you and what inspires you to reach higher levels of awareness. Ask until there is nothing more to ask, and then incorporate the memories and wisdom of these things into your life and share them, with the blessings of your Elders, as the sacred knowledge of your people.

Gannet
Focused Breathing

Gannets are seabirds and are a familiar sight off the southern coast of Australia. Also known as the 'Booby', the sea-faring Gannet hunts by diving from heights of 20 metres or more in a vertical free fall motion. It has no nasal passages; all breathing is accomplished via the mouth. Coming to shore to breed, the Gannet spends the majority of its life on shallow coastal waters hunting fish and squid.

Breath doesn't just refer to the mundane act of respiration; it's a potent instrument of life that provides for energy, wind, stamina and vigour. Breath is a comprehensive force. It is the epitome of life. For thousands of years yogic teachers have espoused the belief that focused breathing can ease pain, manage emotions and improve physical health. It is a fact that most people don't breathe properly. Poor posture and stress are among the reasons why many of us are denied the benefits of a full, deep breath. Focused breathing greatly influences the productivity of the human mind and body. It improves physical, mental and emotional health by instilling a sense of relaxation, soothing anxiety and ensuring a greater flow of oxygen into the body. Gannet honours its breath; so much so that it has evolved in salute to the sacred act. Having no nasal passages means it can dive to great depths at amazing speed, with no threat of hindering its ability to breathe when it surfaces. By ignoring the importance of breath, we effectively disconnect from each another and ourselves. Without breath we are devoid of Spirit. Breathing, when practised with awareness, is vital for the attainment of higher levels of awareness, growth and healing. It inspires creation by affording the healthy flow of energy through our bodies. When birthing a child, for example, the obstetrician or midwife will remind the soon-to-be mother to breathe. Pregnancy activates change on all levels; physically, mentally and emotionally. Focused breathing is highly beneficial to both the mother and child, therefore, as it helps to alleviate the stress caused by such change. Gannet Dreaming promotes correct, conscious and focused breathing, with the understanding that when breathing is maintained and disciplined, health, wealth and happiness walk hand-in-hand. It calls for us to be mindful of our breathing so that we may know calmness, clarity and a greater degree of energy and vitality.

Gull
Correct Behaviour

Gulls are closely related to Terns, Auks, Skimmers and Waders. They are relatively large birds, usually grey or white in colour with black markings on the head or wings. Most are ground nesting birds. Both carnivorous and opportunistic by nature, Gulls will take live food (such as Crabs and small Fish) or scavenge from trash cans, rubbish dumps and picnic grounds. Gulls are both resourceful and highly-intelligent. Most demonstrate complex methods of communication and highly-developed social structures. Whether during territorial defence, mating ritual or parent/chick interaction, Gulls exhibit complex behaviour, intricate body language patterns and calls that are multifaceted in both form and function. Gulls trying to woo a mate, for example, may perform a 'threat' display, but in a modified sequence that alters the meaning and intention of the display.

Gull offers tutorage in acceptable and expected protocol; invaluable lessons when joining any new group, community or association. We have all attended a dinner party and felt unsure as to which knife or fork to use first, for example. We all remember our first day at a new school or job, and the awkward feeling of not recognising anyone. And worse still, most of us know the horror of making a social mistake that makes us look and feel silly; an experience made worse by stress and uncertainty. Just as it casually glides over the rough waves, assessing the torrid sea below before descending to the surface to fish, Gull infuses composure to calmly observe others, to read their body language and study any control or hierarchical programs that may be being played. It alleviates stress by bringing us up to speed on the propriety of an unfamiliar setting or the dynamics of any new group so that we don't mess up socially or tread on toes. Put simply, Gull allows us to assess the lay of the land before artlessly blundering in. It coaches us in the subtle art of cues and signals so that we appear aware of the correct behaviour to display in any clique or situation.

Hawk
Messages

Hawks belong to the raptorial bird of prey family; a relationship shared with Eagles, Kestrels, Kites, Hobbies and Falcons. Hawks are diurnal carnivores, regularly seen hovering motionless over fields watching for movement in the grass below. They perch on power lines and fence posts, watching for Rats, Mice, Insects, small Birds and Rabbits. They occasionally feed on carrion when it is available. They are agile flyers, with some species capable of reaching great speeds, while others deftly take prey while on the wing. Although some Hawks swallow their catch while flying, others swoop down, snatch their prey and carry it to a vantage point, where they quickly dispatch it and tear it into bite-sized pieces.

According to Aboriginal legend, the Kestrel is the protector of the warrior spirit. It is said to have risen from the blood of a tribal war that ended in a great bush fire. It vowed to forever watch and protect the people against further attack. An Ancestor Spirit to some tribes, the Hawk is a messenger of Creation; the bringer of good tidings, healthy change and victory. The Hawk is celebrated as one of the Great Solar Birds that is supposedly able to stare directly at the sun without squinting to lessen the glare. To look directly into the sun without having to look away is symbolic of being able to look directly at an issue and see what needs to be acknowledged and addressed – for the self and others. To witness a Hawk in flight, to hear its cry or to find one of its feathers, suggests you are about to receive a sign or a gift from Spirit. Hawk's cry may indicate a bountiful harvest or an impending time of abundance, while the finding of a feather sometimes portends the birth of a child or a spiritual gift about to awaken within the receiver. Hawk puts us on alert for signs that may fruitfully guide us to the next phase of life. It asks us to remain vigilant and willing to act at a moment's notice. It assures us that it is okay to ask for signs indicating when messages are about to come so that we do not miss them. For example, asking Spirit through meditation or prayer that the messages be pre-signed by the appearance of, for example, a woman wearing predominantly yellow who will ask to take your photograph, is an obvious and precise way of knowing exactly when to be at your most attentive. Ask that the Spirit of the Hawk carry this request to Spirit with the clear understanding that as soon as a woman presents herself, dressed predominantly in yellow and asks to take your photo, Spirit will send an obvious message, sign or omen that will help you to see your future clearly; free of the usual emotional blockages or physical obstacles that have hindered your path in the past. The woman will act as your trigger; your signpost that tells you when to literally stop and listen for Spirit's guidance.

Heron / Egret
Watchfulness

Graceful and proud, Herons are wading birds also referred to as Egrets or Bitterns. Though not biologically distinct from Herons, Egrets are usually so named because of their typically all-white colour and more decorative plumage. Herons congregate in wetlands where they prey on Fish, Frogs and other aquatic creatures. Some species nest communally in trees, while others prefer reed beds. Considered highly intelligent, Herons display incredible skill, dexterity and adaptability to acquire food. They employ shadows to their advantage, often hunting along river banks or the edges of marshes where trees and reeds provide shade. When trees or reeds do not grow, however, some species are known to intentionally cast their own shadows over the water by holding their wings outstretched, a technique known as 'canopy feeding'. The Fish apparently mistake the bird for a shrub or a clump of reeds, so approach assuming it is safe. All that is required of the Heron at this point is to bow its head and snap up the Fish.

For me, the Heron personifies the hierophant: the monk, spiritual teacher and healer. The religious role of the hierophant has always been to enlighten the masses by offering a path of truth and devotion; a way deemed holy. The word hierophant comes from the Ancient Greek, *ta hiera*, meaning 'the holy', and *phainein*, 'to show'. In Tarot, The Hierophant (card number 22 of the Major Arcana) has come to signify the one who guides the people to a place of realisation, knowledge and wisdom. In a reading, it often represents a priest or minister, academic, counsellor or teacher. Ever patient and ever watchful, the Heron symbolises the teacher who waits patiently for potential students to appear and for the correct questions to be asked. The Heron is the wise-one, mentor and Elder; the one who provides guidance, helping others with their spiritual and emotional problems. Heron advocates being ever open to opportunity and willing to learn life's lessons. It suggests we find a level of stillness within ourselves, and nurture it so that we can remain forever receptive to the plethora of belief systems that are bound to present as we grow and develop. With outstretched wings, Heron welcomes us and grooms us for learning. It humbly heralds the appearance of a teacher, while announcing us ready to be offered sacred knowledge. Put simply, Heron teaches us how to access and interpret life's esoteric knowledge and its associated mysteries, as well as the best ways to integrate it meaningfully into our conscious lives.

Honeyeater
Nectar of Life

Honeyeaters belong to the family of songbirds equipped with flat, brush-like tongues, which they use to extract nectar and pollen from flowers. Many species of Australian plants require Honeyeaters to help them pollinate their flowers. The family includes the three species of Wattlebird. Of the approximate 170 species of Honeyeater, 65 are native to Australian shores. They build small cup-shaped nests, usually suspended in forks of branches.

Honeyeater Dreaming energetically opens our hearts to the joy of life, the gifts of Creation and the beauty that surrounds us each and every day. It reminds us of the joy found in 'being', and the abundance that comes when we surrender control over the 'hows, whys and whens' that dominate and limit our prospects. Honeyeater calls for us to dance in the sunlight and sing praise from the heart for the good things currently happening in our lives. In doing so, the little image we hold dear; the image of our yearned-for future, will have a chance of becoming reality. Put another way, by surrendering control of how, when and where our imagined future will come to fruition, we effectively guarantee its emergence. We welcome the nectar of life to flow freely our way, filling our life with opportunity and abundance. Alternatively, because many indigenous flowers rely on Honeyeaters for their reproduction, Honeyeater also encourages us to explore the heart of Australia's medicinal flowers and healing flowers, especially when we feel our health and passion for life waning. Honeyeaters fly from one plant to the next, tasting their nectar and awakening their essence, thus ensuring the survival of medicinal plants and flowers for generations to come. In doing so, it effectively spreads the message of Creation and life itself. There are now many vibrational essence-based remedies on the market created from plants and flowers indigenous to Australia. Harnessing the absolute energetic core of the plant or flower, essences are typically developed as alcohol-based tonics or tinctures best taken in drop form directly under the tongue. Honeyeater embodies the true essence and beauty of life by instilling within our consciousness the healing song of the medicine flowers. Its Dreaming literally translates as the Elixir of Life. It is its responsibility to generate a sense of freedom by awakening the prospect of abundance, good health and joy, and it is our responsibility to recognise it as such; to honour its wisdom by blissfully and freely integrating it into our life, while resisting the urge to limit it by worrying about the 'hows, whys and whens'.

Ibis
Sacredness

Ibis are characterised by long, scimitar-shaped bills grooved above from base to tip which it uses to probe Ant nests, Spider holes and muddy river beds for the tender morsels hiding there. They live in large flocks and feed mainly on Fish, Frogs and Lizards. Ibis breed in colonies in warm regions, sometimes with other water birds such as Spoonbills, Herons and Cormorants. Their nests are generally built as rough platforms in tree tops, but they will also breed on low bushes in reedy marshes.

The Ancient Egyptians revered the Ibis as the incarnation of Thoth, the god of knowledge, magickal words and writing who was said to shoulder the head of an Ibis. It was thought that he created the world by hatching the World Egg while speaking the sacred words of Creation. Ibis Dreaming nurtures the search for wisdom and the keys to 'real' magick. It literally coaches us as we probe the ancient mysteries for the secrets to our own purpose. It expands our responsiveness to the more sacred forms of healing, for example, as well as revealing ways of safely accessing the magickal arts. Ibis opens the gates of awareness by illuminating our inherent spiritual strengths and abilities, while confirming our once imagined past-life experiences as true. Such information can be accessed through meditation, silent contemplation, journey work and automatic writing – a skill easily mastered by invoking the spirit of the Ibis and, in turn, the energies of Thoth. The Encyclopædia Britannica describes automatic writing as 'writing produced involuntarily when the subject's attention is ostensibly directed elsewhere. The phenomenon may occur when the subject is in an alert waking state or in a hypnotic trance, usually during a séance'. At first, the writer may simply produce a succession of seemingly unrelated words, but when proficient, may generate substantial bodies of quality information. It has happened that such writings have formed the basis for book manuscripts, poetry, music, song lyrics or limericks. In rarer circumstances, directions to help find items lost (among other forms of guidance) are revealed, as are messages from the dearly departed or channelled interactions from heavenly bodies, such as Angels, Spirit Guides and Extra Terrestrial life forms. Those 'probing' for the deeper mysteries and wonders of Spirit, therefore, would do well to invoke the Ibis as their teacher, guide, channel and protector. The sacredness found will change your life forever.

Jabiru
Vigilance

Australia's only true Storks, Jabirus stand about a metre and a half tall. They have black necks, white shoulders, black wings and red legs, hence their other name: 'the Black-necked Stork'. Jabirus mate for life and share the responsibility of raising the young. The sexes can be distinguished by the colour of their eyes: the males have black eyes, while the females have yellow eyes. Jabirus mainly eat fish, but will take most things from the water – including Crocodile hatchlings!

When considered symbolically, both Storks and Cranes proffer similar meaning. When in flight, for example, both are said to embody the souls of the recently departed. Flying in triangular formation, with the stronger birds leading and the younger and weaker birds allocated to the centre, both Cranes and Storks are considered emissaries of birth and death. As Australia's only Stork, the Jabiru demonstrates how change, release and surrender may be harnessed and integrated as viable options, and how, once realised as gifts of power, they can quickly reveal a chance to start over. When referring to change, the word 'death' is often taken literally, forming images in the mind of emotional upheaval, funerals and cemeteries. So, when the word is used in a divinatory or symbolic way, it must be understood that it more often than not refers simply to a necessary ending: a transition or the closing of one door so that another may open. Death and rebirth are interrelated. One cannot exist without the other. They go hand in hand. 'Death' leads to freedom. It represents a period we must surrender to in an attempt to liberate ourselves from suppression, depression and hardship. In order to assure change of any kind, we must prepare for it and see ourselves worthy of it. We must vigilantly prepare for its arrival…and be ready to work with it at a moment's notice. By welcoming 'death' (in the form of a long-awaited and necessary ending), we essentially herald a new phase of life. The fact that Storks are also famous for their ageless, romantic relationship to newborn babies and children should come as no surprise. Having asked our parents as little kids, 'Where do babies come from?' many of us were undoubtedly told that Storks deliver them (like the Stork that delivered Walt Disney's Dumbo the Elephant to his mother, Mrs Jumbo) from Heaven. They are bringers of light; ambassadors of new life; symbols of fertility, promise and confirmation. After a time of confusion, Jabiru guarantees a time of clarification. Jabiru Dreaming primes us for new beginnings; awakenings that can only be described as breakthroughs or periods of rebirth. So, as ambassadors of both birth and death, it is unsurprising to learn that Jabirus are also called Policeman-Birds, a title that goes a long way to authenticate their sacred role as vigilant protector of souls – old and new / here and beyond / past and present.

Kingfisher
Halcyon Days

Kingfishers have large heads and powerful bills. They feed mainly on small fish and aquatic creatures. They build their nests in tunnels dug into riverbanks and lay pure white eggs. Kookaburras are the largest members of the Kingfisher family.

Winter solstice, or 'midwinter' (December 21 / 22 in the Northern hemisphere; June 21 / 22 in the Southern), transpires as the shortest day and the longest night of the year. It literally marks the beginning of Winter. It is renowned as a festival of light and rebirth, where people gather together and engage in rituals and other celebrations. The seven days before and after the winter solstice are known poetically as the 'Halcyon Days'; days known to be both quiet and still. Legend has it that the Kingfisher, or Halcyon, builds its nest on the ocean during the seven days leading up to the Winter solstice, when the waters are serene, and incubates them during the seven days thereafter, after which time, it is said, they grow and develop, marking fourteen full days of tranquillity. Kingfisher heralds a time of emotional peace and quiet, when clarity will be yours and answers to difficult problems will become obvious. The emotional pool of life will be stilled and light will be shed, affording time and opportunity to address tumultuous issues troubling your heart and mind. It gently prompts us to shed aspects that no longer serve and to literally start afresh. Kingfisher opens a fourteen day window of opportunity to peacefully handle emotional situations, to speak from the heart or to openly deal with grief, pain or suffering. Inspiring peace and gratitude, Kingfisher suggests taking time out to rest, celebrate and simplify life. Kingfisher rekindles memories of good times past, of childhood fun, old friendships and lost love. It brings to mind our own Halcyon Days, and provides solid reason to reminisce and speak fondly of years gone by. In doing so, Kingfisher welcomes healing and closure, answers to questions never asked and old scores settled. It compels us to appreciate more deeply the beauty and innocence of our own children too, by reminding us that their time as little ones will pass too quickly and, before we know it, they will be grown and gone forever. Kingfisher asks that we celebrate life – and do what we can to ensure we never look back with regret. It asks that we stop and smell the roses occasionally, to appreciate the little, magickal moments that only come once in a while. To find solace in the heaven-sent times of peace and tranquillity, those times of stillness that only come about every so often, is to welcome the true meaning of 'Halcyon Days' and the wisdom of the Kingfisher.

Kiwi
Surrender

The Kiwi is indigenous to the shores of New Zealand. It grows to a height of approximately 18 inches, has a little plump body, small round head and brown plumage with streaks of white. Its plumage enables it to camouflage itself by literally blending in with the light and shadows of the undergrowth. The Kiwi feeds on worms, insects and berries, which it finds with its strong legs and long, slightly curved beak – a powerful tool used to probe rotten logs and the ground litter that covers the forest floor.

According to legend, the Kiwi once had brightly coloured feathers and powerful wings. One day the Creator noticed that bugs were eating the forest's plants. If something was not done, there soon would be no forest left. Someone had to become the 'Official Bug-Catcher'. So, all the birds were called together and asked if they would leave the forest canopy forever to live on the forest floor to guard the forest's plants by destroying all plant-eating bugs. One after another they refused, nervously offering lame excuses for why they could not help. The Creator feared that all would be lost, until it came down to the last bird – the Kiwi. Realising the position he was in, the Kiwi willingly volunteered. Kiwi knew that the role meant great sacrifice: the loss of his colourful feathers and powerful wings. He knew that if he did not offer, no one would, and the forest would be lost forever, and all the birds and animals would eventually die out. Kiwi selflessly surrendered his wings for the betterment of all and, as a reward, was gifted with a long, powerful beak and the title of 'the bravest and most famous bird'. Kiwi calls for us to surrender. By surrendering, we can expect to be pushed forward. Surrendering does not mean 'giving up', but rather 'giving in'. Giving up suggests defeat. It is deemed weak. Giving in, however, is to surrender with strength and a willing heart. It is to accept the fact that we cannot possibly know 'how' things will proceed or come to fruition. It is to focus on the desired outcome and to surrender the 'how' aspect over to Spirit. So long as we have a clear picture of 'what' we desire, we can surrender control over the 'how'. Quite literally, before we can further our lives on any level, we must first be willing to give something up – be it a tangible person, place or thing, or just a thought, belief or fear. Fear, when surrendered, transforms our view of life. Always worrying about the 'what ifs' limits our potential. Kiwi encourages us to surrender all limiting behaviour and beliefs so that we may welcome abundance and success into our lives. Kiwi instils this understanding by carrying us during tough transitional periods. It asks that we examine our lives and decide what – if anything – needs to be surrendered for the betterment of ourselves and others.

Kookaburra
Healing the Self

As the largest member of the Kingfisher family, Kookaburras have solid, thickset bodies, square heads and powerful beaks. Cavity nesters that take advantage of tree hollows and hollowed out termite mounds, Kookaburras inhabit forests, open woodlands, farmland, orchards and grassy plains. Kookaburras use their strong beaks to catch Fish, small Snakes, Frogs, Lizards, Rodents and Insects. Relying on the wait-and-pounce hunting technique, they find a vantage point, and wait for prey to pass by. When it does, they drop from their perch and grab it in their beak, bashing it against a tree or rock until it is dead.

Taking responsibility for your own healing is probably one of the most confronting things you can do, especially if the intention is to acknowledge and release pent-up pain, confusion and resentment, which are common by-products of years of postponed healing. In our times, it is common for people to live their entire lives without ever truly healing many of their past painful experiences and long-held resentments. Most of the time these individuals do not realise there is an alternative to the internal suffering caused when we ignore the need for healing or fail to see that there is healing to be done. It is often ignorance rather than denial that prevents healing from taking place. Kookaburras have a distinctive call that strongly resembles human laughter, thus earning it the title of 'the Laughing Kookaburra'. Many assume therefore, that the message of the Kookaburra is that of lightening up and learning to laugh at yourself. It may be true that its laughter inspires others to laugh along with it, and this rather obvious assessment of Kookaburra's Dreaming is sometimes relevant. But the truth of the matter is that Kookaburra calls for us to probe far deeper than its superficial laughter for meaning. Among their regular prey, Kookaburras catch Snakes by plunging down, seizing them behind the head, flying up high into the air and dropping them to their death. Snake is the harbinger of healing on all levels. Kookaburra therefore, as a bird that hunts Snakes, is telling you to take responsibility for your own healing and to stop laughing it off. Although you may have never spoken of your desire to see your own healing fulfilled, those around you will have sensed the need. Verbalising your need for healing to these people will not only be a relief for you, it will result in a collective sigh from those around you. 'That explains so much ...' will be the general consensus. Kookaburra awakens us to our inner truth and, thus, the dawning of a new day. So remember, that to witness a silent Kookaburra is Spirit's way of restoring faith in our quest for personal healing.

Lapwing / Plover
Eagerness

Lapwings are relatively large, ground-dwelling birds that inhabit open grasslands and swamps, feeding on Earthworms, Insects and their larvae. They nest on the ground in a rough scrape made in the earth, which they edge with pebbles and twigs. Found throughout Australia, their unmistakable call (a loud 'kekekekekekekek') is often heard at dusk.

So enthusiastic to hatch and get on with life, Lapwing Chicks are said to dash eagerly from their nest with egg shells still wedged on their heads. Lapwing encourages us to approach everything we do with a sense of excitement, vitality and passion. It doesn't know doubt or trepidation – in fact, its approach to life is almost one of barefaced impatience. Lapwing primes us to move at a moment's notice; to be alert for windows of opportunity and to never hesitate when it comes to embracing them. Hesitation (no matter how slight) may result in the window closing forever, with the opportunity being lost or offered to someone else. Once in a lifetime, opportunities come along that are worth their weight in gold. To ponder on their potential is to doubt your ability to bring them to fruition or your worthiness to accept them as yours. Uncertainty may be construed as weakness on your part, with propositions revoked as a result, opportunities lost and, worse still, future openings offered to the next in line instead of to you. Lapwing advocates the decision to welcome opportunity whenever it knocks, and to hastily accept any offers that come your way. You can always change your mind later and pass the torch to someone more befitting, should you choose to. It is better to say yes and reconsider later, than to miss out completely and risk never being asked again.

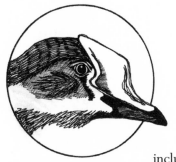

Lotus-Bird
The Cosmos

The Lotus-Bird, or Jacana, is built for its specialised life spent walking on the floating flora of Australia's tropical and subtropical freshwater wetlands, including lagoons, billabongs, swamps, lakes, rivers, ponds and dams. Their long toes help to balance their body weight as they walk across the lily pads and other water born vegetation. Lotus-birds eat aquatic insects, taken from the floating vegetation and directly from the surface of the water.

A powerful, protective charm, the perfume of the Lotus is said to protect those who inhale its scent, and if carried, will bring good luck and blessings from the gods. A sacred flower, the Lotus blossom epitomises what it means to live a 'spiritual' life. Rooted firmly in the mud, for example, it ascends the gloomy waters of the swamp to pierce the surface and emerge. In doing so, it symbolically rises above the mundane world and the physical body, to secede the world of physical yearning and the emotions, enter the rational realms of thought and inspiration to finally comprehend true spiritual enlightenment, growth and clarity. Chakras (pronounced 'shack-ras') are energy centres found within the human body. The term 'chakra' (from the Sanskrit word for 'wheel' or 'disk') can be found in ancient yoga philosophies and Indian tantric texts, with many Eastern religions incorporating chakras into their traditions, often depicting them as perfectly formed, appropriately coloured Lotus flowers. Chakras are anchors, filtering energy from the environment and drawing it into the body. They ensure that there is an even, harmonious flow of energy within the body at all times. It is important that the chakras are in balance with one another, so that the energy flows smoothly between them. When a chakra is completely in harmony, it is described as being 'fully open' like a Lotus in full bloom spinning freely and in perfect balance. To quote a good friend of mine, Anita Ryan-Revel: 'The study of chakras dates back many centuries, and as such, is considered an integral part of holistic health. They are esoteric and vibrational energy forces intrinsically linked with the human body and physiological wellbeing and are considered keys to enjoying a beautiful life. By consciously working with your chakra energy and the issues that relate to each zone, you can bring your life into balance and experience a deep sense that 'all is right' with your world - in particular the seven essential facets of life: security, abundance, self-ownership, love, truth, trust and joy. The chakras are located roughly near the glands found along the vertical meridian of the human body. The name of each chakra loosely describes its location'. According to Anita, the major chakras and their life-aspects are listed as follows:

1. Base (Security)
2. Sacral (Abundance)
3. Solar Plexus (Self-ownership)
4. Heart (Love)
5. Throat (Truth)
6. Third Eye (Trust)
7. Crown (Joy)

Lotus-Bird reminds us that we are a part of the Cosmos, and not apart from it. It calls for us to acknowledge the place we hold within the Universe, and what we can do to make it a better place. Lotus-Bird speaks of Spirit, the Circle of Life and Creation itself. It reminds us that before we can heal the planet or any one else, we must first concentrate on healing ourselves by improving our life and view of the world. We can begin to integrate this knowledge by working in harmony with our chakras. In doing so, we will learn to deal with life's issues on a deeper, more meaningful level, and in time, reconnect on a conscious level to the Cosmos and the realms of Spirit.

Lyrebird
Genetic Memory

Lyrebirds are famous for their ability to mimic sound. Mixed in with their own calls, Lyrebirds have been known to incorporate sounds of chainsaws, horns, alarms and even human speech. They call throughout the year, vocally marking their territory while defending it from other Lyrebirds. Ground dwellers during the day, Lyrebirds roost in trees at night. Lyrebirds are approximately the size of a medium-sized Chicken, with a spectacular tail of fanned feathers. When the male spreads its tail during courtship, it strongly resembles a lyre: a traditional musical instrument of ancient Greece.

Lyrebird supports the concept of genetic memory through its ability to remember the forest sounds of over 200 years ago. Flawlessly mimicking repetitious sound, the older birds pass the sounds they were taught by their parents onto their young, thus literally handing-on sacred lineal knowledge to the next generation. The young instinctively learn the sounds almost as if they are hearing them through their Ancestor's ears. Awareness of genetic memory is often confused with that gleaned from past lives. The notion of past lives advocates that we have all had life experiences in other time periods. It also lends itself to the possibility that we may have lived lives of notable people from history. Many speak of recalling their past lives, remembering firsthand their lives as a famous person in a familiar historical setting. Accounts of children recalling life memories outside the realms of physical possibility are being documented more and more these days. Lyrebird invites us to ponder the thought that, instead of these being personal memories, might they not be the memories of our Ancestors? Experiences passed on genetically for us to access and to learn from in our current lifetime? Within every individual cell that collectively makes us whole, reside the keys to the unlocking of the memory of past experiences passed from one generation to the next. Such memory is inherited and genetic in nature. Genetic memory represents all that we have ever been. It embodies all that we have ever experienced, all that we have ever encountered and all that we have ever understood. It represents all that our body inherently recognises without explanation; knowledge that cannot be justified or rationalised. It is a fair argument, therefore, that suggests our body remembers the memories of everything ever witnessed by us since the beginning of time. Lyrebird primes us for a time of great remembering. The Ancestors are calling to us from the Void to remember a connection shared or a lifetime had in a period long gone. Such effort will provide deeper understanding of the relationships and responsibilities we have now, enabling us to put them into context, thus affording us greater clarity and personal direction.

Magpie
Balance

Magpies are named after the unrelated black and white Magpies found in Europe. A common sight in most Australian backyards, Magpies readily take food scraps from human hands, pet food bowls, picnic baskets and bird-feed tables. Magpies (also known as Flute-birds, in recognition of their melodious song), rise early in the morning and carol to affirm territory and to herald the new day. They occupy parks, gardens and open bush land. During their breeding season, Magpies become very aggressive. They are known to swoop and attack passers-by, launching their attack from behind, clipping ears and swooping heads.

Magpie is the bringer of balance – the yin-yang of the bird world – an agent of awareness, the embodiment of 'the opposites that are equal' and the force that champions the attainment and correct use of esoteric knowledge. She demonstrates that spiritual knowledge, and the power that comes with it, must be approached with a committed, objective mindset. It cannot be attained overnight, or bought with money. Information gleaned during a weekend workshop, for example, can only ever be considered a foundation on which real learning, learning that comes with experience and practice, takes place. True wisdom must be deserved. It must be gathered over a lifetime of study and embraced as a way of life. It must become a path of the heart, explored with unquestionable devotion. Before questing for spiritual attainment, for example, we must first dedicate ourselves to becoming a whole person; a process that involves surrendering our familiar self to Spirit, so that our authentic self, hidden deep within, can emerge reborn. We must be prepared to face our fears and conquer them and turn our weaknesses into strengths and our darkest hours into gifts of power. In becoming a whole person we embark on an expedition to reclaim inner balance and authority and, in doing so, find ourselves stepping out of our comfort zone into the unknown. Magpie is a doorkeeper to other realms; a guardian who lets only those willing to honour the sacred balance between the good and bad, light and dark, and feminine and masculine in all things to explore her world. It guides us to a place of awareness, showing us how to better understand the innate marriage between the opposites that are equal and the duality within all things. If you are drawn to investigate Magpie Dreaming, you are being primed for a deepening of purpose and a broadening of perception. Magpie heralds an obligatory confrontation of fears, the reshuffling of thoughts, review of values and a loosening up of everything that has offered sustenance and strength up until now. It means being ready to walk a path of the heart to find a place of inner freedom: a quest for a better understanding of the poise that resides within you and everything of nature.

Magpie Lark
Life Force

The Magpie Lark is neither a Magpie nor a Lark. It derives its name from the Magpie-like colouring of its feathers and its musical Lark-like call. It is also known as the 'Mud Lark' or 'Peewit'. Magpie Larks build their nests from mud collected from the edges of streams and dams and from under dripping garden taps.

The Dreaming of the Magpie Lark represents an ancient alliance between humanity and mud: the nurturing, life-giving 'blood' of the Earth Mother herself. For centuries, mud has played varying roles in tribal ceremony, particularly those that involved the ritualistic re-enactment of the birth, death and rebirth cycle. Participants smeared their faces and bodies with great clods of mud, for example, to demonstrate their willingness to reunite with their inherent life force and dormant connection to the womb. A fine example is the Sweat Lodge ceremony – a ceremony practised by many cultures, but made famous by the Native American people. As the 'masculine' pre-heated stones are placed in the womb-like central pit of the lodge, the act of Creation is made complete when cold water is poured over the stones. Hot steam billows and those in the lodge sweat heavily, lying on the cold earth to escape the heat. As they exit, they fall to the ground, exhausted and covered in mud (symbolic of the blood of our mothers' womb) – pink and weak like newborn babies. They emerge as if reborn, so deeply humbled by the magnitude of the experience that their life is never quite the same again. On a different note, while keeping to the theme of 'new life', mud found in constantly moving rivers and streams is often rich in nutrients (namely nitrate and phosphate), particularly where tall, leafy plants overhang and line the riverbanks inviting an abundant community of fish and waterfowl. In many parts of the world, crops are regularly flooded with water from nearby rivers so that they may benefit from the fertile silt. It forms a preparatory 'blanket' that returns life force to the tired soil and encourages healthier growth and yield. Mud is also celebrated in the beauty industry for its therapeutic qualities, particularly mud derived from mineral rich areas around natural springs, moors, peat lands, volcanoes and oceans. Such mud is said to hold medicinal qualities potent enough to treat varying forms of rheumatic, skin and digestive problems. Because mud is soluble, the healing nutrients in it are easily absorbed into the skin thus ensuring the detoxifying, softening and firming process. To me, the fact that Magpie Larks use mud as their main nesting material strengthens its symbolic sacredness. Its cup-shaped nest is feminine in form – receptive, nurturing and fertile. As such, it is reminiscent of the womb. The Magpie Lark gathers the mud while it is damp, and moulds it into shape. When dry, it is strong and lasting, inspiring a protective energy that cradles the young until they are ready to fledge. Magpie Lark Dreaming embodies the true essence of life force. It invites us to explore our soul and to celebrate life itself. It calls to us to recognise the sacredness found in all things – to recognise the essence that runs through nature and to celebrate the presence of Spirit. Magpie Lark reminds us of the fertility present in our life; the power of which is evident in our intent, hopes and desires, but also tangibly in our blood and the mud of the Earth Mother herself. Life force is Spirit – it is what inspires a healthy mind, body and spirit; it inspires us to strive, dare, dream and yearn. It is the essence and cycles of life itself, found too in our sacred rites of passage that provide foundation for a long, whole and productive life.

Malleefowl
Efficiency

Malleefowl are large, ground-dwelling birds (around the size of domestic Chickens) that roost in trees at night. Timid and mostly solitary by nature, Malleefowl inhabit dry mallee-eucalypt scrub and open woodland, building nest mounds of sand and ground litter. They scrape leaves, branches, twigs and bark into a heap and, as the ground litter decomposes under the warmth from the sun, the heat generated within the mound incubates the eggs.

Effectively freeing the Malleefowl from the tedious role of traditional incubation, the nest mound affords them more time to search for food, while allowing them to roost in the trees at night away from predatory Foxes, Dingoes and Goannas. Malleefowl Dreaming is all about efficient time management and organisation. It models a system that provides for both personal respite and dutiful attention to day-to-day responsibilities. It coaches us as we set about making our life smarter and more efficient, striking a harmonious balance between business and pleasure, work and play and responsibility and fun.

Mistletoebird
Vows

Mistletoe is a parasitic plant passed from one host tree to another by Mistletoebirds (among others). They eat the berries and wipe the sticky remnants from their beaks onto the tree's branches. The seeds in the sticky mass take root and assimilate themselves into the growth pattern of the host tree, drawing on its nutrients and moisture to survive. Diminutive and vibrantly coloured creatures, Mistletoebirds (or Flower-peckers) are mainly found in Southeast Asia, with one species indigenous to Australia. Adult Mistletoebirds feed on berries and supplement their offspring's diet with insects caught on the wing.

Common wherever mistletoe is abundant, the Mistletoebird is the keeper of vows and promises – especially those inspired by love. It embodies the pledges we make when we first declare our love and devotion for another, including those we forge with ourselves. It can suggest that a reconfirmation of vows, a meaningful show of affection or deeper appreciation for another is in order. No one enjoys feeling as though they are undervalued or taken for granted. Your lover, spouse or life partner needs to know they are loved and appreciated – and hearing it from you will only strengthen the bonds you share. It is said that if you kiss your true love beneath a spray of mistletoe, the love you share will last eternally. Love, trust and commitment are among the greatest gifts anyone can offer another. Mistletoebird reminds us that to know true love is to know what it means to be alive. So, however that love manifests, it must never be taken for granted. Love should be continuously strengthened, reaffirmed, kept alive and revisited, for once it is weakened, it is hard to reclaim, but once lost, it is usually gone forever. Interestingly, placing a sprig of mistletoe in a newborn baby's crib is said to guard against Faeries. Folklore holds true the belief that babies are sometimes kidnapped by Faeries and substituted with 'changelings'. Placing mistletoe in your baby's bassinette, therefore, will deter such Faerie-fascination, keeping him or her safe from harm.

Nightjar
Assurance

At dusk, the Nightjar stirs and begins hunting for insects, taking them on the wing just as a Hawk might take birds and other prey. The Nightjar has a wide-set jaw and bill, long, pointed wings and tail, huge, round eyes, weak legs and tiny feet. A nocturnal bird, the Nightjar spends the day sitting motionless on the forest floor, its eyes closed to slits; their dull, motley plumage offering perfect camouflage, blending it seamlessly into the textures of the leaf litter and ground cover.

Just as a Chihuahua might see itself as a Great Dane, the Nightjar refuses to be held back by physical shortfall or fear. So much so, its confidence and sense of self has earned it the title of both 'Night Hawk' and 'Moth Hawk', names that might inspire imagery of birds of much greater size and strength. Despite its healthy sense of assurance, the Nightjar is also equipped with forethought enough to know when to back off or lay low. And with this in mind, Nightjar is typically the totem of those who shun the belief that they are 'too small' to play with the 'big boys'. Nightjar coaches us to view ourselves as capable, worthy and central to the betterment of the planet. It refuses to see itself as insignificant and encourages us to follow suit. It helps build a soapbox from which we may be heard or a setting in which we may be seen. It supports those who reach out and encourage others; those of us who feel the calling to inspire, mentor and teach. Nightjar builds a sense of confidence, assurance and solid foundation. Promoting belief in oneself, Nightjar says, 'Puff out your chest, hold your head high and feel proud'. It helps us find our voice so that we may begin seeing ourselves as capable of anything and worthy of everything.

Owl
Deception

Owl is the common name for the family of nocturnal birds of prey, made up of two distinct groups: the Typical Owls, of which there are about 122 species, and the Barn owls of which there are about 12 individual species. While there are some anatomical differences between the two families, all Owls have nocturnal vision, silent flight and a carnivorous diet.

Some of Australia's indigenous people believe that Owls embody the souls of women. They are therefore considered sacred. The Owl is a silent flyer, due to the velvety surface of its feathers, making the element of surprise the strength of its assault – its victim is usually completely unaware of it, until the moment of attack. The first that the unwary Mouse knows of the presence of an Owl, for example, is the pain of sharp talons felt in its sides. The Dreaming lesson here is that of deception. Today, according to its pooled spiritual teachings, the Owl warns us not to assume that all is well all of the time. People and situations we trust may not be completely trustworthy, but Owl has the ability to see what others may miss. The gift of this Dreaming is to be undeceived by external appearances and to discover the truth beneath them. A bird that chooses to hunt at night, the Owl is up until dawn. She is one of the few creatures that actually waits for the sun to come up before retiring for a well-earned rest. She literally welcomes the sun as it illuminates and warms the horizon each morning. As such, she symbolically sheds light on those areas of our life that are being deceived by camouflage, fraudulence, pretence or duplicity. Owl's wisdom allows us to know when we are stuck in the content of our own lives, oblivious to the fact that we are wandering aimlessly through life. Owl sheds light on these moments, so that clarity may be retrieved and stability salvaged. By helping us to find light at the end of an otherwise pitch-dark tunnel, Owl promises a time of approaching lucidity, new beginnings and promise. It cautions us when we are perhaps being deceived by the apparently innocent motives of another. Owl may come as a warning that you need to quickly ascertain the integrity hidden behind these motives and to determine how they may affect or influence your view of the world. The Owl has been gifted with clear night vision which, when employed with the right intent, affords us the ability to see what others may miss.

Oystercatcher
Concealment

Large, sturdy wading birds, Oystercatchers are often seen feeding along coastal edges hunting for molluscs, limpets, dogwhelks and muscles. With black or pied plumage, Oystercatchers have incredibly strong, long, flat and slightly up-turned bills, which they use to pry open shellfish with greater ease than other waders.

A symbol of supreme Mystery according to Christian tradition, the pearl is metaphorical of truth and wisdom. A beautiful seabird with a powerful bill used for prying open oysters, the Oystercatcher has plumage apparently stained with a mark that strongly resembles the sign of the crucifix. Christian tradition has it that the Oystercatcher once concealed Jesus under a mass of seaweed when it learned of the danger he was in. Out of gratitude for its selfless act of concealment, the Oystercatcher was marked thereafter with the sign of the cross to venerate its Dreaming. So long as you are not intentionally lying to anyone, including yourself, and no harm comes to anyone, including yourself, all is as it should be. Oystercatcher is not a supporter of the concealment of truth as a means of controlling others, but rather as a way of protecting one's sense of security and self-esteem. Choosing not to reveal a truth is not necessarily lying. If the topic never arises, one does not have to speak of it. It is no one's business but your own, so long as it does not interfere with or damage another's view of the world. If you look at your life and realise that a portion of yourself is being repressed for reasons that no longer serve you, turn this aggravating grit of sand into something precious. Open up and reveal it as your Pearl of Wisdom – the aspect of yourself that you yearn to have seen as sacred and worthy of public scrutiny. Oystercatcher asks what side of yourself you are concealing from the world, either intentionally or inadvertently. What aspects are you attempting to hide from yourself? What facets of your life would you like to see revealed and honoured by all? You are being reminded that there is a time and a place for everything, and that if it seems appropriate to conceal the truth of whom or what you are, then do it, but if it now seems inappropriate, then stop.

Parrot
Colour Therapy

There are approximately 300 different species of Parrot found throughout the world, with 56 species indigenous to Australia. Only five of the species common to Australia are found elsewhere in the world. They are best known for their brilliant range of colours, which include every hue of the rainbow. Parrots have two toes on each foot that face forwards and other two that face backwards, enabling them to hold their food when eating. Parrots have hooked bills, short necks and legs, round heads and stocky bodies.

Generally speaking, Parrot Dreaming is mainly centred on the vibrant, healing energy of colour. Recognising and integrating the subtle, vibrational properties of colour forms the basis of Colour Therapy. Colour Therapy supposedly reinstates a sense of wellness and equilibrium to our body's internal energy centres by honouring the ancient observation that our body's systems and organs resonate favourably to certain colours and poorly to others. Colour therapy is said to stimulate our inherent ability to heal our physical and spiritual body and to repel illness and dis-ease. Monitoring how we are feeling emotionally, physically and spiritually on a day-to-day basis, and responding accordingly by choosing the most appropriate colours to dress in, is a simple way of introducing 'colour therapy' into our lives. Bright, cheerful colours will help reduce negative feelings, for example, while being more specific with your choices will greatly influence how those feelings are affected and why. Blue, for example, inspires open and constructive communication, while yellow helps to awaken our intuitive abilities. Red is a passionate, determined colour, while green attracts new beginnings and nurtures positive change, growth and abundance. White promotes a sense of honesty, purity and trust, while Black has always indicated a contemplative, deep thinking, serious nature. If you are inspired to explore Parrot Dreaming, you may also consider studying colour therapy in any one of its many forms. Parrots are traditionally considered solar-influenced creatures. They are said to correspond vibrationally to the energies of the Sun, with such association marking them emissaries of change and the cyclical process of birth, death and rebirth. As such, Parrots herald new growth, new ideas and the dawn of a brand new day. Many species of Parrot can be taught to mimic human speech. They can therefore be considered envoys of the animal realm, linking their world with ours through the power of communication.

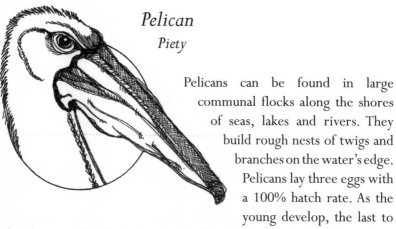

Pelican
Piety

Pelicans can be found in large communal flocks along the shores of seas, lakes and rivers. They build rough nests of twigs and branches on the water's edge. Pelicans lay three eggs with a 100% hatch rate. As the young develop, the last to hatch is expelled from the nest by the other two stronger chicks at an early stage. As the chicks begin to fledge, the strongest, and usually the first-born, attacks the other chick until it topples from the nest to its death. The remaining hatchling is always the most dominant and ensures that a strong bloodline continues.

One legend has it that the Pelican kills her young by smothering them with committed but excessive love. Another blames the mother for killing the chicks because of their persistent habit of striking them with their wings during feeding. The tale continues by saying that she mourns their death for three full days before, using her sharp bill, she pierces her heart and nourishes them back to life with her own blood. This account mirrors the sacrifice made by Jesus, who piously gave of himself for the betterment of the people, shedding his own blood as a promise of eternal life for those who honoured his life and his teachings. The Dreaming of the Pelican embodies goodness, godliness, forgiveness and faithfulness, as well as the categorical love of one for another. A sea-faring bird that maintains endurance by riding the atmospheric updrafts, the Pelican also instils a strong sense of balance as it confidently navigates the ocean's ever-changing waters. Pelican offers support to us as we contemplate the best way to handle life's ups and downs. So, apart from its lessons in piety, Pelican also instils a sense of buoyancy by encouraging optimism and endurance to handle any situation.

Quail
Family Protection

Members of the galliforme family, Quails come in a plethora of shapes and sizes. Typically squat little birds, with round heads and short legs, Quails are found all over the world. Australia has several species of native Quail, including the Button Quail and the King Quail.

According to folklore, Quails apparently post sentries; watchmen whose role it is to protect the rest of the flock by alerting them to the presence of danger. The sentry on duty apparently stands on one leg while clutching a stone in the other. Should they fall asleep, he or she will drop the stone onto the other foot, it is supposed, waking themselves instantly. True to the legend, Quails live in close-knit family groups called 'bevies'. On cold nights, the entire bevy will huddle together star-shaped for shared bodily warmth, with their tails pointing inward and their heads facing out. When threatened, the flock will burst into flight, fleeing in all directions. In doing so, they confuse their enemy while allowing all members to escape. Appearing unstructured with no thought of direction, the get-away is in fact well planned and rehearsed. Quail celebrates the joy that comes with knowing family and the protection and comfort it affords. It also celebrates the sacred responsibility of being the provider and protector of the family circle. It readies us in times of emergency and other unexpected situations by reminding us to have in place familiar and practised emergency plans to suit any circumstance (in times of house fire, for example). It also instils a sense of calm and group co-operation potent enough to deflect disaster and disarray should such a state ever arise.

Raven
Magick

Ravens are highly intelligent, black-feathered birds that share their family with Crows. Legend has it that Ravens communicate using a primitive form of 'language'. They have been observed, for example, 'calling' to larger predatory animals when they stumble across fresh road kill. Their call may attract a Fox, for example, or another creature strong enough to penetrate the road kill's hide. They will wait for it to eat its fill and then swoop down to feast on the exposed intestines and smaller portions of overlooked meat. Ravens eat carrion, rodents, insects, reptiles, Frogs, seeds, berries, fruit, nuts, acorns and eggs. They are a common sight around rubbish dumps, foraging in large flocks after the garbage trucks have upended their loads. Ravens have long been deemed 'evil' and considered 'bad' omens, with ties to dark witchcraft and the devil.

As messengers of the Void, Ravens guide us to a place of healing and wholeness. They reconnect us to Spirit by reminding us of the sacredness of prayer. Prayer sustains and enriches us. It is to converse with the divine energies of the Universe with the understanding that, in order to realise our wants and needs, all we need do is harness these divine energies in honour and remembrance of our innate connection to Spirit. Magick is the ability to communicate our needs and to channel our purpose by sitting within the silence, ceasing the inner chatter and reconnecting with the Universe. It is to seek the assistance of Great Mystery and to delve into the Void for answers – to call to Spirit and ask for help. Magick and prayer are similar. Prayer offers us the chance to talk to Spirit, while magick represents the results that come when we demonstrate perpetual faith in the power of prayer. Raven asks that you honour your innate ability to create magick by participating in the sacred act of prayer. When you pray you must do so with a reverent appreciation of Spirit, in gratitude for the life given to you at the time of your birth. Our prayers must be made in honour of the Earth Mother and in recognition of all the living creatures, and they must be made with the firm belief that all people shall someday look to Spirit and find the courage to walk as one. When you pray, you should ask for the best way to personally honour the ways of Spirit and to seek blessing for those close to your heart. When you finish you must spend a little time in silence to honour the Void, for the silence is sacred and no words are necessary. By embracing the Dreaming of Raven, you not only strengthen your line of communication with Spirit through prayer, you also better understand the deep wisdom that comes with knowing your purpose and the magick that comes with learning how to administer it. Raven offers inner peace that will eventually lead to a deepening of your soul essence and a balancing of the self. Your self-perception will begin to strengthen when you open your heart to the wisdom of the Raven.

Robin
Aspiration

Robins are related to Flycatchers and Chats. Common garden birds, Robins are known for their aggressive character and melodious song, especially during the Winter when they sing well into the evening. They nest in cracks in stone fences and walls and in chimneys. They will even take advantage of overturned flowerpots stored in garden sheds, and the discarded nests of other birds. Robins are relatively unafraid of humans and will venture close to a busy gardener, especially when digging is being done. The possibility of snatching up worms and insects disturbed by the activity makes it a risk worth taking. Beatrix Potter (in her tale of Peter Rabbit) made famous the now familiar image of a Robin perched on the handle of a spade stuck in freshly turned, snow-covered earth – an image depicted also in the children's story, 'The Secret Garden'.

A bird of the 'greenwoods', the Robin is said to embody the intrepid character of Robin Hood, the hero who stole from the rich to give to the poor. The appearance of the first Robin for the year is said to welcome new growth, rebirth and new beginnings. Wishes made on the first Robin are said to come true, or at least proffer good luck for the next twelve months. Robin represents those who 'wear their heart on their sleeve'; those able to convey their emotions without restraint and who are not afraid to do so publicly. They 'cry for the people' and the plight of the world, courageously voicing their sadness for all to hear. Robin people are easy to read because they cannot hide how they feel. With cheeks blushed with frustration, they say what they think and do what they deem to be right. They are unafraid to act on their feelings. You can always tell what they are thinking from their body language and facial expression. Robin people are inherently positive, optimistic and resilient. They are easily taken advantage of, though, when it comes to issues of the heart. They become 'accidental martyrs', falling victim to those exhibiting the 'bleeding heart'. Robin warns against sacrificing our own sense of wellbeing when helping others, thus guarding against being taken advantage of. Those drawn to investigate Robin Dreaming are often 'rescuers' or warriors-types prepared to fight battles that do not concern them. Robin reminds us that there will always be people out there who relish in being 'damsels in distress'; victims who petulantly demand that others take responsibility for their wellbeing because they can't or choose not to. When invoked productively, though, Robin becomes a potent ally in helping us realise our aspirations. It is a harbinger of new life and deliverer of dreams. It nurtures the chance to start over by affording support and opportunity to repair a wounded or broken heart. It primes us for change, realisation, endurance, wisdom, drive and healing. Robin asks if are you feeling over-sensitive. Have you been acting irrationally or feeling emotionally pressured? Do you need to free yourself from the burdens of others? Robin encourages us to 'toughen up' and to welcome positive change for ourselves instead of constantly trying to provide for others. Alternatively, Robin Dreaming offers support to those who, due to emotional abuse or overload, have cut themselves off from the world as a way of preventing further heartache. The Robin, perched on the shovel left standing in the snow, encourages us to dig deep and consult our heart of hearts. It helps us find the courage to thaw any 'frozen' or suspended emotion that needs to be surrendered, released and allowed to flow in a healthy, productive way. Robin restores faith in our feelings. It provides a soapbox from which we may learn to express ourselves openly and freely. It strengthens us as we learn to take risks, dare to dream and believe that our wishes can and will come true.

Sandpiper
Earthing Your Energies

Sandpipers are wading waterbirds. Some species have long, flute-like, slightly up-curved bills, while others have down-turned ones. Sandpipers inhabit muddy rivers and streams, mangroves, salt marshes, beaches, mudflats, swamps, lakes and estuaries, probing the sand for crustaceans and other aquatic creatures.

Most people are familiar with the tale of the 'Pied Piper of Hamlin'; a man employed to rid London of millions of Rats. Armed with nothing more than a magickal flute, he played an enchanted tune, charming the Rats to pursue him. Unable to resist the melody, the Rats followed the piper willingly into a fast flowing river where they met their inevitable demise. Rat Dreaming encourages us to act instinctively on our feelings, especially those that trigger agitation and dis-ease. It warns us when to take necessary action, when to leave and when to let fate take its course. Integrating both the legend of the Pied Piper and wisdom of the Rat into its Dreaming, Sandpiper encourages us to stand our ground, to earth ourselves and initiate practical steps that will see us stabilise the difficult, emotional situations that may be plaguing us at this time. Sand is made from trillions of tiny stones that were once pebbles, rocks, boulders, even mountains that crumbled helplessly into the sea over many years. Sandpiper encourages us to earth our energies and ward off emotional erosion by individually addressing our issues one after another, no matter how large or small they seem. In doing so, we can gradually move a mountain of problems one at a time, instead of feeling overwhelmed and blocked by the magnitude of their collective bulk. Sandpiper instils a sense of inner strength, thus building endurance and resolve to shun the familiar tendency to put off until tomorrow what needs to be addressed today. It helps us see life's issues for what they are, thus helping us to avoid making rash decisions. Sandpiper offers the strength to navigate the murkier waters of life, to regain clarity and probe for those things that promise to nurture our soul.

Spoonbill
Filtering

Spoonbills are large, mostly white-plumaged wading birds. They have naked heads and distinctive yellow or black, broad, spoon-shaped bills. Spoonbills slowly patrol shallow steams and rivers, swamps and estuaries, moving the submerged tip of their bill from side-to-side, filtering the water for small creatures, suspended aquatic plant-life and fish.

Spoonbill Dreaming embodies the act of 'filtering'. It helps us decipher life's messages to reveal our own sacred code; the ancient tongue that only we understand; the language of our Ancestors and the messages it contains that, when interpreted, will reveal our personal destiny here on Earth. It embodies the heartfelt search for, and the realisation of Universal wisdom, purity and truth. The white feathers of the Spoonbill symbolise wholesome inspiration, the energies that filter down from the Angelic realms nurturing undeniable clarity and faith. The golden bill of the common Spoonbill suggests the 'lightning bolt' attainment of higher knowledge, while the black bill of the Royal Spoonbill lends itself to the quieter, more personal, contemplative quest for inherent wisdom. Spoonbill is an emissary of creation and change, responsible for the maintenance and 'spoon feeding' of spiritual knowledge. 'A spoonful of sugar helps the medicine go down' is a famous line personified by the Spoonbill, who gently filters Universal truth, breaking it down to manageable levels of attainment. It represents the alchemical transformation of pure energy into physical form, as purity and truth become inspired forms of healing. It makes the integration of difficult concepts, emotional issues and confronting values that much easier to swallow, gently broadening our perception of the world. Spoonbill helps us filter and weigh up the purity of our own heart, so that we may become more aware of what will support us spiritually and what will not.

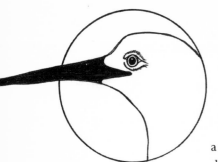

Stilt
Intimacy

Also called the 'Cobbler's Bird', the Stilt is a long-legged wading bird, with a slender bill that strongly resembles a cobbler's awl, the pointed boring tool used by shoemakers. In most species the bill is straight, but the Avocet (a close relative), has a slightly up-curved bill. Stilts use their bills to probe the sandy, muddy ground for aquatic creatures. They patrol the shallows of lakes, estuaries and swamps, hunting for crustaceans, molluscs and aquatic insects. Stilts take their prey with quick head motions, jabbing their bills deep into the sand.

According to folklore, the female shoe has long been linked to sexual intimacy and female fertility. An ancient Greek wedding custom, for example, held that to promote marital intimacy, the couple should insert a dagger (or other phallic-shaped object) into the bride's shoe. Cinderella's tiny glass (breakable) slipper was symbolic of her virginal state, while the 'old woman who lived in the shoe' embodied the supremacy of female fertility (a belief endorsed by the fact that she had so many children she did not know what to do). Even to this day, it is customary among some cultures to throw a pair of shoes at the feet of newlyweds to encourage intimate sexual relations and fertility, or to tie a pair of shoes to the towbar of the car before they depart for their Honeymoon. Another more barbaric tradition is the now outlawed Chinese custom of foot-binding. It was believed that for a woman to be sexually attractive, she must have tiny feet. Tiny feet were symbols of untainted purity. After years of binding, the disfigured feet were said to resemble Lotus Flowers, sacred symbols of life. Stilt Dreaming is all about intimacy. It celebrates the coming together of two people who have true feelings of affection and longing for one another, while bringing into healthy balance the emotions of love and lust. It reminds us of our inherent fertility and the new life and awareness that may spring from such intimate encounters, both literal and metaphorical. Surrounding the sacred act of creation is what is known as 'Great Mystery', the essence of all that is known to be unknowable. Creation imprints the core mysteries of life; birth, death and rebirth. It deems 'masculine energy' as typically metaphysical in nature, an essence force that cannot be contained or held in the palm of one's hand: sunshine, lightning, passion, sexual energy and war. All these are masculine in form. 'Feminine energy', however, is very physical and receptive in nature and can be touched, seen and felt. The womb, the Earth herself, the bearing of the children, the growing of the crops and human nature are feminine in form. Since ancient times it has been said that without the darkness of the feminine force (represented as the Great Mother's Womb and the nurturing energies of our Mother Earth), combined with the masculine light of the Grandfather Sun, the tiny acorn can never be expected to grow into a mighty oak. Life is harmonious when there is balance and the intimate union of the masculine and the feminine is honoured. Trouble and strife only appear when we experience imbalance, when intimacy is replaced with detachment.

Sunbird
Humanity

I once read an article that suggested the father of the Sunbird may have been a sunbeam and that its mother was perhaps a flower; a poetically suitable beginning for such a beautiful little bird. Sunbirds or 'Spider-hunters' are tiny passerine (perching) birds that feed largely on nectar, which they collect while hovering like Hummingbirds. Sunbirds will also occasionally hunt insects and Spiders especially when they have young to feed. They lay up to three eggs in suspended basket-shaped nests. Having only short wings, the flight of the Sunbird is both quick and direct. Sunbirds inhabit the tropical regions of Australia.

The males typically have iridescent plumage, while both sexes have long thin down-curved bills and brush tipped tubular tongues, which enable them to collect nectar from flowers.

A solar-influenced creature, the Sunbird holds archaic association with a cross-like symbol that spans the primordial globe, in one form or another. A symbol adapted by many cultures and traditions, the cross was said to harness the energies and protective qualities of the four directions, the creative force of the elements and the four races of man. Found in burial mounds of North America and cited in eastern folklore (among others) was a stylised, cross-shaped motif that, in one case, featured in its design four long-billed birds. The Sunbird Cross, as the bird-design came to be known, is linked by legend to the Greek Titan, Prometheus and the mystical Garuda, who both stole fire for the benefit of mankind. According to Greek mythology, Prometheus (a name that means 'forethought') was credited for stealing fire from Zeus. He apparently carried the fire in a stalk of a fennel and gave it to the mortals to use. As punishment for his crime, Zeus ordered Prometheus be chained atop Mt. Caucasus, one of the pillars said to support the world. The legend states that an Eagle (an emissary of the Sun) visited Prometheus every day to eat his liver, but because he was immortal, his liver grew back. Despite being immortal, though, the experience caused him immense pain. Prometheus was both bright and shrewd; a man who loved humanity. Even to this day, the term 'promethean' describes an innovative, intellectual and courageous person. Sunbird sheds light on dreams and aspirations that promise to change the course of history for the individual and humanity as a whole. Though difficult to achieve without support and sacrifice, Sunbird sponsors those thoughts and proposals intended to stand apart from the rest, particularly those destined to make a difference to the planet. Sunbird heralds achievements that promise to warm, heal and bring hope to mankind. It offers a way of reclaiming power; a way to direct mankind back to a place of unity and wholeness. Feeding occasionally on Spiders (symbols of choice and destiny), Sunbird integrates the power of regeneration, commitment and creative thinking.

Swallow / Martin
Soul Connections

Swallows are small passerine (perching) birds known for their swift flight, aerodynamic bodies, pointed wings, forked tails and very short bills. They are small migratory birds indigenous to Europe, Asia, Africa, North America and Australia. They have dark blue-black plumage, a white chest and a red throat. They inhabit open farmland and nest under eaves, on rafters and over doorways. They are often found in areas heavily populated by small insects and where Horses and Cattle are kept. Their call resembles a gentle, twittering 'tweet-e-weet'.

Swallows were celebrated as symbols of rebirth, resurrection and new life, as their cyclic homecoming was a sign of Spring's return. They were thought to protect and inspire the lives of people during Spring, Summer and Winter and return to Heaven during Autumn. Believed to represent lost souls made flesh, Swallows were once said to be birds of Heaven, sent to Earth as emissaries of the Angelic realm. According to ancient Roman folklore, the souls of dead children were said to visit their parents as Swallows. They were, therefore, revered as sacred messengers of the gods. Portents of new beginnings and love, Swallows were also considered symbols of the goddess. So much so, it was considered sacrilegious to kill a Swallow or to rob its nest, evoking as much shame as stealing from a church would today. As the goddess waned in popularity, though, the Swallow's forked tail was said to resemble the barbed tail of the devil. As a result, it was spurned by the church and renamed the 'Witch's Chick'. As the Swallow swoops here and darts there, its spontaneity worries depressed, dormant or heavy energy that may be lurking in the shadows. Its presence in or around your home comes as a good sign, suggesting hope and promise. Its anchor-like tail effectively secures, deactivates and disperses negative energy, cleansing the mind, body and spirit. Swallows work in much the same way as spiritual guides, inspiring, teaching and healing those who seek their counsel. I have known them to bring people together who have karmic lessons to address or soul connections to be healed, strengthened or realised. They guide people to understand their potential and to live deeper, more meaningful lives. It is my experience that Swallows point to positive change, new life and opportunity.

Swamp Hen
Pretence

Swamp Hens are seen on riverbanks, farm dams, lakes, marshes and swamps. Walking with a characteristic 'bob', the Swamp Hen has long, naked legs with wide, flat, elongated toes that help it appear to walk on water. In reality, though, it relies on the aquatic plants (such as lilies) for its stable foothold.

Swamp Hen embodies the nurturing, fertile role of the mother. The Swamp Hen watches over and protects her brood, offering emotional support and strength to those around her. She represents a trusted person, a mother figure, close friend or charitable person who works from the heart. Although she promotes taking people in need under the wing, she warns against weaving a veil of pretence while in the process, no matter how noble our intentions. She warns against smothering those we yearn to protect by making life-changing decisions for them and overly compensating for their situation. Swamp Hen reminds us that although it is a good thing to do what you can to help another, it's only beneficial to them when they are forced to remain responsible for their future, liable for their past and committed and dependable in the present. We create a façade; a false sense of security when we take away the power to choose, because with it goes the power to learn. If they never have to take responsibility for their actions and reactions, they will never learn from their mistakes – and they will never grow. Swamp Hen's 'water walk' trick may also expose a teacher of sorts; someone who may be about to offer a lesson contradictory to the one originally expected. It points the finger at those we want to trust;

people who outwardly display honourable motives, but in fact have clandestine reasons for appearing supportive. Such 'teachers' usually only ever demonstrate how NOT to do things rather than what they initially claim. In such cases, Swamp Hen proffers a warning to avoid false prophets, self-nominated gurus and plastic shamans – 'teachers' who claim to be qualified by blood, position or academic achievement, but who are in fact only practised in the art of pretence.

Tern
Outburst

Terns are gregarious, noisy seabirds closely related to Gulls. Enjoying worldwide distribution, Terns are medium to large birds with grey or white plumage, black cap-like markings on their heads, pointed bills, webbed feet and long narrow wings. They also have long forked or wedged tails. Most Terns hunt fish by hovering and diving, while others also eat insects. Terns will often be seen with Gulls, gathering in large mixed flocks on lakes and beaches.

Merrows are Merpeople indigenous to Ireland, easily distinguished by their feathery caps. Their caps are said to propel them through the depths. Should they lose their cap, legend has it they must remain in the shallows forever. If the female of the species has her cap stolen by a mortal man, however, she must marry him and stay faithful until the cap is recovered. Only then can she return to the ocean. The females are shy and gentle and are apparently very beautiful. Like other Mermaids, they are said to warn fishermen and sailors of approaching storms. The males, however, are quite ugly, baring green teeth, green hair and red noses. Both sexes are extremely cheerful. Terns, like Merrows, are known for their little feathery 'caps'. Like the female Merrow, too, they symbolically herald approaching trouble, emotional strife, 'storms', upheaval or angry outbursts. Knowing that trouble is brewing, though, is no reason to avoid people with whom you have unresolved issues. In fact, Tern Dreaming endorses the complete opposite. Sometimes clearing the air (no matter how loudly) can prove more advantageous than allowing animosity to fester. Tern encourages communication, with all dealings allowed to flow smoothly and contact kept merry and charming. In doing so, you will disperse all forecasted 'storms', ensuring blue skies and celebration. Tern discourages the compromising of morals or of making excuses in order to maintain peace and harmony. It encourages, instead, correct, honourable conduct, courteous transactions and reciprocally beneficial discussions. Keeping one's flow of communication light-hearted will ultimately guarantee that things remain hospitable, flexible and insightful. Lose your cap, though, and you may end up losing more than you bargained for.

Thick-knee
Resistance

Also known as 'Stone Curlews', Thick-knees are able to resist the natural temptation to flee in the face of danger. Instead, they drop level with the ground before appearing to 'turn to stone'. When retreat is necessary, however, they slowly turn and casually walk away taking deliberate steps, keeping their eyes defiantly focused on their aggressor. They are relatively large wading birds, with strong bills and large yellow eyes. Their name refers to their prominent knee joints. Although classified as waders, most Thick-knees have a predilection for sparse, arid environments. Largely nocturnal, their loud wailing call is generally heard at night. Thick-knees eat insects and lizards, and lay two to three eggs directly on the ground. They defend their young and their eggs enthusiastically.

Thick-knee's stoical approach to life and apathetic attitude to danger offers the strength to resist panic and never go weak at the knees.

It affords the willpower to face all fears front-on and to overcome weakness. It supports those striving to rid themselves of the word 'can't' and the limiting mindset that nurtures the victim archetype. Thick-knee's 'bring it on' attitude forces us to see the wisdom in every experience. It demands that we stand our ground, speak up and see ourselves as worthy of power. Thick-knee coaches us in the art of resistance and endurance, while demonstrating how to shun the desire to give up. It promises the demise of personal demons (both inner and actual), and guarantees an abundant future. Although the Thick-knee exhibits a resigned face and chooses to live a minimalist life, it champions the emotional wellbeing and physical bounty of others. Thick-knee Dreaming helps us overcome a 'fear of the dark' by teaching us to joyfully welcome and embrace the unknown, while hinting at the possibility of a new venture, school, job, home or relationship.

Treecreeper
Reverence

Treecreepers are small dull plumaged, woodland birds that build their nests in hollows or behind bark. They have stiff tail feathers that support their weight while they scale vertical trees, usually following a spiralled route. They have thin pointed down-curved beaks, which they use to probe the bark for insects.

Many cultures are known to have revered trees, perhaps the most well known for us being the Druidic priestly order of ancient Celtic society. They sanctified nature as a whole, including the sun, moon and the stars, consulting them religiously for signs and omens. They venerated other aspects of the natural world, too: the orchards and woodlands, mountain tops, valleys, lakes, rivers and streams. Some plants were considered sacred as well, including the ivy, mistletoe and holly. Trees like the oak, willow and rowan, though, sat at the centre of the Celtic tradition, with countless myths and legends espousing their healing and magical properties. Other cultures throughout history have looked to the trees with equal respect, incorporating them into their myths and legends, ceremony and ritual. They celebrated the cycles of nature and the trees, particularly the suppleness of their boughs, their endurance and their receptiveness and the cyclic decomposition and restoration of their foliage. They recognised them as potent archetypes; symbolic links that coupled man directly with the natural world. Almost every culture observes a custom of hanging objects from the branches of a tree. Many do this to establish a relationship between themselves and the tree. Throughout Europe, for example, offerings of flowers, streamers and flags are hung among branches to incite healing, curses or good luck. Prayer flags are strung across the Himalayas, often from bare limbs of ancient trees, as blessings to the countryside. In India, it is not uncommon to hang rags from certain trees that double as shrines to the village deity, while others associate the trees with spirits thought to be responsible for good weather and a successful hunt. So close was the bond between the ancients and the trees, that some even associated a man's health to the wellbeing of a particular tree, and vice versa. It was commonplace for a newborn to be allocated a sapling to which its life would be bound. A belief that goes back at least 3000 years holds true that a man who recognises his Life Tree will fall down dead the moment the tree is felled. Sometimes such trees returned the favour by waning or dying in response to the man's failing health or eventual demise. 'Touch wood' is a saying still used today in reply to a spate of good luck and the desire to see it continue. It exists as a reminder of the ancient spiritual history man has always shared with the trees and the spirits said to inhabit them. As the Keeper of the Groves, Treecreeper fortifies the ancient relationship between man and the trees by silently and diligently tending to their needs, meticulously cleansing them of parasites and protecting them from harm. The Treecreeper waits for us to remember the sacredness we once recognised in nature. It calls for us to awaken our ties to the world around us, and to integrate its wisdom back into our lives. For those of us who relish in it already, Treecreeper encourages us to teach others so that they may follow suit. She calls to us to once again dance the Spiral Dance in honour of the tree nation; the Circle Dance once danced by the ancient cultures to ensure personal endurance, spiritual unity, community strength and global togetherness. Because not until we return to the Old Ways that saw the Earth as our Mother; not until we begin to treat her with the reverence she deserves, and honour the animals, plants, stones, trees, rivers and mountains as our brothers and sisters, teachers and healers; not until we are prepared to support her unconditionally can we honestly expect her to continue to support us the way she has up until now.

Wagtail
Motion

The Willie Wagtail is one of the most recognised birds in Australia. It inhabits most environments, except open grassland and dense forest. The Australian Wagtail is totally unrelated to the Eurasian species (family *Motacilla*), the genus name of which literally means *moving tail*. The plumage of the Wagtail appears black on top with white underparts. It has a long black tail, which it fans out while hunting insects and wags from side to side. Wagtails flit about restlessly snatching insects while on the wing one moment, and bouncing across the ground searching for terrestrial prey the next.

The Wagtail speaks of motion. It doesn't mind how it is executed, so long as it has meaningful purpose. Its message is simple – forward movement, no matter how slow, steady or uncertain, is powerful. Everyone can stand still, sidestep or delay necessary progression, but not everyone has the strength or willpower to push forward against the odds. Not everyone can say they have succeeded in life when everything and everyone suggested the opposite. So long as all movement is progressive and productive, life will be balanced, planned and fruitful. Some people are constantly on the move, though, flitting from one activity to the next, never finishing tasks properly before starting something new. Some people start hobbies or recreational activities, but never complete the entire program or have half-finished projects dotted throughout their house, while others jump from one course or weekend workshop to the next, but never stay long enough to graduate or qualify in anything. Instead of focusing on one thing at a time, they waste their energy in a futile attempt to make themselves look busy, important and productive. They wonder why their lives are confused, why communication seems ineffective and why nothing ever gets done. Wagtail Dreaming awakens the cadenced timing of the internal metronome. It coaches us in time management and dedicated effort. It explains that just as its tail moves rhythmically from side to side, we too can find the balance within to move effectively from one activity to the next. When we master the art of efficient timing, we not only find all tasks being completed efficiently and well, we also find ourselves working in harmony with the ebbs and flows of nature, the rhythms of life and the ups and downs of all our relationships. Life becomes easier, manageable and enjoyable again, as we find quality time to spend with the people, places and things that make us the happiest.

Wattlebird

Essence

A member of the Honeyeater family, there are three species of Wattlebird indigenous to Australia: the Little Wattlebird, the Red Wattlebird and the Yellow Wattlebird, found only in Tasmania. Classified as a songbird, the Wattlebird feeds primarily on nectar found in blossoms and flowers, which it removes with its long brush-like tongue. It also takes small insects from flowers, or while on-the-wing. Wattlebirds are responsible for the pollination of many plants.

Resembling little orbs of golden sunlight, wattle blossom in all its glory is an uplifting sight, joyous enough to raise even the dullest of spirits. As its ambassador, the Wattlebird wakens us to the essence of Spirit and the wonder of Creation itself. Each perfectly rounded little yellow flower is reminiscent of the original fire sent to Mother Earth by Grandfather Sun at the beginning of time; the original spark sent to ignite the fire of life and all new beginnings. It is a sacred fire, a fire that roars in the midst of the inner landscape; the Father Fire, the Fire of Spirit, the essence that links our Inner Fire to the Great Fire of Spirit. Wattlebird guards the fundamental nature of this Inner Fire until our memory of it returns and we are once again ready to live an interconnected life dedicated to Spirit. Wattlebird knows that when the time is right, the people will remember their source. Only then will humanity awaken to its potential. Only then will the individual essence of humanity's Inner Fire radiate out and breathe life back into the fires of its brothers and sisters. Like all members of the Honeyeater family, Wattlebird energetically opens our hearts to the joys of life, the gifts of Creation and the beauty that surrounds us each and every day. It reminds us of the joy found in 'being', and the abundance that comes when we surrender control over the 'hows, whys and whens' that dominate and limit our prospects. Wattlebird calls for us to dance in the sunlight and sing praise from our heart for the good things currently happening in our lives. In doing so, the little image we hold dear; the image of our yearned for future, will have a chance of becoming reality. Put another way, by surrendering control of how, when and where our imagined future will come to fruition, we effectively guarantee its emergence. We welcome the nectar of life to flow freely our way, filling our life with opportunity and abundance.

Whipbird

Comprehension

The 'whip-crack' call of the Whipbird is often mimicked by the Lyrebird. Foraging in pairs, Whipbirds are perching birds easily recognised by their white neck stripes, black throat and white-tipped tail feathers. There are three species of Whipbird, all native to Australia.

The word 'whip' inspires thoughts of hard work, control and domination; of Lion-tamers, slave-drivers and Cattle-ranchers. As the only one capable of redirecting your life, though, you and only you are responsible for the 'wielding of the whip' when it comes to motivating yourself to initiate new direction, break old patterns or learn new skills. Whipbird symbolises taking control of your life – with an air of serious dedication. It declares that now is the best time to 'get cracking' with life and explains that if you aren't prepared do what it takes to realise your potential, no one else will. Its whip-crack call signifies the mastery of new skills and harnessing of new-found power. Whipbird demands that we 'get cracking' when it comes to starting a new job, venture, journey, way of thinking or relationship, and surrender outworn concepts, morals, values and beliefs that may hamper our progress. Whipbird asks, too, that you look at your life and check that you are in control. Are you free to make your own decisions, or have you given your power over to someone else? Whipbird primes us to 'just know' what needs to be done and how, without being forced or cajoled. It ensures we truly comprehend the power of the moment; the power that comes with realising that, with commitment and effort, we are destined for a productive future.

Woodswallow
Celebration

Woodswallows are dull-coloured songbirds that delicately flit about, hunting insects while on-the-wing. Despite their brush-tipped tongue, they seldom gather nectar. They are gregarious birds that often congregate in large flocks, inhabiting heath and spinifex woodlands, farmland and open forests. In flight, they resemble large, stiff-winged Swallows. Woodswallows are agile flyers able to soar – a rare thing among perching birds. They are essentially nomadic by nature, constantly moving in pursuit of flying insect swarms.

The Woodswallow or 'Summerbird' heralds the beginning of summer, or Beltane – the time of year when the richness of the Earth and its fertility are celebrated. Beltane traditionally marks the beginning of the Summer season, when livestock is moved to the greener mountain pastures. The festival once included the lighting of ritualistic bonfires on the eve of Beltane and the hanging of May Boughs on doors and windows. 'May Bushes' were also stood in farmyards, constructed from branches of either rowan or hawthorn trees, which both bloom during summer. The May Bushes were then decorated with flowers, ribbons, garlands and coloured egg shells. Beltane is a cross-quarter day, marking the point when the Sun sits exactly halfway in its journey from the vernal equinox to the summer solstice. It is thought that Beltane was originally celebrated on the full moon nearest this halfway mark, being that the Celtic year once incorporated both the lunar and solar cycles. Lucy Cavendish, my very dear friend and mentor, describes the summer solstice (June 20-23 Northern Hemisphere, Dec 20-23 Southern Hemisphere) as being 'the day of longest sunlight, a day of midsummer madness and delight. The ultimate expression of sun power, it's a time of celebration, ripeness, warmth, joy, sharing, heat and sensuality. It is the time when the Goddess is swelling with her unborn child, when she glows with the radiance of expectancy, and a serene joy at the expression of her powers of creativity. Her pregnancy and bliss symbolise the satisfaction we feel as a dream or ambition conceived earlier at Beltane moves towards its own birth, or realisation. As Beltane (May 1 Northern Hemisphere, November 1 Southern Hemisphere) is the ancient Celtic fire festival that celebrates physical pleasure, marriage and sexuality, we can expect our project to create a time of abundance, physical wellbeing, love and happiness'. It is a time to celebrate fertility. It is when the animals are mating, the birds are nesting and the fruit trees are rich with blossom. Children conceived during this sacred holiday were never deemed illegitimate, but rather revered as 'children of the god'. Woodswallow welcomes the time in our life when we can expect to find ourselves thriving, happy and at peace. It marks our life as being 'pregnant with possibility', when nothing is inconceivable and potential is ripe for the picking. Woodswallow calls to us to celebrate our creative, intuitive and fertile nature, and to channel our gifts and abilities into building an abundant, rich future. Woodswallow reminds us that we can only ever expect to reap what we are prepared to sow with Beltane, the power time of the Woodswallow, indicating a potent window of opportunity. Woodswallow also encourages us to reconnect with nature, by camping in the forest, picnicking on the beach, visiting farmland or hiking through the mountains. By celebrating the fertility of the land and the abundance that surrounds us every day, we will eventually become one with its energy and welcome it into our life.

Wren
Ambition

'Wren' is a generic name describing members of the insectivorous songbird family. Wrens weave basket-like nests from twigs and grasses, suspended from branches too delicate for larger predatory birds to reach. The males are easily recognised by their brilliant blue feathers, while the females are generally an all-over dull brown colour.

Wrens appear in folklore all around the world, in stories that include intelligence, strength of mind, endurance, ambition and bravery as themes. A fable once told of a competition between members of the bird kingdom, for example, held with the intention of discovering who could fly closest to the Sun. One after the other, the birds took to the air. Everyone fell back to Earth exhausted, dehydrated or burned black from the sun's rays. All the birds knew that the only one truly capable of the task was the Eagle, who majestically stood back waiting his turn. Circling ever higher the Eagle soared, until it was evident he had won the competition. The other birds declared him the victor and on calling him back to Earth, he was surprised to hear a tiny voice above him say, 'What about me?' The Eagle was shocked. He looked up to see the Wren frantically flapping his wings, sweat pouring down his cheeks, his feathers fraying from the heat. The Eagle knew the little bird could never have flown that high without help. But where had it come from? On his return, the Eagle asked the Wren to reveal his secret. No one had noticed that the Wren had not had his turn. No one noticed the little bird hiding among the Eagle's feathers. The Wren knew that he had taken a huge risk. He had trusted that the Eagle, as an emissary of Spirit, would not eat him to hide his defeat. The Eagle recognised the Wren's bravery however and awarded him the title of 'bravest and most ambitious bird'. Wren heralds the coming of new challenges. It charges us with an unwavering faith in our ability to achieve any goal. Carrying the torch of the East: the beacon of illumination, intuition and the intellect, Wren embodies the ability 'to know'. It offers clarity potent enough to shun confusion and despair forever by acting as the metaphoric light at the end of the tunnel. Wren allows us to trust the vision of the future we have forged since childhood, to have faith in ourselves and our abilities and our right to dream. It maintains mental lucidity and the knowing as to when we should close old doors so that new ones may open. It allows us to feel brave and ambitious, no matter how small we perceive ourselves to be, while celebrating every step we take that moves us further away from our established comfort zones.

introduced / 'feral' birds

Blackbird
Song

Blackbirds inhabit woodlands, parks and backyards, scratching up garden beds and compost heaps in search of insects and worms. Male Blackbirds are (as their name suggests) black, with yellow eye-rings, legs and beaks. The females have brown feathers but lack the yellow features. Indigenous to Europe, Blackbirds are considered pests by many. A songbird and member of the Thrush family, male Blackbirds are often heard singing in the early morning, late afternoon or early evening, serenading their mate as she sits on their eggs. They only ever sing at certain times of the year, and then only during set hours of the day.

Also known as 'Rhiannon's Bird' and 'the Black Druid', the Blackbird was revered in Celtic tradition as the gatekeeper to the Other Worlds, including the realm of Faeries. It is said that their song invites us to enter, explore and follow a deeper, more spiritual path that will, without doubt, expand our consciousness and perceptive knowing. Blackbird sings its praise in response to our commitment to living a meaningful, productive life. It rewards us further by opening our consciousness to the world of spirit – a path it knows will reveal a more fulfilled level of wholeness and knowing. Blackbird's sacred gift is potent enough to ease mental, physical and spiritual dis-ease. It offers a unique way for us to reconnect with others, the Universe and ourselves. Song has long been considered a powerful healing tool, especially when accompanied by rattles, drums, flutes, bells, chimes and didgeridoos. Sometimes those directed by the Blackbird to sing a healing song are shown to place their mouth directly on or over the body and to 'sing' into the dis-ease. The instruments (rattles, drums, and so on) are employed to ground and reassure the one receiving the song. Both the vibration and the melody resonate through the body, carrying with them strong healing potential. It is essential, though, that the song be delivered with pure intent and a controlled ego. When people receive a healing song that is expressly performed for and around them, the experience can be quite overwhelming. The realisation that the song is unique to their energy and their requirements often invokes tears of gratitude. They may cry from a very deep place or find another way to release their pent-up emotions. Either way, the healing medicine of Blackbird's song will have served its purpose. It is important to remember that healing songs do not require any type of musical aptitude; it's all about tapping into your own soul song and being confident enough to release it with little concern for 'how it sounds'.

Mynah
Manners

Common Indian Mynahs were originally introduced into Melbourne in 1862 to control insects hindering market gardens. Instead, they became a nuisance. Despite the idea failing though, the Mynah was still introduced into other parts of Australia for the same reason. They are now firmly established as a feral species throughout the world. Common Mynahs are social and raucous and, like the Starling, are highly invasive. They build their nests in tree hollows and cracks in buildings, and will even steal the nest sites of other birds. They have dark brown bodies, black heads and tails, bright yellow bills and legs, and a patch of naked yellow skin on the cheeks and patches of white on the wings and tail tips. In its homeland of India, the Common Mynah is referred to as 'the Farmer's Friend' because it feeds on insects that destroy crops. They are also celebrated by the people as symbols of undying love, because they mate for life, while the derivative, 'Maina', is an endearing nickname often given to young girls.

Despite its impolite, unhelpful nature, Mynah Dreaming espouses the observation and development of first-class manners. It proffers a fairly obvious trade-off: when you treat others with respect, you will be treated likewise. The moment you move in and invade another's territory, though, or treat their space with disrespect or dishonour, you cannot expect to be permitted to stay or welcomed back. Such behaviour will see you shunned; pushed out of the social group and left to your own selfish devices. Putting pressure on others, although a natural trait of the Mynah, is something it teaches us to avoid. Trying to make others act or perform in ways against their will is both abusive and unfair, and only marks you as a bully and oppressor. Be aware, too, that not only could such behaviour scar your reputation, it may also lead you to trouble with the law. Instead of always wanting more, Mynah reminds us to be grateful and thankful for the wealth and beauty already present in our life and what may yet come our way. Jealousy, greed and avarice are traits unendorsed by Mynah Dreaming. Although it is socially inept, the Mynah inherently knows its flaws. It teaches by its mistakes. So, with time and practice, who knows? Maybe it will learn to walk its talk.

Ostrich
Liability

The flightless Ostrich is the largest living bird on earth. Male Ostriches have black feathers on their back and white primary feathers on their wings and tail. Females and young Ostriches have brown feathers (instead of black) to aid in protection against predators. Living for 40 years or more, Ostriches are gifted with powerful vision and agility. Equipped with extremely well-developed leg muscles, Ostriches can reach speeds of up to 50 kilometres per hour, but contrary to folklore, they do not bury their heads in the sand.

They do, however, swallow stones and pebbles to aid digestion, and for this reason are considered both grounding and nurturing influences for people wandering aimlessly through life. Both sensible and earthy, Ostrich promotes practicality and responsibility. It equips us with endurance and strength enough to confront opposition and work through our complications to grow, prosper and succeed in life. It calls for us to stand our ground and protect what we hold dear. It demands that we hold true to our convictions and never compromise our beliefs or values in our search for truth and knowledge. Ostrich only ever sanctions retreat when we find ourselves hopelessly backed up against a wall. Only then should we consider backing away from a situation, because surrendering is an honourable act that calls for inner strength and some degree of courage, while giving up or denying liability doesn't. The Ostrich rejects cowardice, unreliability and inconsistency. If you pledge to do something, for example, or have willingly involved yourself in activities that portend potentially negative consequence, Ostrich Dreaming expects you to honour your promises and participation in a noble and responsible way. Ostrich encourages us to be more practical, grounded and responsible on all levels, particularly when concerning commitments and promises involving other people.

Sparrow
Self-Reliance

Sparrows seem to exist wherever people gather; suburban gardens, shopping centres, picnic grounds and parks. Common in and around major cities, they are not so common in rural areas. Male Sparrows have grey heads, charcoal cheeks and dark grey underparts, black throats, chests and brows. The females have predominantly brown plumage, as do their young.

Sparrows were revered as symbols of protection by the peasants of medieval Europe, who lived under intense oppressive rule. So much so, they were thought to embody a deity once believed to protect homes and family. During the Middle Ages, feudal communities were established around a ruler or lord and his personal package of land; communities that usually comprised of a castle, church, village and surrounding farmland. The lord who owned the land offered grants only to the most eligible and faithful of his landed gentry, producers, manufacturers and men of the church in return for their allegiance and defence. The common villagers and peasants (those at the lower end of the food chain) lived on and worked the lord's land in exchange for his protection – and nothing more. The term *feudalism* was birthed in the 17th century from the Latin *feudum*, itself adapted from the Germanic *fehu*. 'Fehu' became the first rune in the first aett of the 'Elder Futhark' system; a runic alphabet commonly used throughout northern Europe. It indicates livestock and prosperity, property won or earned, retribution and fortuity, wealth, currency, sanguinity, accomplishment, reputation, power, awareness, lucidity, fertility and happiness. Its contradictory meaning, however, refers to property lost or stolen away, poor self-respect, discontent, hedonism, conflict, apprehension, imprudence, adversity and tyranny. Depicted in many stories as victorious and strong, Sparrows were often shown deposing other, more powerful animals such as Bears, Wolves, Boars and Eagles – symbols of the aristocracy of the time. Sparrow defiantly shuns the negative interpretation of 'Fehu'. It does this so that we might develop the strength to follow suit, welcoming the more positive aspects of its meaning into our life. It is Sparrow's ambition to see us all realise self-preservation and autonomy. Sparrow Dreaming offers us a voice and the strength to express it. It empowers us to stand on our own two feet and to see the world as a blank canvas waiting for us to paint it. It rejects waiting for others to provide for us, or needing the strength of another to make us safe. Sparrow offers the keys to self-reliance by removing the 'abandoned child' archetype from our consciousness forever. It lifts us out of the mundane world and ordinary modes of thinking, and delivers us into a wondrous world where the extra-ordinary is possible.

Starling
Adaptation

The European Starling, or Common Starling, is found throughout Australia. It is a squat, medium-sized bird that offers a distinct triangular shape when in flight. They have glossy black feathers with iridescent purple and green aspects, reddish legs and a yellow bill.

European Starlings are omnivorous by nature and are highly adaptable. Preferring to nest in tree hollows, Starlings will often invade the nests of other birds, driving away the adult birds and killing their hatchlings.

One of the hardest things about moving house is being forced to make new friends and establish a fresh support network. And depending on how far we move, our kids often have to change schools while we have to find a new job – pressures that only add to the stress. Starling embodies the importance of adapting quickly to new settings, developing new skills and acclimatising to different ways. When Starling lands in foreign territory, for example, it wastes no time in introducing its customs, while expecting the other creatures to conform. Appearing ruthless and threatening, the Starling does what it considers necessary to survive. The totem of migrants, drifters and tourists, and those who move regularly because of work or personal reasons, Starling helps build the strength of character needed to make it in a new and unfamiliar land. It helps us adapt quickly to new settings. It calls for us to be observant, opportunistic and nimble-minded, so that we don't waste time in establishing a support network of allies, loyal friends, workmates and acquaintances. Starling people are quick to learn new customs, languages and traditional ways. It is their nature to adapt; essential elements if their integration is to be as subtle as possible and their presence causing as few ripples as necessary. Starling helps everyone else adapt, too, to the unfamiliar customs, beliefs and values of their new community member. It nurtures acceptance, tolerance and a community spirit that will see everyone get along peaceably.

Thrush

Love

The Thrush is a common garden bird known for its melodious song. It is indigenous to almost every continent, except Australia. Affectionately referred to as 'the friend of the gardener', the Thrush is an omnivorous ground forager that preys on worms, insects and fruit.

Legend has it that the Thrush prefers to build its nest among the branches of the Myrtle tree, weaving the nest from its twigs and lining the nest with its leaves. Traditionally, the Myrtle inspires long-term love and good luck, particularly for those who have one or more growing in their garden. Its wood is sacred to the goddess Venus and, when carried as an amulet, is said to attract romantic fascination and unconditional love. Thrush is the emissary of devotion, fertility, peace, abundance and eternal youth. Its Dreaming has long been considered the harbinger of love. The Thrush is the totem of writers, poets, singers and songwriters – a connection that goes back to when the Greek poet Homer was given a caged Thrush after reciting a beautiful poem. Thrush Dreaming helps us remember the ancient language of love, trust and empathy. It opens our heart to the possibility of love and the romantic potential that lays in store for us. It affords the strength of character to shun fear, anxiety and doubt when it comes to embracing affairs of the heart, and coaches us as we build the courage to ask Cupid to aim and shoot his arrow with dexterity and precision. In doing so, Thrush ensures a content, charmed, happy and abundant life.

introduced / domesticated birds

Canary
Sensitivity

The domestic Canary is a descendant of the Wild Canary, a small songbird indigenous to Madeira and the Canary Islands. The Canary is named after the islands, and not the other way round. Members of the Finch family, Canaries were first bred in captivity in the 1600s, and are today bred all over the world. Miners once used Canaries as an early warning system for the detection of lethal but odourless carbon monoxide in their mines. Three or more birds were lowered into new shafts, and if one or more died or responded negatively, the shaft would be declared unsafe.

Yellow is a colour reminiscent of the sun. It symbolises new beginnings, clarity and the easterly direction on the Wheel of Life. It is in the east that the sun rises each morning. With each new dawn comes the chance to start again, to wipe the mind clear of yesterday's experiences and to start afresh. It is also the colour said to embody the solar plexus chakra. Pronounced 'shack-ra', a Sanskrit word meaning 'wheel' or 'disk', the chakra system embodies the seven main energy centres that maintain health and harmony within the human body. Coloured golden yellow, the solar plexus is the home of 'gut feelings' and intuition. As an ambassador of the solar plexus, the Canary's sensitive nature inspires us to listen to our heart of hearts and trust our inner knowing. It offers the chance to see each day as a chance to have a go and strive higher than ever before. The Canary inspires open communication; interaction that inspires ownership of our present circumstance and the role we played in bringing it to fruition. Extremely receptive to the welfare of others, Canary people are usually very receptive to the support afforded by counsellors, welfare workers and healers – those trained to gently get to the guts of a problem by dredging up feelings and triggering emotional responses that may inspire growth, change and responsibility. Gifted with melodious song, the Canary is also the totem of music teachers and serious students of song. Canary's confidence to sing from the heart coaches us to follow suit, to speak our truth and 'walk our talk'.

Goose
The Sabbats

Geese are a frequent sight in rural Australia, with domestic varieties kept on farms and country properties for their eggs, meat and watchdog-like qualities. There are several domestic strains of Goose available, none of which are indigenous to Australia; breeds that include the Chinese or Swan Goose, Graylag, Sebastopol and Ebden. Feral populations are common, too, with crossbred 'farmyard' Geese often found on park lakes, rivers and isolated dams. Australia is home to the native Maned Goose (or Wood Duck), Magpie Goose (which isn't a 'true' Goose at all) and the Cape Barren Goose.

St. Augustine, the first Archbishop of Canterbury was believed to have demoted the sacredness of the Winter solstice by declaring that the Goose heralded the 'The Great Freezing'. He assumed that when a harsh winter beset the land its intention was to worry or thin the Snow Goose population; a battle that symbolised the constant tug-of-war between all that was feared and perceived as evil and all that was good and wholesome. Although it was revealed that evil could never be banished entirely, it was believed that God would always triumph. Snow Geese, it seemed, were considered emissaries of the devil by Augustine, because legend had it they offered their backs as vehicles for witches wishing to travel to and partake in the winter solstice celebrations. The winter solstice is recognised as the shortest day of the year, with the sun at its lowest and weakest. In the northern hemisphere it usually occurs around December 21, while in the southern hemisphere it transpires around June 21. According to ancient teachings, all of life's natural processes are recognised as being cyclical. The passing of time, the succession of birth, life, degeneration, death and rebirth, and the progression of the seasons all follow a cyclical, circular motion. The Wheel of the Year is a calendar of sorts, providing a way of recording such progress – especially the changing of the seasons. It comprises eight festivals, spaced almost evenly throughout the year. These festivals are known as sabbats. The eight sabbats, including the winter solstice, are traditionally split into four lesser and four greater festivals. The lesser are 'solar' festivals, timed by astronomical events. The four greater, or 'cross quarter' days, fall between the solar festivals. Called Samhain, Candlemas, Beltane and Lammas, they are celebrated according to the changing of the seasons. Some parts of Australia have seasons governed by their own unique environmental factors, which results in an altered sequential or 'natural' progression of the seasons. In Australia's tropical regions, for example, the locals often only experience a wet and a dry season. To celebrate the sabbats in the south, the northern hemisphere dates are adapted and shifted six months. Samhain, or Halloween, is when the veils between the worlds are deemed to be thinnest. It is considered to mark the beginning of 'the dark time' of the year, when the sun gets lower in the sky each day and begins to weaken in vitality. Winter solstice marks the shortest (and darkest) day of the year. It is a time to celebrate the anticipated rebirth of the sun and approaching end of winter. Candlemas is celebrated as a festival of lights, falling approximately halfway between Yule and spring. Candlemas is when spring is first felt in the crispness of the air and the warmth of the sun as it grows ever stronger. Spring equinox marks the heart of spring, when day and night are of equal length; the time when Earth bursts back into life after the dormancy of winter. It welcomes new growth and new life. It is celebrated as a time of equality; of balance between the forces of nature and of man and woman. Beltane heralds the old fire festivals during which fires would be lit marking the coming of summer, and when stock animals would be moved to greener pastures. It is when the animals and people would come together in honour of the god and the goddess in fertile union to welcome new life to the land. Summer solstice marks the longest (and lightest) day of the year, when the Earth is closest to the sun. Summer solstice heralds the heart of summer, when the fields are green with new crops. Lammas marks the first harvest of the year, when the first breads made from the early grains are shared among the people. It is a festival of sharing; a celebration of the harvest and its bounty, of gratitude for friends and family and thankfulness to the god and goddess for their love and support. Autumn equinox marks the heart of autumn, when day and night are of equal length. It is when the sun starts to wane in vitality and the days begin to grow shorter; when the full bounty of the year's harvest is brought in and stored against winter, in preparation for spring. By celebrating the sabbats, we awaken to the beauty and bounty of nature, the magick of creation and the keys to life as demonstrated by the changing of the seasons. When we partake in the sabbats, we begin to see ourselves as connected to all things, a sacred part of the cycles and progressions that make up the world around us. We become part of the natural world, instead of separate and alone. The sabbats welcome us home to a place of interconnectedness and remembrance. They offer a chance to rejoice in the wholeness of life and the richness found in the appreciation of the entire journey. By noticing the changing of the seasons and honouring the waning and waxing of the sun and the moon, we better appreciate the growth and development of our children, for example, our role as parents and the experienced had during our own childhood. We stand witness to our own progression and in doing so, we become more accountable for the sacred place we hold in the greater scheme of things.

Guinea Fowl
Forewarning

Guinea Fowl have naked necks and heads and charcoal-grey feathers uniformly spattered with white dots. Guinea Fowl are indigenous to the grasslands, forests, wooded ravines and hillsides of Africa, where they feed on fresh blossoms, seeds, bulbs, insects, snails and ticks. Travelling in flocks of several hundred monogamous pairs, Guinea Fowl are incredibly noisy birds, emitting a rapid, ear piercing 'clack clack' call at the slightest hint of danger. Naturally wary of strangers, they warn landowners of Foxes, Dogs, and other predatory animals, as well as human trespassers. They are also a common sight in orchards and vineyards where they help keep insect populations down. Earthbound during the day, Guinea Fowl roost in trees at night to avoid predators.

The Greek playwright Sophocles (496-406 B.C.) once poetically noted that the African Guinea Fowl wept tears of amber. Although a beautiful notion, amber is in fact a natural resin formed between fifty and seventy million years ago; the fossilized sap of pine trees often containing insects and prehistoric plant follicles. It is prescribed by new age, vibrational healers as a powerful tool capable of deterring chronic depression and suicidal tendencies. By remembering its sensitive association with amber, however, Guinea Fowl protects those of us feeling weighed down with responsibility and warns of impending emotional or mental collapse. Its loud clacking call forewarns of approaching negativity, depression and emotional darkness. It essentially targets it as it would prey, takes hold of it and cleanses it by transmuting its essence into awareness. Its feathers, for example, may be carried as a charm, with the intention of altering the negative affects of pessimistic thought or intention, while shoring up those who feel powerless and out of control. A god's eye crafted from pine needles and decorated with Guinea Fowl feathers, when suspended over a bed, will vibrationally warn of approaching illness or banish that already infecting the house. Armed with an aggressive, no-nonsense attitude, Guinea Fowl enhances mental clarity, while validating, grounding and affording stability to those who seek its counsel.

Peacock
Integrity

Members of the Pheasant family, Peacocks are best known for their impressive upper tail feathers and dazzling colours, which they rely on to attract a mate during courtship. Peacocks are incredibly noisy birds that eat insects, worms, maize and wheat. In their native land of India, they are welcomed into the villages because they naturally target and kill venomous snakes.

According to mythology, the Peacock is a symbol of the goddess's vigilance and her all-seeing eye, particularly the Roman Mother goddess, Juno, who weighed its tail feathers against the hearts of men to determine their integrity and their worthiness to travel to the Otherworld. In Hindu belief, the Peacock is a soul-bird; a heraldic bird of good fortune, protection and watchfulness; an oracle of truth and purity. Hearing the mournful cry of the Peacock was once somehow deemed an indicator of man's fear of being forsaken by God. Christian superstition marks the Peacock as a bringer of bad luck, claiming it to be the only creature arrogant enough to permit the devil access to paradise. Another legend champions the Peacock, though, declaring it both watchful and full of integrity. It was its vigilance that enabled it to recognise and restrain the devil as he set about infiltrating paradise. The Peacock apparently swooped down, grabbed the devil and swallowed him whole, regurgitating him some distance away. It is from this story that the expression 'it came like a bolt out of the blue' originated, signifying bad luck that seems to land 'out of nowhere', with 'the blue' perhaps hinting at the blue throat of the Peacock. Another tale depicts the Peacock as being superficial and frivolous and only concerned with the grandeur of his own appearance. It suggests the Peacock screams in reaction to his unattractive legs; a shock response to the indignity of being cursed with such ugliness. Peacock warns that, quite possibly, your integrity may be in doubt; that perhaps you have allowed your ego to get in the way of truth or that you have negatively compromised your values and beliefs in some way. Perhaps you have been so focused on reaching a target that you have lowered your standards to fulfil your goal? Perhaps you have told some white lies of late to make you look or feel better? Have you sold out a friend or relinquished your loyalty in order to better yourself? Peacock is a bird of integrity. It always tells the truth. It cannot lie, and it warns against trying. Liars must have good memories in order to maintain their charade, for if they don't, their duplicity will eventually be revealed. Peacock ensures our hearts always weigh pure by making sure we only ever speak the truth and never judge others for their perceived weaknesses. In doing so, it will keep watch for impiety in its many guises as it tries to permeate your personal paradise. Peacock teaches us to hold our head up and be proud of who and what we are and to deem ourselves (inclusive of all our perceived weaknesses and flaws) 'perfect' in its purest form.

Pheasant
The Aficionado

There are 48 breeds of Pheasant recognised today, some of which are commercially bred here in Australia for their meat. Many other ornamental varieties are kept by bird enthusiasts as exotic additions to garden aviaries. The stunning plumage and tail feathers are favoured by hat designers and fly-fishermen all over the world.

A solar influenced creature, the Pheasant is considered a sacred symbol of light, truth and magnificence in China, believed to bring both good luck and accomplishment. To the Japanese, however, it is a symbol of thunder. Believed to have the ability to harness and direct passion, energy and desire for change, the Pheasant is a creature said to display true commitment and devotion. It symbolises the unconditional and protective love a mother feels for her children, the fondness we may feel for a friend, and the wonders that can be achieved when we shower ourselves with love and dedication. It can afford the strength and endurance to better yourself through study and scholarly accomplishment, for example. Pheasant is a bird that mates for life. It demonstrates devotion to its partner while honouring its own need for happiness and wellbeing. It is a bird of balance; of harmonious union and equality. Pheasant may herald new relationships or positive, fruitful connections with other people. It may indicate a karmic bond shared with another; a soul connection, perhaps, that must be explored or better understood. A bringer of fertility, the Pheasant often portends a new workplace, home, friends or some other relationship. It doesn't necessarily indicate a sexual relationship or a partnership driven by sexual attraction though. Instead, it may signify a new relationship shared with yourself: a spiritual rebirthing, the harmonious blending of your yin and yang aspects or the surrender of your familiar self and the embracing of your true self. Before you can honestly attract the devoted love of another, you must first develop a healthy, honest relationship with yourself. You must first learn to love and accept yourself, despite your perceived flaws before you can expect anyone else to.

Pigeon
Homecoming

Pigeons have small heads, short necks, stout bodies, sleek plumage and a waxy bulb at the base of the bill. There are many different breeds of domestic Pigeon; the most popular being the Homer Pigeon. Many people race Homer Pigeons. They release them miles away from home and then time them as they return. Many cities, including Melbourne and Sydney, have resident Pigeons; feral descendants of the Rock Dove.

The Pigeon is uncanny in its ability to find its way home, no matter how far it travels. As such, it can be relied upon for support when we are homesick or forced to spend extended periods of time away from family and friends. It allows you to feel close to those you love, even when you are miles apart. Carrying your prayers and messages of love, it delivers them into the dreams of those you miss. Pigeon Dreaming instils peace and contentment when 'home' offers no fixed address. Pigeon can be invoked when you need to get in touch with someone you have lost contact with. To make contact, sit quietly in a place you know you won't be disturbed, relax and visualise the person you miss going about their business. Visualise a Pigeon perched on your knee, with a note from you secured to its ankle that clearly explains your need to speak to them. Now, imagine the Pigeon flying away, taking the note with it. You should receive a response after a short wait or, at the least, news of their last known movements through someone who knows them well. Pigeon prompts those who have developed the wander-bug to not wander too far, encouraging them to keep regular contact with those back home. Pigeon Dreaming invites us to return home on an innately personal level, too. It helps us reclaim our soul essence and to remember the promises we forged with ourselves as children, but have long forgotten. It welcomes us home to a loving, non-judgemental heart so that we may realise true happiness, inside and out. Pigeon delivers us back to a state of wellbeing, stability, clarity and inner peace, by reminding us we are safe and forever loved.

Rooster / Hen
Resurrection

Almost every breed of domestic Chicken originated from the wild jungle fowl of India. A typical and expected sight on Australian farms, the Chicken is kept as a source of fresh meat and eggs. Today, many of the rarer breeds are raised as show stock by poultry enthusiasts. Chickens are celebrated for their egg-laying abilities.

As the most famous layer of eggs, Hens are symbols of fertility and new life. They embody the male sperm joining with the female egg in the sacred act of creation. Because they welcome the sun's golden rays, however, Roosters are deemed the personification of the sun's warming energy. In Japan, it is the quintessence of the day's first rays of light while, in China, he embodies the five most favourable qualities of humanity. It is a bird of prophecy, positive in character and behaviour: his proud stance and erect comb affords him a sense of power and wisdom. The Rooster's ankle barbs denote an air of military calibre and the courage needed to honourably triumph in battle. The Rooster is revered for his 'goodness'; for it is observed that he distributes his food evenly among his family. Finally, the Rooster represents poise and promise, because of the confidence radiated each time he greets the sun – quite a contrary description to the antagonistic, conceited animal many see the Rooster as being. Rooster symbolises the hero, the guardian and protector of the people. It inspires hope and promise. When invoked with pure intent, Rooster Dreaming holds the potential to bring any dream to fruition (legend says that the Rooster could find an Earthworm in a desert). The downside, though, is that those who carry the Dreaming of the Rooster are usually very extravagant with their money (they would say they were generous), they have difficulty resisting temptation and are usually plagued by bad luck (as observed in the way the Rooster scuffs the ground for his food). Rooster people, when working with their more 'negative' qualities, often deny their flaws by 'crowing', or bragging about exaggerated or fantasised achievements. Rooster people are romantic, seductive and alluring. They love to be admired, despite being very private, proud and protective of their home and family. Rooster is the totem of salesmen, military officers, restaurateurs and hairdressers. As a result, those drawn to explore these careers or, simply, the Dreaming of the Rooster are encouraged to shun narcissism, tactlessness and forcefulness.

Turkey
Shared Blessings

The Wild Turkey, famous for its striking plumage, is indigenous to the woodlands of America and Canada. Synonymous with Thanksgiving, the Turkey has become the emissary of autumn and the harvest. Male Turkeys are often known as Toms, and can be distinguished from the females by their iridescent feathers and beard. The females are generally an earthy brown, to offer camouflage as they nest.

Although capable of fundamental flight, the Turkey is essentially an earth-bound bird, emblematic of the spiritual wisdom radiated by the Earth Mother and the shared blessings she offers. Her blessings come many forms: plentiful crops, healing herbs, minerals, timber, water and animals, to name just a few. Turkey encourages us to honour and give thanks for these blessings, and to use them well. Acknowledging the sacrifices made by another is the message of the Turkey, which readily gives of itself so that others may prosper. With a profusion of handsome feathers and plenty of rich meat, the Turkey honours the 'giveaway' process: a tradition that sees the giving away of things held dear to make the life of another that much richer. Turkey willingly exchanges life for death. It sacrifices its life so that others may live. It honours their lives and strengthens their bond with Spirit and the Earth Mother by giving selflessly of itself. It gives for the sake of seeing joy on the face of the receiver. Giving something away or sharing can be as simple as offering someone a little of your time or your support. A friendly smile can mean a lot to someone who feels alone. Always remember that the more you give of yourself, the more the world will want to share with you.

THE KINGDOM
OF THE
CREEPY-CRAWLIES

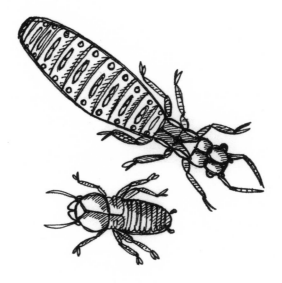

Creatures of the insect world hold the keys to the inner worlds, the spiritual realms hidden deep within our psyche. From the art of stillness to the wonder of personal and spiritual transformation, insects speak of the inner journey, our inherent connection to Spirit and the higher self.

native / indigenous / introduced insects and arachnids

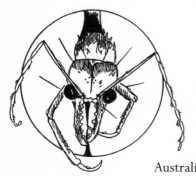

Ant
Strength

There are currently 15,000 described species and subspecies of Ant on the planet, with 1275 described species and subspecies indigenous to Australia alone. Ants are social insects that live in groups known as 'colonies' made up of a single egg-laying queen, workers, eggs, larvae and pupae. The workers form the bulk of the population. Their responsibilities are many, including the construction and maintenance of the nest, collection of food, attention to the eggs, larvae and pupae, tending to the queen and the protection of the colony. Although males do exist, all the workers are female. They are sterile, though, and do not produce eggs. Ants demonstrate a refined system based on cooperation, teamwork and efficient communication; a system that allows them to exploit their environment in ways unrecognised by other creatures.

Ants are able to carry many times their own body weight in their jaws, a skill that makes their industrious lives so much easier. Using their powerful jaws to carry food, their young and the loose dirt created when excavating their intricate tunnels, Ants work as a team, drawing on the strength that comes with pulling together. Oversized jaws are prized not just for their threatening appearance, but also because they make formidable weapons. Efficient fighters, Ants rely on their body strength to overcome their opponents and their strength of mind to anticipate their every move. As dynamic and analytical engineers, Ants know great endurance. Ants work toward all set goals from a communal perspective. In doing so, all tasks are approached and deliberated upon with a cooperative spirit, advanced upon with a common objective and undertaken as a team. Such an approach ensures that all responsibilities are completed quickly and efficiently. They also understand the need for patience, because their diminutive stature makes the duration of projects much longer. Ant asks if you are operating as a team member or as a sole agent. Are you honouring the role of your supervisor or boss? Are you considering the difficulty of their task, especially if there is respect for you as a team member? Are you pulling your weight around the home? Are you expecting others to take care of you? Are you taking care of them? Find the strength to take responsibility for your own life. Do not expect others to sacrifice their values and beliefs to support yours. When you take responsibility for your life, you inspire others to do the same. A web is created in which everyone ultimately supports one another, and assists each other in the ownership of joint responsibility. To understand and harness the power of Ant will see you ultimately become the engineer of your own life. It will provide for the laying of solid life foundations which will pave the way for new opportunities and inevitably lead to success.

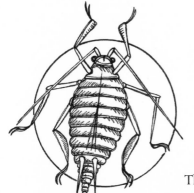

Aphid
Alchemy

Aphids are tiny, soft-bodied, wingless, sap-sucking insects approximately two millimetres in length that appear mainly during the warmer months. They have trunk-like snouts that point down and back. Aphids cover themselves with a wax-like substance in a bid to thwart dehydration. Aphids feed on the developing shoots and flower buds of roses, hibiscuses and peach trees by piercing the plant's outer layer and sucking its juices. They are sometimes responsible for misshaped buds and bloom and foliage loss. They are easily controlled, though, by Ladybirds and their larvae, Hoverflies and their larvae, Lace Wings, and small birds. To ensure a healthy garden, avoid chemical sprays. In doing so, these predatory insects and birds will quickly take up residence.

Greek legend suggests that the first rose emerged from the blood that sprang from the union of the virginal mortal, Psyche and Eros, the fertility god of erotic love and sex. As a result, the rose has become a symbol of the soul, love and the elixir of life, and man's quest to better understand and harness each. When carried, pink rosebuds and their petals, for example, are said to invite friendship, gentle love, romance and self-acceptance, while red rosebuds and their petals are believed to inspire passion, lust, psychic powers, healing, protection and aid in divination. So potent is their power that roses were once deemed vital ingredients in early alchemy – the study centred on the turning of base metals into pure gold. And as an insect that feeds on the sacred flower, the Aphid has become an intimate custodian of the rose's alchemical secrets and other wisdom. It heralds the enhancement and evolution of man's ability to work from the heart, the expansion of the soul and the blossoming of life itself. Aphid instils a sense of promise; that everything will be okay and that the dull, listless energy we carry will soon be transformed into joy, beauty and love. To unlock its power, Aphid invites us to study the roses we have in our garden and interpret the messages they proffer. The blue rose represents ridiculousness, for example, while the golden rose indicates absolute achievement and perfection; the red rose is emblematic of sexual attraction and allure; the white represents purity and wholesomeness, while pink embodies the heart. An eight-petalled rose signifies regeneration, while a seven-petalled rose refers to the seven days of the week, the seven planets, the seven angelic rays and the seven degrees of enlightenment. The number of petals most affected by the Aphid thusly indicates which day, planet, angelic ray or degree to focus your attention on when it comes to unlocking the pure gold your life holds in store for you.

Bee
Potential

Bees are communal creatures that build nests occupied by permanent swarms. Bees, of which there are a few hundred species, create cells within their nests that are made in part from wax secreted by the workers. Collector bees gather the nectar and bring it back to the hive, where worker bees remove it and process it by means of special enzymes in their abdomens that convert the nectar into simple sugars and those simple sugars into raw honey. True Honey Bees and Bumble Bees are the only species in which both larvae and adult Bees consume honey. Since October 2006, reports of a mysterious affliction (known as 'colony collapse disorder' or CCD) causing the death of millions of Honey Bees have been flooding in from all over America. The affliction has decimated commercial beekeeping operations across the country, leaving beekeepers struggling for survival and farmers concerned that their crops will not be successfully pollinated this year. Crops that depend on Honey Bee pollination (including apples, peaches, soybeans, pears, pumpkins, cucumbers, cherries, raspberries, blackberries and strawberries) have been dramatically affected by the mass die-off. According to the Pennsylvania Department of Agriculture, studies have revealed a large number of disease organisms in the affected hives, with no one common environmental agent or chemical yet to be identified as the primary cause.

Images of Bees once decorated the walls of beehive-like tombs. It was believed that Bees were the embodiment of the souls of priestesses who had dedicated their lives to the goddess Aphrodite, whose symbol was a golden honeycomb. Aphrodite's priestesses were known as melissae, which means 'bees'. Artemis, too, had priestesses known as melissae. Artemis' priestesses, though, were accompanied wherever they went by eunuch priests called essenes, which literally translates to 'drone'. The goddess Demeter was often referred to as the 'Pure Mother Bee', while Deborah, a former matriarchal ruler of Israel, was affectionately known as 'Queen Bee' by her people. Bee promotes the celebration of life, the realisation of potential and the ability to make good from every opportunity. Put simply, 'honey equals money', with Bee literally affording the Midas Touch to those who see the value in organised community, dedicated team work and group vision. Bee can be invoked to aid fertility when one is attempting to conceive a child, or in any situation (personal or business) that requires a barren 'seed' or concept to take root and prove viable. If you are birthing a new business, for example, view yourself as the Queen Bee working toward the development of your own hive. Over time, increase the size of the hive to the point where 'drones' are required to eventually run the business on your behalf, leaving you to either sit back and reap the rewards or to establish another one. So, why are the Honey Bees dying? It is my belief that the Honey Bees are dying off because we have forgotten what true wealth is. We have replaced loyalty, peace and happiness with fast cars, high powered jobs and flat screen TVs. We no longer perceive the unconditional love of friends and family as personal wealth, but instead choose to weigh success against the brand of clothes we wear and how much money we can accumulate in a year. Unfortunately, it seems to be the trend today for people in positions of power to spend their time thinking about money and how they can get as much as they can without having to share it. The rich are richer than ever before, while the poor are still poor. To me, Bees represent the global economy and their hives, among other things, the template that holds everything in balance. Honeycomb is an ancient symbol of the Universal Tapestry. Like a perfectly formed jigsaw puzzle, it demonstrates quite literally how one thing supports the next, with each person, creature and thing 'slotting in' in complete harmony with each other. Perhaps the template is breaking down. Let's face it, we have abused it for long enough – we have shunned it and our Earth Mother almost to the point of abandonment, and what one forgets over time simply ceases to exist. It is my belief that the Bees are dying because the web of life may be falling apart. Perhaps the Universal Tapestry is beginning to fray at the edges and that all that we have come to believe to be reality is beginning to falter. To reverse the process, I believe we must heed the Bee's calling to remember their ancient message and return to a place of unity where organised community, dedicated team work and group vision are once again revered as the highest of priority.

Beetle
Misconception

Armoured casings protect the delicate gossamer wings of all Beetles, which come in countless shapes and sizes. They display an equally diverse array of body adornments and patterns. Compare the common Ladybird, with its spotted scarlet wing casings, to the huge antlers of the Stag Beetle, for example. Worldwide, there are approximately 350,000 different identified genus of Beetle and 30,000 species of these are native to Australian shores.

Associated with life, death and rebirth, Beetles have embodied great mystery since the dawn of time. In Medieval times, alchemists were said to have linked creation itself to the Scarab. To this day, dried and powdered Beetles are deemed powerful fertility charms in some cultures; a solar-influenced creature by others, revered as messengers of the sun god in his many forms. In Ancient Egyptian folklore, the Scarab Beetle enjoyed sacred association with the sun god Khepera, who was considered responsible for the sun's journey across the sky. The link was forged by the observation that it rolled dung balls across the ground and the incorrect assumption that only males of the species produced offspring. It was also erroneously supposed the eggs encased within the ball could only hatch (and the young emerge) if the balls themselves were allowed to soak in water. Khepera priests pronounced the Scarab a symbol of the 'one god', and had mammoth statues of the Beetle erected in specific temples. Jewellery depicting the Scarab was worn by wise men, while Scarab-shaped amulets replaced the hearts of the mummified remains of those departed. Over time, belief in Khepera as the sole creator waned, with people realising that in order for young Scarab Beetles to emerge, the dung balls had to lay in the sun-warmed sand for a total of 28 days – the exact time it took for the moon to pass through all twelve zodiacs. This new association bound the Scarab to the energies of 'Mother' Earth and the feminine moon, and saw the 'Mother' reassigned as a co-Creator, with revised images showing Khepera rising from a lotus flower. Beetle comes as a sign that some misunderstanding has been allowed to manifest, possibly resulting in lines being crossed and communication being hindered. It warns that something said has been misconstrued, or that you are perhaps being misled by a false or erroneous belief. Beetle also exposes a gentle soul hidden behind a rough and tough exterior, or a situation that, at first glance, tenders confusion and hindrance, but may in fact turn out to be a gift from the gods. Beetle also suggests that a situation or topic traditionally handled by men could – for one reason or another – be better handled by a woman. Or perhaps approaching life from a more intuitive, caring or nurturing stance might prove more beneficial than the familiar, more physical one adopted before.

Butterfly / Caterpillar
Transformation

Butterflies are insects that enjoy an unusual life-cycle. Beginning as a larval caterpillar, they move through to a dormant pupal phase before experiencing metamorphosis, after which they emerge as the colourful winged adult form we recognise as 'the Butterfly'. Most Butterflies feed primarily on nectar, while others derive nourishment from (among other sources) pollen, sap and fruit. They hold a vital ecological role as pollinators of flowers. Butterflies only consume liquids, taken in by means of their proboscis, feeding on nectar and sipping water from rain puddles, dewdrops, fountains and bird baths.

Butterflies work vibrationally with the number three. Since ancient times, the number three has represented creative power and growth.

'Three' was the first number to traditionally represent the 'whole'. As a symbol, the number three contains an obvious beginning, middle and end. It is the Triad – a term which embodies the Universal nature of the world as Heaven, Earth, and Sea. It is life as a whole, encompassing the three phases of the moon, for example, the three phases of human development (Maiden/Youth, Mother/Father and Crone/Sage) and humanity itself, being made up of the body, mind and soul. In Greek, the word 'psyche' can mean 'butterfly', with the insect's power to transform today extending the word's meaning to include reference to the concept of the self; a notion that encompasses the soul, self, and mind. The Greeks believed that the 'psyche' formed the root of all behaviour. As the Butterfly moves from one developmental stage of life to another (as it moves from the darkness and confines of the chrysalis to the light of freedom), it shows trust in its ability to grow and adapt to new situations. Butterfly promises that when contemplating change, and when the time is right, she will offer three potent windows of opportunity to rebirth, grow and heal on all levels – with each window, augured by 'butterflies in the stomach', lasting approximately one week in duration. Such a period is typically followed by a figurative death, represented by the ending of a job or relationship, a bout of depression, a breakdown or a sudden shift in awareness. Only after the darkness is celebrated can clarity and gratitude be reinstated. When initiating change, wait for the 'butterflies in the stomach'. This is the best time to get things moving. However, if you feel the butterflies in the stomach, but cannot activate anything due to extenuating circumstances, do not fret. Butterfly offers *three* windows of opportunity. Simply wait until the next time the butterflies are felt. But be aware that if the second opportunity is left unheeded, the third chance may very well be the last one offered for some time. A creature naturally deaf, Butterfly encourages us to harness the silence so that we may better hear those around us, both corporally and ethereally; those who may be calling intuitively to us from the heart rather than audibly by means of their voice.

Centipede
The Good Red Road

Despite what their name suggests, few Centipedes possess one hundred legs. They are often confused with Millipedes but can be easily distinguished by their venomous fangs hidden underneath the head. Although venomous, the bite of the Centipede generally only causes localised swelling and irritation. Only one human death – a small child on a Pacific Island – has ever been recorded resulting from a Centipede bite. Prominent in Australia's more arid regions, Centipedes are commonly found under rocks, logs or bark in most backyards and gardens.

Centipede Dreaming incorporates the 'Good Red Road' philosophy of the Ancients: the physical path we walk to ground emotional and spiritual awareness in our quest for truth and interconnectedness. Centipede demonstrates an inter-relationship to the four directions, the four seasons, the animals, birds, plants and stones as well as Sister Sky, Mother Earth and Great Spirit. Its wisdom integrates the knowledge gleaned by exploring all cultures, all directions and all traditions. It encourages us to sample each, extract what works for us and dump what doesn't, before bundling what remains together and labelling it as 'truth'. Each of its legs embodies individual life-lessons, rites of passage and personal stages of development, as well as the many steps we must take as we journey toward wholeness. Centipede walks with us as we trek the Wheel of Life – many times during the course of a day, physically over a single lifetime and, on a karmic level, many times over countless lifetimes. Centipede affirms that it is not until we find harmony with nature and harmony within ourselves that we obtain all four Gifts of Power in their truest form: illumination, innocence, introspection and wisdom. Only when we become whole can we hope to 'shed our robes' and honourably walk the Long Blue Road of Spirit.

Cicada
Cycles

Cicadas are sap-sucking insects that spend up to the first seventeen years of their life (depending on the species) underground. While in nymph form, they feed on the sap of tree roots. When it is time to break free of their nymphal case, they dig their way to the surface and climb the trunk of the nearest tree. It is here that they discard their alien-like outer skin, and wait for their wings to dry. Squeals of fear-tainted delight can be heard soon after, as the empty cases are discovered by curious children.

Cicadas were once kept in grass cages as symbols of resurrection, immortality, eternal youth and control over greed. According to Australian Aboriginal lore, the Cicada offers vitality. As a tribal totem, those from Cicada clans are expected only ever to marry into a Crow tribe. Cicada's unique life cycle illustrates the necessary and healthy balance that must be realised between what is deemed 'darkness' and what is celebrated as 'light'. It is not until this balance is found can we expect to live a fertile life. It helps us find 'good' in 'bad', light in the dark, a positive in every negative, and reason within confusion. It balances the feminine with the masculine, and nurtures us as we navigate life's cycles: as night turns into day, death turns to rebirth, and winter turns to spring and summer to autumn. In fact, it is Cicada's shrill song that heralds the arrival of summer – the season of celebration, new life and abundance. Cicada comes as a wake-up call; a chance to surrender all fear, release all burdens and pains from our past and look forward to a prosperous future. It embodies the harmony found between the yin and the yang; the balance between dreaming, conception and action and the necessary shift from depression to clarity, restraint to freedom and weakness to strength.

Cockroach
Resourcefulness

The Australian Cockroach (or simply 'Roach') is a large, winged species that grows to approximately three centimetres in length. Typically brown in colour, the Australian Cockroach originated in Asia. It is very common throughout the world (except the polar caps), travelling the world via shipping and trade. Capable flyers, Cockroaches travel quickly on land, darting about, scurrying into small cracks and under furniture when disturbed. Cockroaches are opportunist feeders and scavengers. Unafraid to venture indoors to look for food, they prefer the outdoors, inhabiting dry bush land, hiding under bark, rocks and logs or in damp leaf litter where they feed on rotting leaves.

Starring American-born actor, Michael T. Weiss as 'Jarod', *The Pretender* was a very popular television series that aired between 1996 and 2000. It followed the exploits of a highly intelligent man with the uncanny ability to become anyone he chose. By adopting the personality and character role of others, he would seamlessly 'pretend' to be (among others) a doctor, police officer and pilot. Following a similar theme was the movie *Catch Me If You Can* (2002). It tells the true story of Frank Abagnale Jr., a young con-artist who impersonates an airline pilot, doctor, assistant attorney general, and history professor – all before his nineteenth birthday. While not suggesting for one moment that we impersonate other people in order to better our life, or break the law by pretending to be trained or qualified to perform specialised roles or tasks, Cockroach Dreaming does allow us to slip into any setting and situation with ease – to the extent that others may assume we have always been there. New occupations, positions and ranks, locations, acquaintances and relationships are made that much easier to adapt to with the help of the resourceful Cockroach who coaches us to acclimatize and assimilate quickly and flawlessly. A survivor under harsh conditions, Cockroach heightens our sensitivity to any environment, cultivating a sense of belonging and trust in others. It helps us choose the best face to show; to superficially be whom and what is expected under any circumstance, even if it seems to contradict who and what we truly are.

Cricket
Good Fortune

Crickets are related to Grasshoppers. They have flat, black bodies and long antenna. Crickets are best known for their chirp, although this is something only the males do by rubbing their forewings together. They make two different chirps: a calling chirp and a courting chirp. To hear the calls, Crickets have ears located just below the knee joint on each of their front legs. They usually sing at dusk on warm, dry nights.

Crickets are considered good luck in China, where they are sometimes kept in grass cages as unique pets. The chirp of the Cricket is said to herald rain or financial gain in some parts of Brazil, but in others, it portends illness (especially if it is black) and even death. Grey Crickets are said to attract money, green ones are said to welcome hope, while never-ending chirping is thought to signify pregnancy. The song of the Cricket is also believed to resemble the chanting of Buddhist priests, a chant that usually indicates hot weather the following day. Cricket Dreaming inspires movement and activity – particularly when his song is heard on a warm, sunny day because the sun is a symbol of strength, courage and new beginnings. Cricket sings in a bid to make us cheerful and excited about life. So, when his chirp is heard, luck is on our side. Cricket calls to us to embrace his chant, to reconnect with its rhythm and to join in its song. When celebrated, the chant of the Cricket delivers us into a place of beauty and inner harmony. It helps us find the inner silence so that we may live in the now. It suggests that whatever we put our minds to while in this state, will surely come to fruition. If nothing else, we will be gifted with unexpected good fortune.

Dragonfly
Illusion

Dragonflies are commonly seen flitting about over lakes, ponds, streams and swimming pools. Their larvae, known as 'nymphs', are aquatic. Although they rarely sting humans, they will bite if handled roughly. Not only beautiful to look at, with their iridescent colours that shimmer in sunlight; they are also profoundly useful in controlling Mosquito populations. Dragonflies eat Flies, Bees and Butterflies.

According to indigenous Australian folklore, the Dragonfly – like the Butterfly – embodies the regenerative powers of rebirth. After mating, Dragonflies deposit their eggs in water, where they hatch and develop into ferocious aquatic larvae before transmuting into adult Dragonflies. The Dragonfly emerges from a fully aquatic lifestyle, to a creature capable of full aerial flight, no longer restricted to the confines of the pond or river into which it was initially hatched. Dragonfly experiences a symbolic death at the midpoint of its life. After a period of obligatory dormancy, the Dragonfly re-emerges as an apparently completely new creature, with deceptively iridescent wings that seem to glisten with the changing light – a transformation Dragonfly is yearning to see you do today. As children we may be taught values and beliefs that are based on cultural or family tradition and morals that may be simply regarded as outdated in today's society. These illusions seem so real, though, that we accept them as our reality. As we mature, these ways often contradict our self-discovered principles and we learn to adapt them accordingly. However, depending on how deeply these beliefs are ingrained, sometimes we cannot shake them in order to make way for our own. When this happens we find ourselves in turmoil because we feel as though we are dishonouring our culture or family by trying to follow our own truth. Dragonfly urges you to break through self-endorsed limitations that hinder your development and growth. Look at yourself and acknowledge the illusions you may have woven around yourself as a form of protection. Ask yourself if these illusions were put in place to prevent you from seeing a truth or to prevent others from seeing the real you. Have you started to believe your own deception and a falsity originally instigated to protect your sense of insecurity or low self-esteem? Your view of the world may be restricted by your tainted perception of what is real and what is not and as a result, the view the rest of the world has of you may be unfairly tainted also.

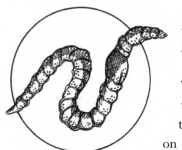

Earthworm / Worm
Sustainability

Terrestrial Earthworms range between two to three centimetres and two to three metres in length, depending on the species. For example, the Giant Earthworm of Gippsland, Victoria, has been known to reach several metres in length. The clearing of native vegetation and the introduction of foreign, more dominant species of Earthworm has negatively affected the number of indigenous species once common in gardens, orchards and farm paddocks. The mouth of the Earthworm opens directly into the digestive tract. They are best known as decomposers of leaf and plant matter. Earthworms are able to replace or reproduce lost portions of their bodies; an ability that varies between the species and the individual degree of injury. It is even thought to be possible to grow two whole Earthworms from a single bisected creature.

As an ambassador of the Earth Mother, Earthworm champions the importance of efficient recycling and sustainable living. It reminds us that if we expect the Earth Mother to continue to support us, we must be prepared to honour her more deeply. Earthworm lives in harmony with the Earth, teaching us to 'walk gently' upon her back by using only what we need and wasting nothing. It encourages us to integrate self-sufficiency and permaculture-based philosophies into all our farming, household and gardening practices. Earthworm also works energetically with those forced to make decisions that divide, test loyalty and, perhaps, demand displays of favouritism. Children of broken homes, for example; kids required to choose one parent over another, or made to live with one and shun the other, are fortified by the wisdom of the Earthworm. Earthworm sustains those who feel their hearts being torn in two. Perhaps you're secretly in love with a married man, or your ex-wife (a woman you still have feelings for) is seeing someone new? Earthworm Dreaming shores up those of us forced to grin and bear it when it comes to emotional issues or affairs of the heart. It teaches us to dig deep and find the strength to deal with feelings of confusion, anger and resentment by instilling flexibility, compassion and staying power. It helps us maintain composure and a sense of maturity so that we don't snap and emotionally fall apart.

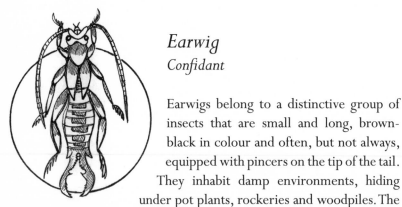

Earwig
Confidant

Earwigs belong to a distinctive group of insects that are small and long, brown-black in colour and often, but not always, equipped with pincers on the tip of the tail. They inhabit damp environments, hiding under pot plants, rockeries and woodpiles. The name 'Earwig' comes from a misconstrued belief that the insect has a penchant for human ears. In truth, it more likely comes from the descriptive 'ear wing', which refers to the shape of the Earwig's hind-wing. Although capable of flight, Earwigs rarely take advantage of the ability.

When the issues that haunt our mind are serious enough, the consequences can be crippling. Emotionally, we may find ourselves frozen, unable to operate efficiently on any level. Our communication is hampered, as is our ability to be honest and open with those close to us. Sometimes we find ourselves stretching the truth or blatantly lying in a bid to ignore the core issue. Earwig Dreaming centres on the ear, and our ability to hear what needs to be said. Perhaps you are being called to act as a 'sounding board' or confidant for another, or alternatively, you may need to find someone to hear you out. It suggests the need to get something off your chest, to unload or 'confess' to something that burdens you emotionally. Earwig welcomes the bouncing around of ideas and the seeking of advice.

Flea
Frivolity

Anyone who owns a Cat or Dog will be familiar with Fleas; small parasitic, wingless insects that cause their host to scratch uncontrollably. Hopping from one host animal to the next, fleabites cause itchy skin irritations and localised swelling. Flea larvae begin life as grub-like creatures usually found where host animals commonly rest.

Fleas personify all that is distasteful, dishonourable and tactless in regard to behaviour and attitude. People who only commit to things that benefit them, for example, more often than not work with the energy of the Flea, a creature that sanctions frivolous behaviour, inconsiderate actions, selfish motives and insensitive words. Although it personally practises what it preaches, its presence comes as a warning for us to avoid following its example by not taking responsibility for our actions. Flea, by its very nature, portends bed-hopping and disloyal behaviour. Although it deems its conduct as fun and frivolous, the truth of the matter is it hurts, causing discomfort and pain to those who bare the brunt. Flea bleeds others emotionally, while nurturing its own needs, making itself feel fuller, stronger and content. Is this how you want others to describe you, or is this how you feel about someone you know? Flea prompts the questions, are you sharing company with someone driven solely by their own desire? Are you guilty of draining others of energy? Are you a pawn in another's game of chance? If so,

Flea warns that your integrity may be in question or that your sense of security has been frivolously breached.

Fly and Maggot
Awareness

Blowflies lay Maggots in the carcasses of road kill, which assist nature by removing the decaying bodies of the dead. In this way, Flies help to control disease. Apart from this, scientists know little about the true 'purpose' of the common Fly. Australia is famous for the Black Housefly, Horsefly and Blowfly. Prevalent in warm summer months, Flies cannot survive the cold seasons. They die out in winter, to be replaced by young in the spring and summer.

Associated with demons and plague in early writings, Flies have long been deemed vehicles of death, decay and destruction by the Hebrews and envoys of evil, sin and pestilence by the Christians. Some African tribes celebrate a Fly-god, with the Fly itself revered as the embodiment of the soul. As such, the Fly is honoured and never killed. Here in Australia, Flies swarm in the thousands. Seen by many as uninvited guests at barbeques and outdoor gatherings, Flies bother babies and animals and those who work outdoors. They literally turn up everywhere, and are difficult to dissuade. Extremely familiar facets of life, Flies have crept into colloquial conversation. Sayings like 'One hundred million Flies can't be wrong', or 'I'd like to be a Fly on the wall when *blah* finds out about that…' and, 'there's no Flies on you, mate' are familiar phrases indicating varying levels of awareness and insight. Such clichés highlight the Fly as a creature of awareness. Shape shifters and bi-locators, Flies observe, unseen, eavesdropping and soaking up knowledge not intended for their ears. Always alert, Fly pinpoints depressing energy, particularly in areas where they're most likely to swarm; areas described as negative in vibration. Such energy must be removed or cleansed as soon as possible by means of burning sage and allowing the smoke to waft thoroughly throughout. Fly Dreaming may also warn of people who carry dark-side entities or who welcome them into their spiritual practise. Fly encourages us to enhance our awareness so that we may become learned in the darker aspects of creation, more aware of the less obvious and develop our shape shifting abilities so that we can 'be' in two places at once.

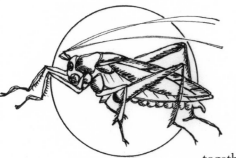

Grasshopper
Success

Grasshoppers belong to the same family as Locusts, Crickets and Katydids. Grasshoppers chirp by scraping their hind leg and forewing together. Best known for their powerful hind legs used for jumping great distances, Grasshoppers begin life as wingless nymphs before metamorphosing into winged adults.

Grasshopper empowers us to move forward with confident, purposeful strides. In fact, it inspires us to take giant leaps of faith when it comes to our progression and personal growth. It dares us to step outside our comfort zone and explore what life has to offer on a more expansive level. It helps us find the inner strength to realise levels of success never before thought possible. Associated with lightning in Aboriginal mythology, Grasshopper Dreaming charges us with emotional strength and energy to get any job done. It propels us forward with lightning speed, so that we may fulfil whatever we set out to achieve. For those harbouring new ideas, Grasshopper comes as a positive sign and blessing. It offers a warning, though. If you are starting a new business, keep it small, or better still, go it alone. Grasshopper knows only too well the damage an excessively large group can do to a bountiful crop when control is poorly managed or when the harvest is too willingly shared. Sometimes it is best to take forward leaps alone, especially when the journey has only just begun or the potential outcome remains uncertain.

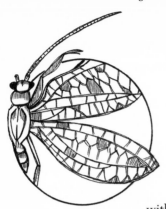

Lacewing
Ceraunoscopy

Lacewings possess four membranous wings, criss-crossed with delicate veins. They have chewing mouthparts and most (but not all) are predatory. Lacewings undergo complete metamorphosis, with the larvae showing obvious physical differences to the adults. Grub-like in appearance they are known as 'Lion Ants', sporting large, protruding vice-like pincers.

Nature offers a plethora of subtle signs and omens for those sensitive enough to notice. A champion of these sacred forms of communication, the Lacewing (also known as the 'Storm Bug', because its appearance often portends approaching rainstorms) encourages the ancient study of (among other forms of divination) 'ceraunoscopy'. Those who practise Ceraunoscopy draw omens by scrutinising the shape, movement and repetition of pattern of lightning and the sound of thunder to confirm a suspicion or circumstance yet to happen. The term 'Ceraunoscopy' derives from *Ceraunos*, a Pagan god of lightning. Apart from Ceraunoscopy, there are many other ways to access the secret codes of nature. Some include:

Aeromancy - a form of divination that looks at cloud shapes
Apantomancy - a form of divination based on chance meetings with animals
Astrology - a form of divination that analyses the interaction of celestial bodies
Austromancy - a form of divination that studies wind movement
Geomancy - a form of divination that scrutinises patterns found on the ground and the influence of the Earth's vibrational 'currents'
Hydromancy - a form of divination that looks at water, including its colour, ebb and flow.

Nature offers us a veritable library of secret languages that, once translated, represent unique opportunity; sign-posted prospects and keys potent enough to unlock doors to transformation and healing. We can learn much about ourselves, our world and the many realms of Spirit by simply looking to nature for guidance. So, apart from possibly heralding an approaching 'storm' in the form of emotional shake-up and eventual cleansing, Lacewing suggests we broaden our subtle awareness to include the signs offered by nature, and to (according to our element, perhaps) decide on a natural divinatory form to study and become adept at.

Leech

Vampirism

Leeches, with their long cylindrical bodies, are best known as blood-sucking parasites that inhabit damp, dank, swampy environments. Like Earthworms, Leeches are members of the Annelid family. They have no obvious 'head-end' to their segmented body – a characteristic common to their clan.

Individuals that emotionally, spiritually or physically absorb the energy or self-esteem of others, more often than not personify the vampiric qualities of the Leech. In similar fashion to how a Leech drains its victim of blood, Psychic Vampires are people who energetically feed on the life force of those around them. Many cultures speak of mystical people who feed on the energy of their victims – the Tiger Women of Asia, for example, and the Fox Women of Japan, the Incubus and Succubus of Judaeo-Christian mythology and the 'Powaqa' of Hopi tradition: a parasitic being that preys on people in need. It pretends to offer help and support, only to weaken its quarry more by feasting on their essence. Instead of assimilating the life force of others, Spiritual Vampires are typically only interested in nourishing themselves physically and financially. Spiritual teachers, groups and larger organisations that financially, emotionally, physically and even sexually prey upon the vulnerabilities of those in search of enlightenment, truth and personal empowerment, are fine examples of Spiritual Vampires. No matter what form of Vampire they may be, anyone who constantly takes with little thought of giving back; people best described as sticky beaks, gossips, close talkers; those who 'fish' for personal information or constantly ask leading questions; those who dump responsibility or repeatedly seek advice, assistance or counsel with little or no intention of offering thanks, compensation or remuneration, are all cases of people gainfully tapping into Leach Dreaming; people who are, in my humble opinion, best avoided or approached with a guarded mind.

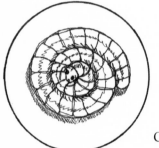

Millipede
The Labyrinth

Although 'Millipede' means 'thousand feet', in truth it only has about 30 pairs. Timid for invertebrates, Millipedes, unlike Centipedes, do not have venomous fangs with which to protect themselves. Instead, they roll themselves into tight spirals to discourage predators, and then discharge a foul smelling, distasteful substance.

In its coiled state, the Millipede personifies the labyrinth: an ancient symbol that, by uniting the circle and the spiral, invites us to explore its depths in search of spiritual enlightenment and wholeness. Unlike the maze, a puzzle that requires left-brain logic to solve, the labyrinth is a right-brain task that involves intuition, creativity and imagery. It is a journey that leads us back and forth, turning us 180 degrees every time we enter a new circuit. As we change direction, we shift awareness from left to right brain, thus inducing a receptive state of consciousness. When walking a maze, an inquiring mind is needed to find the centre, but the passive labyrinth demands one simple choice: to enter or not. The labyrinth, like the spiral of the Millipede, has one well-defined path that leads us to its centre and back out again. The choice to walk the labyrinth is based on our desire to know ourselves better and to explore a spiritual path. It is a metaphor for the voyage we all must take if we are serious about developing spiritually – a journey to our deepest centre that eventually leads to our return; a point that marks our emergence as wiser beings equipped with a broadened understanding of who we are. The labyrinth, as a tangible archetype, can easily be walked with the index finger around a drawing on a small piece of paper, or bodily, using a life-size representation. Similar to the concept of the Medicine Wheel, the labyrinth is a symbol of our life journey – a symbol that creates sacred space, tempers our ego and encourages us to safely journey within. To walk the labyrinth is to quest for ancient knowledge and spiritual awakening. It represents a voyage that is unique to the self and our soul. During the walk, try to relax, meditate and seek answers to private questions, but most importantly, be warned that the labyrinth encourages the facing of fears and the necessary defeat of personal demons. To walk the labyrinth is to connect with God or Spirit and the Creative Source, which is considered the most inevitable aspect of life, but one typically reserved for the end of our earthly life. Sometimes the walk may finish quickly, seeming to take no time at all, while other times it may take longer as we stop and rest and ponder the next course of action. As with any journey, though, it is not unusual to feel lost at times and unable to retain direction. If this does happen, try to remember that unlike the maze, the labyrinth offers a three phase journey that includes a definite beginning, middle and end, with no dead ends or trick turns.

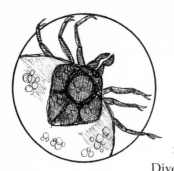

Mite or Tick
Exploitation

Mites and Ticks belong to the Arachnid family, a relationship shared with Spiders and Scorpions. They range in size from microscopic to one centimetre in length. Diverse in appearance, some juvenile Mites and Ticks only have three pairs of legs, gaining a fourth pair with their first sloughing. They do not have antennae and appear as a single body mass.

The term 'vampirism' alludes to the custom of drinking the blood of a person or animal. Because blood is a recognised symbol of life-force, vitality and creation itself, drinking another's blood bears little difference to stealing their soul or draining their life force. Although certainly a facet of some spiritual beliefs, popular culture and folklore insinuates that supernatural powers may be gained by drinking the blood of humans. In zoological terms, vampirism is used to describe Leeches, Mosquitos, Mites, Ticks and Fleas and some species of Bat – in fact any organism that relies on the bodily fluids of another for its survival can be described as a vampire. As an archetype, the vampire is embodied within those who thrive in unbalanced, abusive, exploitive relationships and situations. It is particularly obvious when these individuals, like a Tick or Mite that has gorged itself silly and dropped off its host, decide they have nothing more to gain from exploiting their partners and friends, and so leave, inexplicably packing up their belongings and moving on to their next gullible, love-starved victim. As well as latching onto their host and feeding mercilessly on their blood, Mites and Ticks are also known to spread blood-borne diseases. Anyone who has ever acquired a sexually transmitted disease or other illness by exchanging bodily fluids with someone who knew of their communicable condition, therefore, knows only too well the unhealthy, selfish, parasitic Dreaming of the Mite and Tick and the nature of those who inherently champion its cause. Mite and Tick people take until there is nothing left. They seem to have little or no conscience, being more than happy to drain their family and friends of every resource they have, and then when nothing remains, do not think it rude to never offer thanks or reimbursement. People plagued by Mites or Ticks need to consider the major relationships in their life, be they personal or professional, and ask themselves: Do my relationships take more than they give? Are they balanced and 'two-way' in nature, or do they demand too much of my time and energy? And finally, do these relationships exploit my good nature? Mites and Ticks, by their very nature, bear witness to one-sided, exploitive relationships. What you do about yours is up to you, of course. If you wish to remain the host of a parasitic relationship, Mite and Tick are happy to oblige.

Mosquito
Living Family Spirit

Notorious as bloodsuckers, Mosquitos belong to one of the largest insect families in the world; a family that includes Midges, Sand Flies, Houseflies and Blowflies. They are known to spread blood-transmitted diseases such as malaria, particularly in underdeveloped countries.

According to the Ainu people, the indigenous hunters and gatherers of northern Japan, Mosquitos were said to have risen from the ashes of a hobgoblin, an imp that was, according to legend, killed and burned by an Ainu hero. Traditionally, the word 'goblin' means 'spirit', while a 'hobgoblin' describes the spirit of the hearth or hob; a domestic ghost or Ancestral Guardian of the fireside. It was once common practice to bury the dead under the central fire pit of the home. It was here that the people believed the ghosts of the family members inhabited and protected the home and its inhabitants. Even after Christian rule decreed the dead were to be allocated specific burial sites away from the home, the belief remained that the spirits of the dead protected the family via the hearth. The hearth formed the hub of the home.

It symbolised the heart of tribal life; its warmth and glow enhanced by the living family spirit that radiated from its core. The hearth pit became the religious centre of the family, as well as an active portal or pathway to the Underworld where the spirits of the Ancestors were thought to reside. Conceding its blood-related fascination and connection to the people, Mosquito Dreaming embraces the ancient Ainu legend by embodying the 'Living Family Spirit'. It reminds us that our Ancestors walk with us, watch over us and protect us from harm. To experience a Mosquito under unusual circumstances (out of season, for example, in plague proportions, or in strange setting like an aeroplane), comes as a sign that the Living Family Spirit is alive and well, and that someone may be trying to communicate or resurrect his or her position within the family from the other side.

Moth
Lingering Energy

Like Butterflies, Moths undergo complete metamorphosis: from the egg through to a larval (caterpillar) stage, pupa (cocoon) and adult. Many nocturnal creatures, such as insectivorous Bats and Owls, rely heavily on the Moth as a food source. Moths belong to the same family as the Butterfly but, unlike them, have feathery antennae. Most Moths are coloured a dull shade of brown, although some day-flying species are brightly coloured.

According to Maori belief, the Moth is the embodiment of Spirit. Moth's obsession with and attraction to light forms the core of its Dreaming. The way they bother street lights, ceiling lights and table lamps represents our inherent (and probably unrealised) desire to unite with God, Spirit or 'the Light'. I like to believe that when the Creator was making the animals, there was energy left over that, instead of being returned to the Universal Source, was shaped to become the Moth. Since then, Moth has never felt as though it truly belongs. So, it spends every waking moment trying to return to The Light, deemed by some to be the source of all life. Moth urges us to put our fears and indoctrinated beliefs aside, and to reach out and reconnect with Spirit and invite the warm glow of its presence into our hearts. Many people are afraid to trust their innate connection to Spirit. Many have long forgotten their birthright to communicate directly with God. Because of life circumstance, many people believe themselves forsaken by the Creator, and so put little faith in having their prayers heard, let alone replied to. Moth puts our fears to rest, by inviting us to give God another go. Often the problem lies with us when it comes to our prayers not being heard. Offering prayer is one thing, but believing ourselves worthy of a response is another. A fear of Moths indicates a fear of, once again, being ignored by God. It suggests a lack of faith in our right to have our prayers heard. Moth asks that we put our fears and limitations aside and speak to Spirit without expectation ... and then wait to see what happens. Moth also comes as a warning that your space may be clogged by residual or lingering spiritual energy – both 'good' and 'bad'. It suggests we cleanse our space, our aura, home, workplace, car, self and family regularly, ridding it of built up or residual energy. This is particularly important when you have just moved house, or have moved your bedroom or office into another room. Before you take up residence, it is wise to spiritually evict the previous tenants and the vibrational essence they have left behind. In my opinion, smudging is the best way to cleanse space as it calls in the energies of the Earth Mother. By burning the clippings of herbs (like sage and lavender) – herbs collected and dried specifically for this purpose – the smoke produced will set about banishing lingering energy forever. To 'smudge' yourself, gather the smoke in your cupped hands and 'wash' it over yourself, as you would water. Such an act is known to prevent nightmares in children and to ease discomforting feelings in certain rooms. Concentrate on areas you feel need particular cleansing and pray to the unseen powers of the plants to cleanse your aura, encouraging the negative energies to return to the Universe or 'The Light' via the smoke.

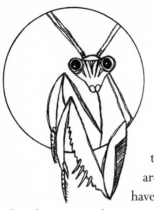

Praying Mantis
Prophecy

The Praying Mantis honours its name as it stands with forelimbs held together as if deep in prayer. Its raptorial front legs are armoured with single or double rows of thorn-like bristles. The males of most species are fully winged, while the females usually have compacted wings or no wings at all. The female Mantis is larger and physically stronger than the male and, like some species of Spider, is known to eat its mate during copulation.

Some African Bushmen hold the belief that the Praying Mantis shares the qualities of the Creator Spirit. With similar respect, devotees of the Greek Priestess 'of the oracle', Mante (meaning 'Prophet', or 'Moon Inspired'), once inaugurated a mystical cult of female worshippers known as The Mantes. Over time, the all-female sect gradually allowed men to initiate until the inevitable day arrived that saw the introduction of a male-only rule. Soon realising their spiritual inadequacies, however, the Priests of Mante apparently condoned and welcomed castration in a vain attempt simulate the unrivalled feminine power of the original sect members. It was believed that the souls of the first Mantes took the form of Praying Mantises between their physical incarnations. Praying Mantis is an emissary of the archaic feminine power 'to know'. She quietens the mind so that tension may be reduced and the inner chatter silenced, thus stilling the mind and opening our consciousness to spiritual insight and prophecy. It coaches us to listen with a meditatively induced and intuitive ear so that we may better understand our transcendental self. Offering no shortcuts or easy paths to enlightenment, Praying Mantis espouses the sacred stillness and sacred prayer as being the keys to the receiving of Spirit and its prophetic messages.

Scorpion
Honour

Scorpions are members of the Arachnid family. Some species reach lengths of up to 12 centimetres. They are commonly found in urban backyards, gardens and under household objects, under bark, leaf litter, rocks or fallen logs. Scorpions have pincer-like forelimbs used for grasping prey and self-defence. Their abdomen tapers into a tail tipped with a venomous stinger and poison gland. Scorpions hold their tails over their bodies protectively, the stinger poised ready to strike. Australian Scorpions deliver a very painful, but rarely fatal sting.

A sword suspended over the head once heralded impending doom for the fated man; a scene mirrored by the stance of the Scorpion. Over time, such ceremonial forms of execution became strictly symbolic in nature, marking the death of innocence while announcing promotion for the individual in question. Brandishing the sword became an act of respect, a ritual that saw the individual rise from being just a man to a respected knight. While the sword still touched each shoulder, it no longer had to pass through the neck to make its point. Astrologically, the sign of Scorpio (October 24 to November 22), the eighth sign of the zodiac associated with intensity, passion, and power is represented by the Scorpion and influenced by the element water; a relationship that seems to support tales of magickal swords and their heroic champions. Rising mysteriously from enchanted bodies of water or held ransom by charmed rocks; legendary tales abound of faerie-honed swords owned by gallant knights sworn to champion truth and honour above all else. Though, the end of the stories invariably sees the swords returned to their creators, marking the death of the hero. On King Arthur's death, for example, Excalibur instinctively returned to The Lady of the Lake. Arthur's famous blade was a revered symbol of honour, permeated with magick and wisdom intended to help bring peace and plenty back to the land. Although Scorpion people are often very attractive, gallant, captivating, intelligent and charming, Scorpion encourages us to wield 'the sting in our tail' in similar fashion to how traditional Buddhist disciples are expected to handle the sword of knowledge. It asks that we express ourselves in humble ways and that we display honour and integrity in our quest for power. Scorpion Dreaming nurtures a sense of pride, spiritual enlightenment, wisdom and nobility of heart, promise, prophecy, bravery and growth. It represents our quest for spiritual truth, while helping us face fears in honourable ways.

Silverfish
The Aura

Silverfish are regularly found in human dwellings, under refrigerators, in drawers and under furniture. They are most commonly found in or near crevices of wood bonded with starch glue, a favourite food source. Silverfish are nocturnal and shy, so aren't regularly seen. They eat anything that contains starch or polysaccharides: glue, book binding, paper, photographs, sugar, hair, and dandruff. They will also feed on books and magazines, tapestries, textiles, cotton, linen, silk and synthetic fibres. Silverfish are known to go a year without eating and are coated with a silver-blue dusty substance that rubs off when handled.

Silverfish comes as a reminder to check the health and wellbeing of your aura. The aura (pronounced 'or-rah') is the energy field that surrounds all living things, the force that radiates life energy from the body. Without realising it, our environment, the people we associate with and our lifestyle choices strongly influence the integrity of our aura. Its subtle energies bear witness to who and what we are. Long before the onset of externally obvious symptoms, for example, the aura provides a readily observed and easily interpreted account of our immediate condition: a detailed record of our health, mental activity and emotional state. Closely outlining the body – and usually no more than half an inch wide – is the pale etheric aura. Looking like a thin layer of smoke tightly hugging the body, it is the easiest part of the aura to see. As we sleep, the etheric aura swells and reaches out from the physical body in order to interact with, and store, the outer auric energies of the Cosmos. Often called the 'vitality sheath', the etheric aura levels and contracts as we wake, forming a dense, protective field around the body. Emanating from the chakras, the main aura is banded around the body in protective layers of colour. Life-force energy is fed from Mother Earth through our feet and into our chakras, in similar fashion to how a plant draws water through its roots. Each of the chakras generates different energy represented by a particular, symbolic colour. Our present physical state and our frame of mind govern the strength and vibrancy of the chakras and how effectively they rotate in balance with one another. Working as one, the chakra centres generate the dominant hue of the aura, mirroring any change within the body with each rotation. Many traditions claim that 'raking, fluffing and patting' will revitalise the aura while repairing any damage or weak spots caused by everyday living. To revitalise your aura effectively, you may require the assistance of a friend, but if you feel able, you can do it yourself. With your fingers splayed and slightly bent (like a rake), begin making quick short, combing strokes, starting at your feet and progressing gradually to the top of your head. Try to keep each stroke about 30 centimetres in length and about 10 to 20 centimetres away from your body. While raking, imagine the aura looking like a large bowl of well-whipped egg whites. This is a good description of what the aura looks like after raking. Now, repeat the process – this time starting at the top of your head, moving down toward and including your feet. Once completed, the aura is ready to be 'fluffed'. 'Fluffing' softens the 'edges' and dislodges stubborn negative energy that may still be lingering. Again, start at the feet and work up by making circular motions using the palms of your hands (with your fingers outstretched), the whole time wiggling your fingers in a gentle manner. Once you have made your way to the crown, repeat the action, this time moving back down toward the feet. Fluffing has a calming effect on the aura, especially after the more rigorous 'raking'.

Imagine that your aura resembles a bag of cotton wool. Now consider this: moments ago, your aura was like that bag of cotton wool, neatly packed in its tight wrapping, but now, after being raked and patted, it looks as though someone has pulled it out, ripped it apart and turned it into an unruly fluffy cloud. Imagine trying to put it neatly back into its wrapping. You couldn't – not without a lot of work. But by 'patting' the aura, you can return it to a near perfect state. Cup your hands and, again, work from your feet up toward your head, moving your hands rapidly in and out from the body, ranging from 5 to 20 centimetres in distance. 'Patting' the aura realigns the energy field. Do it all over. Once you have reached the top of the head, continue back down toward the feet.

A list of aura colours and possible interpretations:

Pink: love, friendship, childlike innocence
Dark pink: love, friendship, being overprotective
Light pink: nervousness
Red: vitality, activity
Dark red: anger, resentment, lust, temper
Pale red: waning energy
Orange: personal power, change, satisfaction, unity
Dark orange: strong ego
Pale orange: loss of control
Yellow: creativeness, intellect, a thinker
Dark yellow: sudden changes, discomfort, worry
Pale yellow: stagnation, disinterest
Blue: a healer, harmony, understanding, empathy, journeys, transition
Dark blue: disharmony
Pale blue: new beginnings, peace, tranquillity, contentment, communication
Green: fertility, nature, wealth
Pale green: new beginnings
Dark green: envy, jealousy, greed, lack of trust
Indigo: potential Indigo / Warrior Child, astral travel, higher knowledge

Dark indigo: karmic issues, lessons

Pale indigo: developing awareness, lessons learned

Purple: developing spiritual knowledge, psychic ability

Dark purple: misuse of spiritual power, desire for spiritual power

Pale purple or violet: balancing karma, spiritual balance

White: guidance, spirit guides, teacher

Bright white: growth, learning, clarity, centeredness, calmness

Gold: success

Dark gold: self-indulgence

Pale gold: developing awareness, self-esteem, buoyancy, poise

Silver: developing psychic ability, the goddess

Grey (and dark silver): depression, apprehension, refusal

Light grey: despair, fear, cynicism

Dark grey: abandonment, rejection

Black: trapped, confusion, grief, anger, darkness, hopelessness,
   psychic attack, ill-wishing

Brown: connection to the Earth, nature, the elementals, faeries,
   animals, plants and trees, grounded, trustworthiness, practicality

Slater
Teeth

Often mistaken for insects, a quick count of their seven pairs of legs quickly reveals their true crustacean identity. They breathe through gills like their aquatic cousins and require a damp, moist environment completely devoid of sunlight. Slaters, or Pill Bugs, are related to Shrimps, Crabs, Lobsters and Crayfish. Easily recognised by their flat armoured bodies, Slaters range in colour from dull grey to pale pink.

Although no one remembers the reasoning behind the association, the 'Pill Bug' is said to offer good medicine to those having problems with their teeth. Dehydrated Slaters were once ground and taken internally (a practise not advised today) as remedies thought to cure toothache, and strung around the necks of teething infants in a bid to ease the pain of teething. Teeth have long held significance as divinatory symbols, particularly when it comes to our dreams. Apparently, dreaming of teeth indicates unpleasant meetings or emerging illness. If, in your dream, your teeth are loose, you can expect failure, while having your teeth filled portends lost items being found. To dream of your teeth being accidentally lost heralds the downfall of general affairs and possible hardship, while seeing your teeth being spat out foretells illness within the family. So, Slater reveals that apart from being responsible for grinding our food, teeth offer insight into our future as divinatory symbols. It also demonstrates that because they come and go, teeth mark our evolution through three of the most fundamental phases of development – the infant (as per our 'baby' teeth), the adult (and the teeth that appear after our milk teeth fall out), and the Elder (when our real teeth are replaced with false teeth or dentures). Slater encourages us to be excited about life, to see each phase as opportunities to grow and prosper. It nurtures us as we make decisions that will ultimately shape our future, and to sink our teeth into the ones that promise the most viable ways to bring our dreams to fruition. It's only warning, though, is to avoid the temptation to bite off more than you can chew. Such behaviour will see your likelihood of success diminished or lacking potential.

Slug and Snail
Resurgence

Slugs and Snails are soft-bodied creatures. They differ slightly in most ways, except that Snails have external shells and Slugs don't. With one or two sets of tentacles on their head, Snails and Slugs both have excellent vision. They glide along on a surface of mucus that is expelled from glands under their foot. They belong to the Gastropod family. Gastropod means 'stomach foot', due to the fact that their stomach lies just above the large, fleshy 'foot'.

It was once thought that Snails slowly wore away their bodies as they dragged themselves across the ground, their remains ending up nothing more than slimy trails. It was also believed that after wearing themselves away, Snails were literally able to rebirth them selves as they inexplicably re-emerged whole from their womb-like shells. Its head appearing and disappearing from the safety of its casing, Snails became ambassadors of the lunar cycle, embodying change, birth, death and rebirth. It promises that after every period of darkness, light must eventually return; that after every night, there must be a new dawn, and that after every 'dark moon', there is always a new and whole one. Snail nurtures the simple truth that after ending we are given the chance to start over; that after an old door is allowed to close a new one must open. It helps us recognise the significance of the cycles being played out in our life, and how we might harness the potential offered by necessary change by simply acknowledging their presence. On a more light-hearted note, Snails were once employed as the most primitive of divinatory aides. Apparently Snails, by climbing the golden crop stalks, announced the best time to harvest around the time of the autumn equinox, while unwed women were once encouraged to seek the predictive services of the Snail when it came to finding a husband. Folklore espoused that Snails could reveal a spouse by spelling his name in slime on a piece of dry slate, thus favourably changing the romantic destiny of the woman forever.

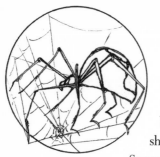

Spider
Weaver of Dreams

Spiders are ancient creatures that have shared the Earth with man since the beginning of time. They are Arachnids, sharing their family with Ticks, Mites and Scorpions. Spiders have two main body parts, eight jointed legs, simple eyes, piercing jaws and abdominal silk spinning organs. Some spin webs that easily trap walking, jumping and flying prey. Many use silk to wrap, subdue and hold their prey before eating them. Some Spiders, known as 'ambush hunters', do not build webs. Equipped with excellent eyesight, they sit in the open, hidden among foliage, flowers or bark, and ambush their prey, grasping it with their strong, spiny front legs before devouring it on the spot.

According Native American folklore, it was Grandmother Spider who sang the Universe into being by weaving the Web of Life. Grandmother Spider wove the first Dreamcatcher, a beautiful and protective web woven within a ring of willow wood. In the centre she placed a single turquoise stone, a symbol of connection to the Creative Force, clarity, peace, communication and protection. It is said that with the aid of a Dreamcatcher, our dreams can be harnessed and brought to fruition. Spider, as the Weaver of Dreams, reminds us that we are the creators of our own lives and that we alone choose the directions we take. Every night the Spider weaves her web and every morning she pulls it apart, fully prepared to reweave it later that night. Her web is symbolic of life. We are all vital strands in the Web of Life. Each of us is imbued with strength and wisdom to make a vital contribution to the planet. Spider encourages us to explore life and to investigate the strands that lead out from the centre of her web. Some will offer reward and others won't. As we journey the positive strands, life seems abundant. A wrong turn though, will present a strand that offers nothing. Life becomes difficult with all attempts to free ourselves proving futile. The Web of Life is riddled with pitfalls, but it also promises greatness to those prepared to take risks and work hard. As the Weaver of Dreams, Spider urges us to explore life and to reweave our web when our path becomes barren. She helps us reclaim our power and to bring our dreams to fruition. She warns, however, that in order to open new doors we must first close old ones by facing our fears and making choices that promise new beginnings. Spider reminds us of our roles as vital strands in the Web of Life. We all yearn to take control of our lives and to make a difference to the world. We all yearn to believe in ourselves, to have faith in our ability to heal and to realise our true potential. Spider nurtures the wisdom to make your healing possible and your life more profuse. Now is the time to acknowledge your vulnerabilities, face your fears and strive to achieve your dreams. Spider calls to us to embrace our Purpose and Personal Power: to reconnect with Spirit and remember that you are not apart from the world in which you live, but rather a vital thread in the Universal tapestry. Without your input, the tapestry will fray and eventually fall apart.

Stick Insect
Guarded Communication

Stick Insects belong to the Phasmatodea order of insects. The term *Phasmatodea* comes from the Greek word, 'phasma' which means 'an apparition or phantom', referring to their eerie resemblance to sticks and leaves. There are approximately 2,800 known species of Stick Insect, with most species common in the world's more tropical regions. The Lord Howe Island Stick Insect, for example, is listed as critically endangered, with captive breeding programs established throughout Australia to help bolster its numbers.

Despite feeling good about ourselves and positive about life, confident that we have taken care of our emotional baggage once and for all, unanswered residual questions associated with past experiences may still be lurking, hidden in the dark recesses of our mind, waiting for their chance to be responded to. Sometimes, without our knowing, unresolved issues subliminally influence the way we act and react to current situations. Our past effectively controls our present. How efficiently we integrate our past affects our ability to communicate openly today. Stick Insect nurtures us as we bravely acknowledge the past and face issues head to head. Although supportive, Stick Insect encourages us to never use our past as an emotional crutch and an excuse for our present limiting behaviour. By forcing us to deal with the past, Stick Insect strengthens our ability to communicate freely and honestly without obstruction, ensuring that our future life-path is kept clear of old patterns and familiar complications. Alternatively, Stick Insect's ability to disguise its appearance also warns (when appropriate) to guard against revealing personal or private information. It steers conversation away from personal or central issues, reminding us to share only the bare essentials with those who are not normally privy to such insight. Thus, it encourages discernment under pressured conditions. By volunteering private information, we run the risk of it falling into the wrong hands and being stolen, passed on or used against us.

Termite
Saboteur

Also referred to as White Ants, Termites only superficially resemble Ants. They live in colonies of up to a million, building giant mounds around rotting logs and stumps, Termites construct their nests from masticated soil, wood, ground litter, saliva and droppings. Termites are major commercial pests that cause serious structural damage to buildings, crops and cultivated forests, but are considered vitally important in the decomposition of organic matter and the recycling of nutrients, particularly in the world's subtropical and tropical regions.

Forming an obvious association, the house is a symbol of security, sense of belonging and foundation. It forms the hub of daily activity, the heart of the family and the base for all communication. And as a creature that readily eats away at that symbol, Termite comes as a warning that someone may be working silently and intentionally to undermine your sense of security. With patience and hungry determination, Termite slowly commits its time to instilling doubt and a sense of insecurity, slowly weakening the foundations you've worked so hard to establish in regard to family and work relationships, friendships and affairs of the heart. Targeting not only the physical home, Termite indicates the presence of a saboteur – someone determined to cause emotional and mental unrest. So, when you suspect the presence of a Termite, get an exterminator – and fast: a private investigator, counsellor or mediator qualified to ease the mind and re-establish a solid base.

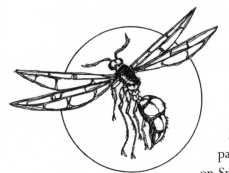

Wasp
Immobilisation

Most Wasps have two sets of wings, a stinger, a few or no hairs (unlike Bees). Many predate other insects, or share a parasitic relationship with them, preying on Spiders, for example, or as reproductive hosts. All Wasps fall into one of two categories: solitary or social. As their name suggests, solitary Wasps live and operate alone and don't construct nests. All solitary Wasps are fertile. Social Wasps, however, tend to live in colonies, build nests and, generally, only the queen and males are fertile, with the majority of the colony consisting of barren female workers. Most Wasps are parasitic whilst in the larval stage, but feed primarily on nectar as adults. Some are omnivorous, but this is rare. Those that are, however, will feed on windfall fruit, nectar and the carcasses of dead animals. Parasitic Wasps paralyse their prey by injecting them with venom. They then either lay their eggs inside the host or arrange them externally. As the eggs hatch, the larvae eat the host. After their first meal, however, the young are left to fend for themselves.

Many people choose a path of addiction to numb the pain and confusion of life. Although initially knowing their choices are harmful, they gradually distance themselves from reality as life becomes increasingly overwhelming and unbalanced. Over time, their dysfunctional world begins to feel normal and they lose sight of their options. According to legend, it was the Spider who first brought the Dreamcatcher to the people, as a gift from Spirit intended to help them weave their own reality. Spider encourages us to reweave our life web, to make decisions regarding our future and to disallow others from hindering us realising our dreams. Unfortunately, though, some of us unwittingly (perhaps) choose to follow destructive life paths, tainting our chances of ever weaving a productive web capable of harnessing the things required to live a good, wholesome, meaningful life. Some of us, for example, have a penchant for drugs, alcohol and/or other addictive substances or activity that, if left uncapped, may very well lead to us never realising life itself, let alone our dreams. When it seems that someone we know is personally at risk or following a path that promises to result in their downfall or demise, Wasp may be (with care) invoked to freeze their reality or put them into a symbolic state of suspended animation – especially when dealing with addiction, abuse, violence or anti-social behaviour, mental illness or suicidal tendencies. Appearing negative at first, Wasp Dreaming hints at abuse of power, control and manipulation. However, when it is our desire to see someone reach their potential, but to realise that dream means having to put a stop to things on their behalf with love and pure intent, Wasp Dreaming can indeed be positive thing, incurring no karmic penance. It must only ever be done to nurture the family unit, to hold it together and to ensure its united healing and growth. Wasp Dreaming is good, but only when the intention is to protect rather than interfere.

THE KINGDOM
OF THE
FINNED & FLIPPERED
ONES

Water symbolises many things: emotions, cleansing and feminine energy. Throughout history it has been linked with the astral plane and the creative forces of nature. The creatures that reside in, on or near water, therefore, can be seen as ambassadors of its energy, guiding our intuition, creative abilities and imagination.

native / indigenous / migratory / introduced fish and other aquatic creatures

Abalone
Grandmother Ocean

Also known as the Ear Shell, the Abalone clings to rocks with its muscular foot. Abalone feed on algae at night. As a group, they simultaneously discharge countless sperm and eggs at breeding time that gravitate together and fertilise. The larval stage lasts approximately one week.

According to the native people of the Pacific Northwest Coast of America, the Abalone shell is inherently feminine in nature, embodying the energies of Grandmother Ocean. As a result, many believe it should only be incorporated into ceremonies that use water, and never fire. Being that fire is masculine in form, some even have issues with it being incorporated into the smudging ceremony, despite its supposed long-standing association. Instead of the shell, they would prefer to see a clay or stone bowl used, a receptacle that features the earth element – a feminine element that better understands the nature of fire. At the end of the day, though, whether you decide to include the Abalone shell into your smudging ceremony or not, is entirely up to you. The notion of the '(Grand) Mother Sea' was first realised with the goddess Rhea, who became Demeter after she birthed Zeus – the goddess responsible for the separation of solid from liquid within the primeval Void of Great Mystery, or the separation of the Earth from the Sea. Put another way, the birth of 'Earth Mother' from *her* mother, 'Grandmother Ocean'. Demeter's name means 'the Sea Horizon', symbolised by the receptive womb-like cauldron. Abalone invites those who are experiencing loss, separation or abandonment to seek the advice, guidance and insight of our Grandmother, the Ocean. Find yourself a comfortable spot away from other people, smudge thoroughly and draw a protective circle in the sand around your body.

Meditatively discuss the issues with the Ocean, and then wait and intuitively prepare for a response that may come to you as a symbol (tangible or not), a gut feeling or spoken word. As one of the many representations of 'the Grandmother', Grandmother Ocean yearns to see you, her grandchild, grow and prosper – as any grandmother would.

Angelfish
Guidance

Luminously coloured, Angelfish inhabit coral reefs, the splendour of their surroundings paling in comparison to the iridescent stripes, bands and geometric shapes that decorate their body. Not to be mistaken for the freshwater Amazonian Angelfish, a member of the Cichlid family commonly seen in pet store fish tanks, Angelfish spend the daylight hours 'grazing' the seabed, feeding on algae.

'*An angel is a spiritual creature created by God without a body, for the service of Christendom and of the Earth. They rescue, guard, keep, protect, bring us messages from God, fight our battles, and carry out God's desires*'
- Martin Luther King

The word 'Angel' comes from the Greek word, 'Angelos', meaning 'messenger'. Angels have long been revered as heralds of God; guiding lights that inspire, heal and fight for justice. Winged human-like beings radiating halos of white light, Angels appear in most major religions, playing important roles in creation. Revered in Judaeo-Christianity, for example, Angels appear in both the Old and New Testaments and are believed to belong to a celestial hierarchy of nine main Orders. According to the New Testament, all celestial beings are grouped into seven ranks: Angels, Archangels, Principalities, Powers,

Virtues, Dominions and Thrones. The Old Testament adds cherubim and seraphim, which, when added to the other seven ranks, comprise the nine choirs of Angels in latter Christian theology (although the number typically remains fixed at seven). According to the book of Revelations, there were seven Angels that stood before God. Who these Angels actually were remains a mystery because different texts quote different Angels. The Angels most commonly agreed upon, though, became known as Archangels: divine messengers that sustained a line of communication between humanity and God while combating negativity in the form of confusion, fear, grief, greed, anger, frustration, abuse, control and tyranny. Very few Angels were referred to by their true name in early sacred texts, as doing so was thought to lessen their power. When called upon, Angels are said to guide, heal and inspire, their wisdom rousing clarity and creativity. Seeking angelic support has been incorporated into spiritual belief since the Middle Ages. Jesus himself was said to have boasted being able to invoke seventy-two thousand (twelve legion) Angels when required. There are many things worth considering when developing your understanding of Angels. Remember, for example, that an Angel only looks like a human with wings because we have grown to expect them to look like that, which means that anyone who inspires us to strive higher, to heal our lives or to respect ourselves more could essentially be an Angel. It is indeed true that Angels appear in many guises. A child who smiles at you from his shopping trolley, for instance, or the lady who picks up your keys as you fumble to unlock the boot of your car with your arms full of groceries; the doctor who saves your sister's life or the school teacher who offers a sense of promise for your child's academic future. All these could very well be Angels. An Angel might take the form of the faithful old Dog that sits with you night after night when there is little chance of visitors calling unannounced, the Cat who wakes his family and warns them of house fire, or the Elephants that lifted people onto their backs and carried them to safety during the Asian Tsunami in December 2004. Angels remind us that we are not alone. They remind us of the ever-loving presence of Spirit. They remind us to be thankful. They remind us of the simple pleasures, the little joys and the beauty found in the moment. They inspire us to not look back with regret or to look anxiously into the future. Angels remind us to appreciate and admire life as it stands at this point in time. They inspire us to stand in the 'now' and just 'be'. They encourage us to live life totally in the present and to walk our path with integrity and respect for all things. Angels inspire a sense of connection, interrelatedness and sacredness. They remind us that we are never alone and that we have nothing to fear except fear itself. They inspire a sense of abundance, by reminding us that we hold within our soul the keys needed to manifest the things we yearn for most of all. Angelfish encourages a deeper, more personal investigation into Angel Dreaming, paving a colourful journey toward peace, balance, healing, transformation and spiritual development.

Archerfish
Truth

Inhabiting fresh water rivers, the Archerfish rises to the water's surface and shoots a jet spray from its mouth at insects that have landed on overhanging branches. The target is predictably hit from its roost and is quickly eaten as it hits the water. Accurate to two to three metres, the Archerfish's aim must be precise to successfully counteract the refraction of sunlight through the water, a natural obstacle to vision.

Archerfish Dreaming embodies the metaphorical arrow, an ancient symbol of truth, protection and fate. A mark of the hero, Robin Hood stole from the rich and gave to the poor with the help of his trusty bow and arrows. On his deathbed, Robin vowed that where his last arrow landed would mark his final resting place. Governed by the element air, flint or obsidian arrowheads were apparently given to Native American youths as tangible representations of the warrior-spirit, as tokens thought to inspire clarity, guidance and support. Arrows are imbued with the blessings of Spirit. They protect us from temptation and emotions that threaten to taint and blur our judgement. To witness an Archerfish take down prey is indicative of receiving the arrowhead of truth. It confirms and blesses our life path, clarifies our destiny and guides us to spiritual enlightenment.

Barramundi
Equilibrium

Barramundi is an Aboriginal word from the Rockhampton area that literally means 'large scales'. Once referred to as the Giant Perch, the great fish is now nationally recognised as the Barramundi. Barramundi feed on Crustaceans, Molluscs and smaller Fish, inhabiting rivers and streams. They journey to estuaries to spawn, the males migrating downstream to join the females who each lay millions of eggs. Most Barramundi mature as male, but change to female after their first spawn. This means that most adult Barramundi are probably female.

> *'Girls can wear jeans*
> *And cut their hair short*
> *Wear shirts and boots*
> *'Cause it's okay to be a boy*
> *But for a boy to look like a girl is degrading*
> *'Cause you think that being a girl is degrading*
> *But secretly you'd love to know what it's like*
> *Wouldn't you*
> *What it feels like for a girl'*
> - from 'The Cement Garden' by Ian McEwan, 1978

Gender roles have long been divided into two categories: male and female. Today, though, these roles are being challenged, with what was once considered typical roles, fashions and habits for men being taken up by women, and vice versa. Barramundi Dreaming enables us to break down the boundaries surrounding gender, literally deconstructing the rules associated with what is deemed masculine and what is considered feminine. It champions what it means for a male to be 'metrosexual', while espousing relational understanding and equality. Rather than describing heterosexual men who look or act homosexual or bisexual as it once did, the term 'metrosexual' now denotes men who partake in activities once considered feminine; men who demonstrate strong concern for their aesthetic appearance by spending time and money on their image and lifestyle. The transformation experienced by the adult Barramundi suggests a conscious shift within the modern male; a step away from the traditional role of doer, hunter-gatherer 'yang', toward the metaphysical, dreaming 'yin'. It shows a calling for males to honour their whole, balanced selves, instead of focusing solely on their more dominant male aspect. Barramundi demonstrates clearly the differing modern impression of how a man should look and act by comparing it to the expected norm of generations past. It embodies the shunning of expectation and the burdens that come with accepted gender roles, and a possible move toward androgyny. Barramundi creates a sense of equilibrium by raising awareness of man's innate feminine characteristics and the ever-growing power of the feminine creative force within all men. While defending what it means to be a full-blooded male, it acknowledges the sacredness of intrinsically knowing both the masculine and feminine aspects of self.

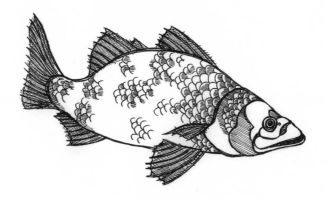

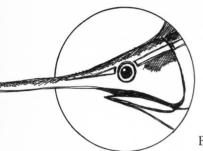

Billfish
Tenacity

Billfish belongs to the same family as the Marlin, Sailfish and Swordfish, all of which sport elongated bodies and pointed bills. Billfish have impressive dorsal fins, with some species displaying two. Very fast swimmers, Billfish prey upon Tuna, harpooning their quarry with their pointed bill before devouring it. Preferring tropical and subtropical waters, the Billfish or 'Grandfather of the Sea' inhabits temperate waters all over the world. They are common in most Australian marine waters. A favourite among big game fishermen, the Billfish makes for a spectacular catch. The thrill of the hunt quickly wanes in comparison, though, with the desperate violence exerted by the Billfish as it fights for its freedom. Sometimes its tenacity pays off, as its struggling dislodges the hook stuck in its mouth or snaps the wire-like line that binds it to the fishing boat.

Demonstrated by its ability to break free from the fisherman's hook, Billfish teaches by example the determination required to see things through and to reach set goals, no matter how unlikely our chances. Tenacity, resolve and persistence are character traits of the Billfish, a creature that personifies the expression, 'It's not over 'til the fat lady sings'. It encourages those of us who struggle with commitment to 'soldier on' and never give up, even when faced with immense adversity. Advocating wholeness, freedom and personal abundance, Billfish explains the subtle difference between 'giving in' and 'giving up'. 'Giving up' means losing faith; it says, 'I can't do this anymore, it's too hard.' And instead of looking for other options, we throw in the towel. We stop in the hope that our original belief was unfounded and that we are better off for giving up. 'Giving in', however, is completely different. It is to surrender control and to trust that all will work out for the best. It says, 'I can't do this alone, it's too complex.' But instead of stopping and losing faith; instead of worrying about the steps that need to be taken to make things happen in our favour, we focus on the final outcome only, and surrender the hows, whens and whys. It is to trust in a higher force. It is to invest in our right to receive. So long as we maintain faith in our desired outcome coming to fruition, and work tenaciously toward realising our goal, why it happens, when and how is irrelevant. It's simply none of our business.

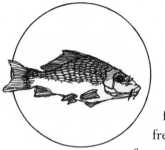

Carp
Reward

The Carp is an introduced species. Their aggressive, territorial ways are responsible for the obvious decline in Australia's native fresh-water fish. In an effort to eradicate them from our waterways, professional fishermen are employed to hunt the Carp. Unfit for the table, though, their bodies are sold to manufacturers of garden fertiliser and pet food.

The Carp swims upstream, against the current, to mate and release its eggs. It faces and overcomes many obstacles on the way, literally 'running the gauntlet' to return to its ancestral spawning ground – a race that takes a great deal of physical energy to complete. As it approaches its mark, the Carp must take a final leap of faith – one last leap that sees it reach its goal. Such a leap is said to take the Carp to 'Dragon Gate', a level of awareness that bestows great power and reward; a stage that affords illumination, passion, introspection and wisdom. People working to complete a period of study or degree of academia or those simply fulfilling life dreams or personal levels of achievement can be likened to the Carp that has successfully leapt to 'Dragon Gate'. For demonstrating resolve and achieving honourably against the odds, the Carp promises rich reward to those dedicated to furthering themselves and bettering their lives.

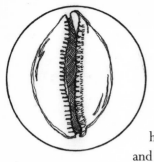

Cowrie
Fecundity

Cowries are Marine Snails found mainly in tropical regions. The shells are generally smooth to touch, although some species have granular shells, and most are patterned and beautifully coloured. Cowrie shells are typically oval in shape with a long, narrow, notched opening. Many species are carnivorous, feeding on Sea Sponges (among other prey). They hunt at night and hide in rock crevices by day.

Cowrie shells are often incorporated into jewellery, used as ornaments or carried as talismans as potent symbols of female independence, feminine fertility, conception and wealth. As one of the world's earliest known depictions of the Yoni, the Cowrie shell's resemblance to the female genitalia is undeniable. Gypsy women have revered the Cowrie as a charm that heightens female fecundity for centuries, while the Ojibwa Indians of North America incorporated the sacred white Cowrie shell into their shamanic rituals and medicine ways. Cowrie Dreaming inspires fertility on all levels – from new beginnings to the profitable start of a business or project. When invoked, the benefits may be witnessed in the form of a bountiful harvest, phenomenal healing, financial gain, deeper spiritual insight, academic success, a new relationship, an employment opportunity or a pay rise. Investigating the spiritual properties of the Sponge might also prove beneficial to those yearning for a more productive life. Most commonly, though, the Cowrie is either worn or carried to stimulate conception and to ensure a viable pregnancy. Those yearning to become mothers would do well to invoke the fecund wisdom of the Cowrie Shell.

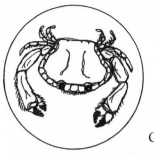

Crab
Diplomacy

Best known for their sideways scuttling, Crabs are covered with a thick exoskeleton, armed with a single pair of claws. Marine Crabs are found all over the world, with many of freshwater and terrestrial species chiefly inhabiting the tropical regions. Crabs are omnivores, feeding on Molluscs and other Crustaceans, Worms, fungi, bacteria and algae.

Cancer is the fourth sign of the zodiac, associated with family and domesticity. Symbolised by the Crab, Cancer is considered a fruitful sign. Ruled by the moon, and influenced by the element water, those born under the sign of the Crab (June 21 to July 22) will identify with its natural tendency to side-step challenging situations. A creature that abhors arguments and feelings of unrest, Crab chooses to follow a passive, compliant, unquestioning path guided by the full cycle of cause and effect. Instead of always addressing our issues front on by speaking up or demanding attention, Crab prefers we cultivate the more diplomatic approach of 'agreeing to disagree' at times, almost tiptoeing around our problems to avoid confrontation. By keeping the peace and trusting in the Universal laws of karma, Crab could be accused of hiding its head in the sand, running from emotional encounters and concealing its true feelings behind its crusty protective shell. And this may be the case at times, but in reality Crab simply champions the adage, 'It will all come out in the wash'.

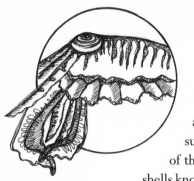

Cuttlefish
Legacy

Cuttlefish are marine creatures that are closely related to the Squid, Octopus and Nautilus. Despite what their name suggests, they are not Fish, but members of the Mollusc family. Cuttlefish have internal shells known as 'cuttlebone', large eyes, eight limbs and two tentacles equipped with suckers, which they use to catch small Crabs, Shrimp and Fish. They are predated by Dolphins, Sharks and (among others), Seals. With a one to two year life span, Cuttlebone, once dried and washed free of salt, is sold commercially in pet stores. Containing calcium, they make natural beak-sharpening devices for caged Parrots.

Many artists, writers and musicians only achieve fame and fortune after they have died, the rewards of their ultimate success coming too late for them to enjoy personally but providing a healthy legacy for their family and friends. And like these individuals, the Cuttlefish only realises its final purpose after its demise. Its legacy: its cuttlebone. It lives a good, whole life, enjoying the simple pleasures afforded by Grandmother Ocean while providing nourishment to many other creatures. But, after being found washed up on the shore, Cuttlefish continues to provide, even after its death. On finding a cuttlebone, you may be notified of an unexpected windfall, inheritance or payment. Alternatively, you may learn of a long-forgotten, clandestine or previously unknown family history, kinship or hereditary condition. Cuttlefish ultimately heralds a legacy or something left in the care of a benefactor; something you're planning on leaving your children, for example, or something being kept in store for you.

Dolphin
Breath

Without a doubt, the most famous Dolphin ever would have to be 'Flipper', the Bottle-nosed Dolphin made famous by the television series of the same name. *Flipper* helped elevate the Bottle-nosed Dolphin to the status of 'the world's most loved Dolphin'. Bottle-nosed Dolphins form groups of about a dozen individuals, often combining to form herds of several hundred. The most abundant of all Dolphins, however, is the Common Dolphin, which come together to form groups of several thousand. Common Dolphins are often seen feeding alongside the Bottle-nosed Dolphin. Both are found in all temperate to tropical oceans and seas, and can reach an average speed of up to 20 km per hour.

Dolphin is one of Spirit's midwives. She is present when we are born; she helps us take our first breath and then pilots us through life in much the same way she guides boats from port, reminding us to breathe as we embark on all creative ventures. The time spent in the womb is sacred. It shapes our view of the world before and after we are born. Realising what life was like for both you and your mother while she was carrying you will help explain why you act and react toward life the way you do, the way you feel toward your family, why you hold your breath in times of stress and why your view of yourself has developed as it has. Your sense of security and confidence, your relationships and even the type of employment you seek, are all determined by the quality of time spent in your mother's womb and the conditions under which you drew your first breath. You agreed to everything as it is, as it was and as it will be before entering this life. What you do with this understanding and how you let it affect you is the key to a healthy, happy existence. Dolphin prompts you to review your life by asking questions that may trigger heartfelt reactions to your time in your mother's womb. Ask yourself what life was like for you and your mother during this time. Consider the possibility that there may be things you are trying to bring to fruition that are unconsciously being blocked by your memory of your time in the womb. Are you symbolically holding your breath as you intuitively remember anxiety, the stress of your mother and your birth, for example? If you draw a blank, talk to your mother or someone you trust to help you remember. Evaluate the details that stand out and see them as a foundation on which to re-map your journey, to check your life's blueprint and to review the sacred contracts you signed before entering this world. See this as an opportunity to reclaim your power, to rebirth and to finally honour the first breath you ever took.

Dugong
Healing the Womb

Dugongs, 'The Madonna of the Sea' or 'Sea Cows', are large marine mammals that inhabit Australia's tropical waters. They graze the water plants of rivers, estuaries and shallow coastal inlets. Once common, Dugongs gathered in large herds. Due to over-hunting for meat and 'oil' and a decline in sea-grass, populations have plummeted noticeably. Their long gestation and slow growth rate don't do much to help their numbers either. As a result, Dugongs are now listed as endangered.

Known and loved as the Manatee in some parts of the world, legend has it that the Dugong was once human in form. No one knows which, but apparently she was transformed into her present form by either a blessing or curse. Belonging to the order *Sirenia*, the melodious call of the Dugong (which is clearly audible to those in fishing boats or walking on the shore), probably initiated early belief in the Mermaid and the Siren of Greek mythology. A creature that gently serenades her young, and suckles them from her pectoral breast, the Sea Cow is archetypal of the mother and the womb. Dugong cradles her young: supporting, embracing and protecting them. Innocuous to other creatures, the lunar influenced Dugong symbolises all energies wholesome, reproductive and motherly. She reminds us to nurture ourselves, to celebrate our roles as mothers and to honour our mother as our primary caregiver. Dugong Dreaming calls to women to heal themselves on levels deeper than the physical. She speaks of the united power of women collective: the cellular memory triggered by a sister's scream, the learning of discernment and lessons gleaned through loss, abuse, oppression and matriarchal neglect. Dugong Dreaming reminds women that their power comes from their womb and that their healing represents their connection to Spirit. It is said that women share sacred genetic memory of all that has gone before them and that which is yet to come. They remember the wrongs exacted upon them by all men, for example, the wrongs they have imposed upon their sisters and the pain their sisters have inflicted upon them, and Dugong states that these are the things women must heal. Dugong speaks of the journey into the memories of the Grandmother Spirit and the need for all women to heal collectively from the womb.

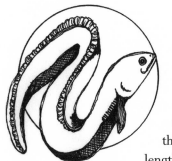

Eel
Breaking of Addiction

Eels spend the majority of their lives in fresh-water lakes, dams and rivers, annually returning to spawn in the waters they themselves were born into. Reaching lengths of over one metre, Eels have long Snake-like bodies, slippery skin, strong tails and dorsal fins.

According to folklore, Eels may be called upon to help purge alcoholic addiction. If one was to drown an Eel in a barrel of wine or beer, it is said, and then if one was to drink that same wine or beer, the result will be an almost immediate intolerance of all alcohol. Of course, simply invoking the spirit of the Eel will offer the same effect. Whenever you feel the need to imbibe, or you catch your friend or family member reaching for a drink, visualise an Eel floating in the liquid, its leaching energy souring its flavour and brutally polluting the experience. So long as no harm comes to them or you, visualise the most negative response you like. The desired outcome, after all, is the decision never to drink alcohol again. Similarly, the spirit of the Eel can be invoked as a means of offering or obtaining healing support. Likewise, due to its phallic shape and Snake-like appearance, Eel's spirit (when carried in the form of a talisman or charm) can be summoned to help sluice sexual addiction and licentious proclivity.

Freshwater Crayfish
Productivity

Freshwater Crayfish are blue or brown coloured crustaceans. Resembling the Lobster (to which they are related), Freshwater Crayfish (or 'Yabbies') are favourites among children who often keep them as pets in aquariums. They are also trapped by fishermen as bait and food. Also known as the Crawfish or Crawdad, Freshwater Crayfish breathe through gills. They are commonly found in flowing rivers and streams, with most species finding polluted water objectionable.

A potent symbol of productiveness, legend has it that the Crayfish helped Spirit in the re-creation of Mother Earth by bringing mud up from the depths of the Great Flood. When threatened, the Crayfish reverses with great speed, backing itself into tight hiding places. Although such behaviour could indicate departure from responsibility or the rejection of one's current circumstance, the large number of eggs produced by the Crayfish suggests inherent knowing, future planning and productivity. Attaching them to the underside of her tail, Crayfish's eggs promise new beginnings, fertility, expectation and potential. On choosing to take flight, though, they become unrealised potential; a lack of faith in our ability to create for ourselves or produce on any level. Crayfish implies that in order to reach set goals, we must thwart the desire to flee by making a concerted effort to push forward. It offers endurance by sharing the advantage of its protective outer shell, nurturing confidence powerful enough to combat our natural tendency to retreat.

Frog and Tadpole
Cleansing

Frogs are amphibians, characterised by powerful hind legs, stocky bodies, webbed toes, bulbous eyes and no tail. They enjoy a semi-aquatic life but, when on land, they jump and climb tree trunks, logs and rocks. Some have suction-like toe pads that allow them to climb glass doors, windowpanes and other smooth surfaces. Frogs are carnivorous. They eat Spiders, Caterpillars, Worms, small Snails, Crickets and other insects. Their call is usually heard at night, but mostly during their mating season (depending on the species). Frogs call by passing air through the larynx, amplifying the sound by means of vocal sacs and expanding skin membranes near the throat and mouth. Most deposit their eggs in or near water so that, when they hatch, the Tadpoles are safe to metamorphose into Frogs. Tadpoles have gills and a tail, which they lose as they develop. Many Frogs absorb water directly through their skin. The permeability of their skin, however, often leads to water loss. Many species are nocturnal to help combat this. By gathering in groups, others limit water loss by sitting closely together, their bodies slightly touching. This reduces the level of air to which their skin may otherwise be exposed.

Frog, as the 'Lord of the Waters' (according to Aboriginal tradition), teaches us to honour our emotions. When its chorus is heard, Frog generally indicates approaching rain. Those who live in the Australian outback, for example, look forward to the wet season because it soothes the earth, making promise of new growth and fertility. Symbolically, it implies a need to settle the emotional dust that prevents the stream of life from flowing in a productive manner. It promises to cleanse our Spirit by stimulating the release of sacred tears and the freeing of pent-up emotion. When we welcome our cleansing tears we are reassuring ourselves that everything will be okay and that all will work out in the end. Instinctively we are preparing our bodies for fruitful new beginnings and the conclusion of emotional barrenness and drought. When we journey through life denying ourselves of emotional cleansing, we grow numb to the possibility of change. We stop looking for opportunity and signs of new growth. We begin to see life as being empty, sterile and deficient and we forget what life was like before the drought. When honoured, though, our tears hold the power to strengthen us and deepen our sense of self-worth. They help us look at life in a bountiful way. Our tears welcome fertility and growth back into our life, but only when they are celebrated. To deny them, or to see them as signs of weakness, is to guarantee a drought that will forever hamper life and any chance of emotional healing. Where there is no love, encouragement or support there is no chance of growth. Without rain, there is no life. Without tears there can be no healing. Frog asks that you embrace your tears and to see them as a chance to rid yourself of emotional, physical and spiritual burden. It reminds you to take time out for yourself, to shun negativity and fear and to release emotional baggage; to welcome and honour your tears and to see them as a healthy way to cleanse the soul of pain, grief, fear and longing. It offers the chance to recharge our batteries and reclaim a sense of balance and healing in our lives, thus affording a fertile new ground on which to start again.

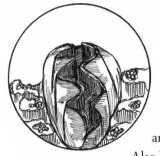

Giant Clam
Inhibition

Securing themselves to the sandy seabed with fragile filaments, the Giant Clams that inhabit Australia's Great Barrier Reef are the largest of their kind in the world. Also known as 'bivalves', Giant Clams lie among the coral with their valves wide open, allowing sunlight to shine on their brightly coloured internal mantle tissue, photosynthesising native algae, which they consume. Images of divers' legs being firmly trapped between the slammed-shut jaws of Giant Clams tell an awful but untrue story. They actually close their valves very slowly and with extreme care.

Giant Clam Dreaming offers the chance to initiate and embrace new growth, deeper understanding, clarity and change. A creature that relies heavily on the sun's warming rays to develop the algae on which it feeds; Giant Clam invites us to be more receptive to new ideas. Veneration of the sun promises longevity. It is warming, invigorating and offers rebirth each morning. It means, however, being candid and approachable and open to change. At the slightest hint of danger, however, Giant Clams slowly close their valves, blocking out the sun. At some time or another, we have all been guilty of 'clamming up', especially when we feel threatened, pressured or under scrutiny. We freeze, unable to express ourselves clearly. For most, these moments are rare; the feelings short lived. When 'clamming up' becomes the norm, however, triggered by low self-esteem or preservation instinct, we inevitably become reticent and forlorn. We find it difficult to open up to new relationships and opportunities. We may even avoid conversation for fear of being judged, ridiculed or overlooked. For some, being asked a simple question inspires such panic that they experience nausea. Giant Clam dares us to face our fears by affording us courage and stamina. It helps us rid ourselves of inhibition so that we may open up. It encourages freedom of speech, emotional expression and the sharing of ideas and constructive criticism. By its very nature, Giant Clam welcomes the healing and revitalising energy of the Sun each morning.

Goldfish
Sanctification

Although members of the Carp family, Goldfish have no barbels on the corners of their mouths like the feral Carp that inhabit many of Australia's rivers and waterways. Domestic forms of Carp include the Koi and the Crucian Carp. Goldfish are among the world's most popular household pet. First domesticated in China, Goldfish were introduced into Europe during the 17th Century. They come in a wide variety of forms and colours and most are hardy enough to live in the most brackish of water. Some of the most popular varieties include the Black Moor, Bubble Eye, Comet, Fantail, Lionhead, Oranda and Shubunkin.

Feng Shui, the ancient Chinese art of placement traditionally practised to achieve harmony with the home or office environment, marks the Goldfish as a symbol of good fortune. When welcomed into your home, Goldfish Dreaming quickly turns a house into a home and, ultimately, a home into a sanctuary. To rid your environment of accumulated negative energy or 'sha-chi', therefore, establish an aquarium in the southeast corner of your home and/or office. Alternatively, place a fishbowl to the inside left of your front door to encourage the healthy inward flow of positive chi. Placing blue or black gravel in the bottom of your aquarium will help activate your career, while green gravel will boost energy, health and ambition. Maintaining a clean, flowing, well-lit aquarium is believed to help transform negative energy. Round bowls are best, especially those fitted with an effective filtration system, bubbling water and low-voltage light. Round objects are said to assist positive chi to flow smoothly through and around rooms and buildings. Support the aquarium by keeping the area around it as neat and tidy as possible, while ensuring a healthy flow of natural light, or simulated light that is not too dim and not too bright. Vibrant, active Goldfish are best because they attract and sustain the flow of positive energy. According to Feng Shui, nine is an auspicious number, so eight Goldfish are favoured, accompanied by a single black one. If keeping nine fish is out of the question, three is also a potent number as it symbolises 'yang' or masculine energy. Purchase two Goldfish to inspire good luck and energy and one black one to invoke security. Black Fish are deemed powerful symbols of protection, either deflecting negativity or absorbing it. Black Fish are said to take in negative chi and release it as waste, thus helping to create a living sanctuary free of energetic interference. If the bowl's water becomes excessively cloudy, the Feng Shui cure is apparently working. If the black Fish dies, the negativity within the house or building is probably extreme, with its death warning of the need for stronger cures. Goldfish are celebrated because they resemble baby Dragons; another favourable creature thought to bring good luck. The Chinese word for fish is 'yu' – a word that can also mean accomplishment or abundance.

Jellyfish
Supernatural Forces

Jellyfish are invertebrates; free-swimming, gelatinous organisms sometimes referred to as Medusas, named after the Gorgon Medusa of Greek mythology, who was one of the three Dragon-like daughters of Phorcys, god of the sea. Medusa was a terrifying mortal creature whose body was covered with golden scales and, instead of hair, her head writhed with venomous Snakes. Each Snake was an individual entity, with its own brain and private agenda. Equipped with long tentacles barbed to hold prey, the sting of the Jellyfish is painful. In a few tropical species, the venom is potent enough to kill an adult human. Like Medusa's Snakes, each tentacle (or zooid) is an individual entity, independent in all ways, but reliant on one another for survival.

The Dreaming of the Jellyfish, or 'Ghost of the Ocean', should only be called upon when all else fails, and only then with extreme caution and deep respect. Floating carefree on the surface of the ocean,

Jellyfish (at first glance) appears harmless, almost fun. Unknown to the observer, though, danger lurks just below as wispy strands armed with venomous barbs weightlessly reach out and ensnare all that wanders too close. Once thought to embody the souls of drowned sailors, Jellyfish indicates the presence of paranormal influence, ghosts and entities. Although difficult to see, they entice curiosity, mystery and purposeful investigation of forces classified as supernatural. When invoked with intent, most spirits are happy to protect, guide and heal. Most are virtuous and kind; pleased to help. But some are not. At first sight, all spirit beings appear harmless. But some are not what they seem. Dark-side entities, for example, have one goal: to disrupt, weaken and destroy. They're generally not above deceiving those who encounter them, usually with the intention of infiltrating and undermining their health and wellbeing, their security and even their sense of reality. Irksomely, many of these spirits are unwittingly welcomed by light-workers as Angels and other light-side entities. Light and dark are present in all things, with the word 'light' not always corresponding to what is 'good' or 'positive' and the word 'dark' not always meaning 'bad' or 'negative'. With this in mind, it is wise to never accept or trust any entity without question. Remember that just as there are forces that only wish to inspire and see humanity prosper and heal, there are apposing forces of equal strength and power that would happily starve us of purpose and see mankind shrivel up and die. So, should you ever encounter an 'Angel', either in the tangible sense or in the non-physical realms of meditation, dream or vision, for example, it is prudent to immediately and ruthlessly quiz it for proof of authenticity. Why? Because, although it is safe and correct to assume that a true 'being of the light' would never betray, forsake or abuse its role as messenger of God, Spirit or 'the Light', a Dark-side entity would. Dark-side entities are driven by one motivation: to confuse, obstruct and dissuade, and they will do whatever it takes to fulfil that goal, even it if it involves 'dressing up' or pretending to be something they aren't. True light-side beings, however, have no reason to deceive: what you see is what you get. Jellyfish Dreaming warns that although it may be fun and rewarding to work with the Spirit World, we should remain ever vigilant of what we invoke, why we invoke it and how. Jellyfish warns that prevention is better than cure, so work with the Spirit realm carefully and respectfully and constantly check and confirm that all is as it should be.

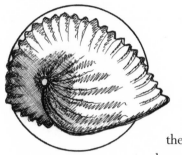

Nautilus
Resilience

Related to the Octopus, the Nautilus is the only member of the family to have an external shell. Born without the traditional suckers, ink sacs or ability to change colour at will, Nautiluses have up to ninety tentacles arranged in circles and, unlike other Cephalopods, theirs are retractable. The Nautilus shell has inbuilt gas (primarily nitrogen, oxygen, and carbon dioxide) chambers designed to keep it afloat. Moving by jet propulsion, they draw water in and out of the chambers with the hyponome, a muscular funnel or siphon into which water is sucked. When water is inside the chambers, the siphuncle – a tissue filament that passes through the shell – removes the salt and diffuses it with the creature's blood. When the water is pumped out, the Nautilus corrects its buoyancy with the gas contained in the chambers. Draining water from the shell's chambers moderates its density, turning it into a kind of flotation device. The Nautilus is capable of crawling onto land or across the sea floor.

The Nautilus' ability to float upright while fully submerged represents optimism, good spirits and light-heartedness. To be light-hearted is to float through life free of inflexibility and arrogance. It is to appear carefree, playful and glad to be alive, especially when we find ourselves in over our heads as far as responsibilities or commitments go. Nautilus affords a sense of endurance and inner strength potent enough to overcome the need for pretence. It stabilises the mind so that we can see the positive in all experiences, whether they be deemed good or bad. Encouraging us to take responsibility for our actions, Nautilus Dreaming does not condone disloyalty or deceptiveness.

Instead, it instils poise and pride, allowing us to hold our head high with confidence. Nautilus encourages us to breathe through testing times so that we may preserve composure and not panic. It imparts a sense of balance, a harmonious foundation on which to firmly establish calm and acceptance. Nautilus Dreaming suggests that to remain buoyant when things get tough is to know enthusiasm and true resilience.

Octopus
Infidelity

Octopuses are famous for their eight muscular arms, typically lined with suction cups. Most have soft bodies with no internal skeleton. The only hard part of the Octopuses' body is the beak, which strongly resembles that of a Parrot. Their soft body allows them to squeeze into very narrow crevices when fleeing their enemies. Some Octopuses have two fins and an internal shell. Octopuses have three hearts: two that pump blood through their gills, and one that pumps blood through the body. They also have fairly short life-spans. Some, for example, only live for six months where as some of the larger species survive until five years of age. After mating, male Octopuses only live a few months before dying, and the females usually die of starvation soon after hatching their eggs because they refuse to eat during incubation.

The number eight is a fortunate number, promising both prosperity and perpetuity. Formed by a single line that forms two intertwined, never-ending loops, the number eight has become a symbol of commitment, eternal life, abundance and fortitude. Despite its obvious ties with the auspicious number, though, the Octopus has chosen to shun its potential in favour of licentiousness and self-indulgence. The cheat of the animal world, the Octopus has earned itself the suspect Dreaming of infidelity. Apart from its ability to change its colour when threatened or stressed, folklore portrays the Octopus as fickle and one of little faith because it flees under pressure and ejects a cloud of ink to cover its tracks. Lustful men and womanisers are described as having 'as many hands as an Octopus', suggesting inappropriate and ill-mannered behaviour. To only ever focus on our shadow side because it is easier than the alternative is to waste our potential and to give up on moderation and dependability. Instead of disloyalty and infidelity, therefore, Octopus Dreaming reminds us of our inherent ability to live long, abundant lives rich with love, allegiance and promise.

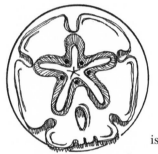

Sand Dollar
Hope

A creature that burrows into the sandy sediment of the sea floor to hide from predators, the Sand Dollar (or Sea Biscuit) is an unevenly shaped Sea Urchin covered in very short, fine bristles. They have five sets of pores used to channel water through their interior, affording locomotion. Tube-feet move food toward the mouth, located at the centre of the star-shaped grooves on the belly. Sand Dollars eat plankton and other organic matter found on the seabed. Adults congregate together and, during reproduction, release 'gametes' (specialised sex cells that fuse with one another during fertilization) into the water. The larvae metamorphose through several stages before the test (skeleton) forms.

Also known as the 'Holy Ghost Shell', the markings on the Sand Dollar are believed to narrate the birth, crucifixion and restoration of Christ. What appears to be the profile of an Easter lily in the form a five-pointed star, for example, is said to personify the energies of the Star of Bethlehem. The slender egg-shaped apertures are reminiscent of the five lesions made in the body of Jesus during his crucifixion, while on the underside of the case is found the familiar shape of a Christmas Poinsettia. When broken open, the shell reveals hidden chambers each containing five unusually shaped granules that emerge resembling birds in flight; birds said to represent the Doves of Peace that purportedly appeared as Angels and serenaded the shepherds the night of Jesus' birth. To find a Sand Dollar is to find much more than a discarded shell: it is to be entrusted with an ancient promise of hope, faith and optimism. A symbol of rebirth and new beginnings, Sand Dollar Dreaming offers freedom and a sense of belonging to those prepared to live a life of devoted belief. To see the Sand Dollar for what its name suggests, a talisman that invokes divine and sanguine wealth, will ultimately lead you to a place of spiritual enlightenment and inner peace.

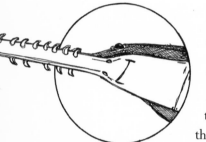

Sawfish
Disengagement

The five species of Sawfish found in Australian waters are members of the tropical Ray family, which is related to the Shark. All species are endangered due to trapping. When dried, the 'saw' is a favoured souvenir and an ingredient in alternative medicine. Found largely in Australian estuaries, the Sawfish has a compressed body and a prominent flat 'toothy' snout that looks similar to the blade of a chainsaw when laid on its side. These toothy protrusions are in fact modified scales and not teeth at all. Preferring life on the muddy seabed, Sawfish hunt small fish and invertebrates such as Crabs and Shrimps.

The Sawfish is the spiritual guide of individuals who constantly find themselves walking a double-edged blade; haunted by the adage, 'damned if you do, damned if you don't'. As we journey through life, we tend to meet people who – for one reason or another – become friends, while others only ever become associates. Among the ones that become friends are those that honour the relationship unconditionally – giving and taking equally, with love and compassion, and those who don't. Some of these take more than they give, despite the apparent closeness of the relationship. They seem to expect attention and demand more than is fair. Worse still are those members of our family who take more than they give, almost expecting continued love and support simply because of blood-ties and kinship. These sort of blatant one-sided relationships are both parasitic and wrong, and Sawfish Dreaming nurtures us as we set about identifying them and lovingly disengaging ourselves from them. It is a sad truth that 'givers' often attract 'takers' and 'takers' draw 'givers'. Whether intentionally done or not, 'takers' tend to deceive 'givers' by making them feel indispensable, while 'givers' unwittingly support the deception by falling victim to the superficial praise. 'Givers' like to think they are needed and appreciated for their generosity and honesty. Their support is genuine and unconditional – and the 'takers' know it. Oblivious to the emotionally manipulative ways of the 'takers', 'givers' are seen as easy pushovers. True 'givers' are kind and considerate, willing to help others with no thought of recompense, often putting themselves out to accommodate those close to them. The moment that a 'giver' does something for themselves, though, or says 'no' to a request, the 'takers' often disapprove, often passionately. They cleverly discourage such ideas with patronising comments like 'Oh, that's great! I wouldn't do it myself, but you go ahead'. The 'giving person', not wanting to disappoint, will often back down. Hearing only 'I wouldn't do it', words intended to dishearten and set back. The 'giver' is subconsciously returned to their familiar comfort zone, vaguely disappointed, disempowered, but secure none-the-less, while the 'taker' climbs back onto his or her pedestal, almost self-toppled by fear of losing control or of no longer being admired or needed for their guidance. And thus the pattern continues, until the controlling factor is recognised, addressed and disengaged by the 'giver'. Sometimes referred to as 'cutting the ties that bind', Sawfish encourages us to reclaim our own power while developing the ability to see clearly the limitations, expectations and manipulation that have shaped our view of the world and the world's sculpted view of us. Sawfish Dreaming helps disengage us from these restrictions. One of the most effective and powerful ways, I have found, is by exercising focused intent via visualisation. Envisage yourself sitting in the basket of a hot-air balloon, about to take off, with anchor ropes trailing down being held securely by those that you love and respect. It is almost time to start and, although it is tempting to ask those holding the ropes to release them, resist the temptation because no matter how hard you ask, they will surely refuse. Although they're fully aware of your need to soar so that you may explore yourself, reclaim lost power, confidence and self-love, not one of them will let you go willingly – even those who love you unconditionally. Fear will prevent those that truly love you from surrendering their hold; fear of losing you or of being alone, and worse still, fear of being forgotten or replaced. Those whose feelings for you are fuelled by control, determination and self-gain, though, will have suspicion as their motivation for holding tighter; suspicion driven by their disbelieving realisation that you have finally woken up to their manipulative ways. So instead of asking them to let go, reach down and cut the ropes yourself, releasing their grip by force. Those who love you conditionally will see you gradually drift away from them, possibly for good, with their presence in your life becoming ever less frequent, important and controlling. Those whose love is unconditional, though, will be pleasantly surprised to see you soar to places their love alone could never have taken you; a love set to deepen over time, nourished with respect and trust. By disengaging ourselves from everyone in our life, Sawfish helps us realise the difference between categorical devotion and restrictive fondness. It gently yet powerfully sets us free by lifting us from the lonely, cold depths of regulation while inviting us to explore the warmer waters of life.

Scallop
Pilgrimage

Free-moving in nature, some species of Scallop fix themselves permanently to rocks just below the tidemark or anchor themselves precariously by a thread to jetty pylons and submerged debris. Circular and fluted, the Scallop shell is hinged with a strong internal ligament. With up to 40 eyes dotting the edge of the shell, the Scallop detects danger and flees by rapidly opening and closing its shell, sucking in water and ejecting it with such great force that the creature is thrust forward. An audible whistling sound is produced when the Scallop propels itself forward.

Celtic Pagans once worshipped at Brigantium, the temple previously dedicated to the goddess Brigit before their religion was violated by the Christian church and the shrine was surrendered to the followers of Saint James the Greater. Scallops have always been popular among the pilgrims who hike the 'Way of St James' on their way to the shrine at Santiago de Compostela in Spain, their hats and cloths traditionally decorated with images of the shell. According to folklore, as the early Christians walked they would present the shells at every house, basilica and fort they passed and, in doing so, could expect a handful of food or a drink for their effort. In this context, the Scallop heralds a quest for truth. It embodies the physical or spiritual journey we might take in search of greater wisdom or deeper understanding. It heralds a time of discovery, growth and awakening by encouraging a personal pilgrimage undertaken with the intention of attaining sacred knowledge. When taken with pure intent and no preconceived expectation, such a journey will surely see you rewarded with spiritual nourishment. Alternatively the 'Birth of Venus' (by Sandro Botticelli c.1483) is a large painting currently on display at the Uffizi Gallery in Florence. It depicts the goddess Venus emerging from the sea as a mature woman on a Scallop shell (a classical metaphor for the female vulva), apparently blown to shore by spiritual passion. On arrival, she is welcomed by a goddess of the seasons who warmly offers her a floral wrap. Venus is the Roman goddess of love, beauty and fertility, comparable to the Greek goddess Aphrodite. She was once revered as the ancestor of the Roman people. The work was painted for Lorenzo di Pierfrancesco de' Medici's Villa di Castello in celebration of the love of Giuliano di Piero de' Medici for Simonetta Cattaneo Vespucci. Unfortunately, Botticelli was also in love with the beautiful Simonetta, who was the model for the painting, but because of his friendship with Lorenzo de Medici, he apparently kept it to himself. From this perspective, therefore, Scallop invites love into our life. It cherishes the romance of true love, and helps us hold tight the joy and inspiration only love can bring. Scallop Dreaming nurtures the feelings of love and devotion we feel for another (even if unreciprocated), while fostering our birthright to be ultimately loved and respected unconditionally in turn. Despite the obstacles presented to us by circumstance, Scallop manages to open a mutual channel through which pure and unadulterated love, trust and acceptance may flow freely from us and back to us in kind.

Sea Dragon
Suppression

There are two species of Sea Dragon indigenous to Australian waters: the Weedy or Common Sea Dragon and the Leafy Sea Dragon. Belonging to the Seahorse family, Sea Dragons differ to Seahorses in several ways. Not only do they have weedy, leaf-like appendages, for example, the Sea Dragon does not bear a pouch like the Seahorse, used for rearing young. Instead, the males carry the young on their tail. Nor do they have a prehensile tail. Unlike that of the Seahorse, the tail of the Sea Dragon is unable to grasp objects. Sea Dragons propel themselves through the water by rapidly moving their ventral and dorsal fins. They do not have teeth or stomachs and feed through a long, tubular snout. Growing to about 30-50 centimetres in length, Sea Dragons generally appear as a green-gold to orange colour, and are ornately delicate.

Celtic tradition offers specific protective qualities to the Dragon. Mystical and magickal beasts, Dragons were deemed the guardians of the four elements: earth, fire, water, and air. Its ability to shed its skin and emerge as a new, transformed being is thought to mirror man's will to dare by teaching us courage, strength and self-knowledge. Dragons encourage us to face and combat our fears so that we might transform them into gifts of inner strength and self-power. The Water or Sea Dragon is said to expose that which has been suppressed or long forgotten, intentionally or not. It raises questions regarding issues from the past, and brings dormant memories to the surface so they may be fruitfully addressed. Usually with good reason, the memories that emerge often frighten and overwhelm as they reveal the reasons behind their initial suppression. Facing these fears with empathy and nerve inevitably brings about greater depth of soul, acceptance and improved health. Although sometimes seen as bringers of emotional inundation and outburst, Sea Dragon heralds a long awaited time of complete balance and stability, as suppressed memories wholesomely integrate with the conscious mind.

Seahorse
Integration / Responsible Fathering Skills on an Emotional Level

Seahorses are so named because of the uncanny resemblance of their head to that of the Horse. Their snouts are long and tubular and their stocky bodies are covered in rectangular bony plates. Seahorses have prehensile tails and the males of some species, after incubating the eggs in a special pouch, take full responsibility for the raising of the young.

The Seahorse is a 'yin' or 'feminine' totem. Its gentle, nurturing energy is both receptive and creative. Ruled by the moon, the Seahorse speaks of nature's cycles while mirroring the ebbs and flows of Grandmother Ocean. Like the Emu, Seahorse demonstrates effective fathering skills, but, instead of the enduring, grounded, practical approach inspired by the Emu, Seahorse presents a gentler, more nurturing approach. It supports us when circumstances become emotionally testing for us (as the father or child), especially when the receptive and protective energies of our (or their) mother is absent. As with the message of the regular Horse, Seahorse provides both strength and direction by helping us realise our passion and, in turn, our source of personal power. Inspired by the element water and its correspondences, Seahorse retains the (possibly single) father's sense of masculinity and practicality, while seamlessly integrating the feminine, nurturing, sensitive and intuitive energies of the mother. Likewise, it affords all men the opportunity to consciously balance their 'yin' and 'yang' aspects by integrating the typically female intuitive ability 'to know' with their stereotypically male trait, 'to do'. Thus, Seahorse provides a figurative anchor and the emotional strength needed to hang on, especially when exhaustion and emotional pain threaten to overwhelm.

Shark
Authority

Sharks are the purest and most efficient killing machines known to man. Their razor sharp teeth are grown in layers so that when one is knocked out, another replaces it almost immediately. Their 'skeletons' are formed almost entirely from cartilage. Sharks must remain constantly on the move, allowing water (and oxygen) to pass through their gills. If they stop swimming and remain still for too long, they run the high and probable risk of drowning. Australia has many species of Shark common to its waters, among which is the most infamous: the Great White, which grows to lengths of up to 12 metres.

Most people are afraid of Sharks because they believe them to be merciless killers. Sure, Sharks are ruthless predators, but strange as it may sound, you have more chance of being struck by lightning than being eaten by a Shark. According to the Australian Bureau of Statistics, less than one person a year (on average) has been killed by Sharks in Australian waters over the past 200 years, 57 over the past 50 years. Shark is the totem of people whose job it is to protect, maintain order and dispense discipline. Just as the dorsal fin of a Shark may pop up unexpectedly behind the unsuspecting surfer, the flashing blue light of a police car can suddenly appear in the rear-view mirror of a motorist. Shark is the totem of those charged with roles of responsibility and authority within the community: police officers, justices of the peace, school teachers, principals, prison wardens, parking officers, judges and magistrates, bank managers and members of local council. Shark demands that we show respect for authority, to see merit in respecting the need for and the maintenance of boundaries within our home and community. So, based on the fact that fatal Shark attacks are rare, a fear of them may not be any more than a superficial excuse that masks a deeper, more personal problem. Perhaps on a subconscious level, we fear Sharks because we inherently relate them to authority. It seems that those who are wary or untrusting of authority share a similar feeling toward Sharks. Those abused, oppressed or neglected may also feel vulnerable around Sharks. Shark confirms that respect must be earned and that those who distrust authority either need to be shown respect themselves or taught how to feel self-respect. For those who do not fear Sharks, the advice is simple: never splash about in waters not intended for you and you will be fine.

Sponge
Accumulation

There are about 6000 diverse species of Sponge recorded internationally; with many more still to be discovered and classified. One of the oldest life forms on Earth, some with no mouth, tissue or any organs, the Sponge left scientists perplexed for centuries, unsure whether to categorize the creature as a plant or animal. Found to feed on fragments of organic material, though, the Sponge was finally verified as an animal.

A naturally absorbent creature, Sponge strengthens memory by affording greater ability to retain and recall knowledge with accuracy and ease. Whether studying for an exam, practising for a rehearsal, coaching for a game or preparing for an interview, Sponge is a powerful aid for those needing to remember information long term. It also affords the ability to manifest wealth or to accrue it in a positive way. It promotes a sense of self-belief and suggests that by having faith and following our dreams, personal and monetary wealth will accumulate. Naturally fortunate, Sponge people are masters of charm, drawing others around with a simple smile or a flick of their hair. They attract fascination and wonder and make friends with the greatest of ease. Sponge supports those who seek security in all they do by schooling them in purity, honesty, willpower and anticipation.

Starfish
Existence

Starfish, or Sea Stars, belong to the class *Asteroidea*. They are stiff-bodied, slow-moving creatures with mouths that face downwards. Tube-feet move food toward the mouth, located at the centre of creature's belly. Starfish eat organic matter found on the seabed. Typically, five arms radiate out from the core of their bodies, each bearing rows of suction caps.

The five arms of the Starfish are symbolic of the human microcosm, five being the number that embodies the nature of the Universe, Creation, Great Mystery and mankind as a whole. It could be said that human existence itself rotates entirely around the number five. With arms and legs out-stretched, the human form resembles a pentagon or a five-pointed star. The pentagon shares the symbolism of perfection and power similar to the circle as, like the circle, it embodies the whole: the five senses (taste, touch, smell, sight, hearing), the five elements (earth, air, fire, water and ether or spirit), the five stages of life's cyclical process (conception, birth, life, death and rebirth) and human growth and development (baby, child, teenager, adult or parent and elder). The five-pointed star also implies individuality, spiritual attainment and education. Since the beginning of human history the circle has represented equality, protection, fertility and feminine wisdom. As Black Elk, Elder of the Oglala Sioux people, once said:

> ' ... *the sky is round, and I have heard the Earth is round like a ball, and so are all the stars. The wind in its greatest power whirls. Birds make their nests in circles, for theirs is the same religion as ours. The sun comes forth and goes down again in a circle. The moon does the same, and both are round. Even the seasons form a great circle in their changing, and always come back again to where they were. The life of a man is a circle from childhood, and so it is in everything where power moves'.*

Starfish Dreaming reminds us that what goes around comes around, that nothing happens by chance and that all things are equal. It tells us that we are not alone; that we walk as part of a whole, a drop in the ocean, a leaf on the Tree of Life. It affirms that we are a vital thread in the Universal Tapestry, an essential ingredient in the greater scheme of things – that our voice should be heard and that our contribution to the planet, no matter how small, is destined to make a difference.

Stingray
Masquerade

Belonging to the Shark family, the Stingray is usually equipped with a whip-like tail and a dorsal fin in the centre of its disk-like body. With less than 20 human fatalities worldwide attributed to Stingray stings (all stings were to the torso), their venom is highly toxic. Generally placid, some species of Stingray have a venomous barb halfway along the tail that is capable of exacting a severe or possibly fatal wound. Stingrays are mostly seabed dwelling creatures that inhabit temperate coastal waters and estuaries. They bury themselves in the sand making them almost impossible to see. Most stings occur when people accidentally stand on them. The most famous stingray-related death to date is the one involving television personality and naturalist Steve Irwin. He died on September 4, 2006 after his heart was pierced by a stingray barb while snorkelling off the far north Queensland coast while shooting a marine documentary.

The Stingray is the totem of those who show one face in order to protect another. They usually have two faces – a public one, and one that only close friends and family know. Very private people, it is rare to get clear insight into the personal life of a Stingray person. They keep to themselves, protecting their family and home from prying eyes. They advertise only the things they feel people need to know, and keep the rest clandestine. They quietly go about their business, often doing wonderful things to better the planet without making a big fuss. A peaceful creature with frightening cousins, the Stingray frequently guides those who display a threatening appearance or gruff personality, if only to hide their true (and often gentle) persona. Armoured with tattoos, body piercings, spiked hair, intimidating speech or menacing clothing, these characters are usually nothing at all like how they appear. They remind us of the adage, 'never judge a book by its cover'. Only ever aggressive when provoked or startled, Stingray Dreaming asks that we always take time to get to know people before forming superficial opinions of them based on their appearance, character, nationality or lifestyle choice. Their initial presentation may be nothing more than an elaborate and protective masquerade intended to throw you off guard, affording them opportunity to step away and blend back into the shadows.

Trout
Health

The word 'Trout' refers to a number of freshwater fish species that belong to the Salmon family, *Salmonidae*. Inhabiting freshwater streams and lakes, some species of Trout (namely the Brown Trout from England and the Rainbow Trout from California) were introduced into Australia by amateur fishing enthusiasts during the 19th century. As a result, many species of native fish are now endangered. In some areas, the Rainbow or Redband Trout still displays the tendency to swim upstream during the winter months to spawn. Trout camouflage themselves by using the reflected sunlight to its advantage. As the sunlight dances on the surface of the water, it blends naturally with the sun enhanced colouring of the Trout's scales.

'My heart leaps up when I behold
A rainbow in the sky:
So was it when my life began;
So is it now I am a man;
So be it when I shall grow old,
Or let me die!'
- William Wordsworth (1802)
From the poem, 'My Heart Leaps Up When I Behold'

The Trout has long been deemed a sacred messenger of fertility and good health. A solar influenced creature, the Trout's ability to leap clear of the water was imitated by ancient cultures in fertility rites as a way of harnessing the energy of the rising sun. The dances were also performed to signify the end of winter and to welcome spring and summer. According to Irish folklore, the Leprechaun hides his famous pot of gold in a most secret hiding place – namely the foot of a rainbow. Rainbows (a phenomenon produced by sunlight passing through beads of moisture in the atmosphere, causing a band of coloured light to appear) are said to mark the cessation of rain, particularly extended periods of heavy drizzle. According to the Bible, rainbows represent the agreement forged between God and man, as well as the promise made by God to Noah that he would never again flood the planet. 'Noah's Thanks Offering', (c.1803), a painting by Joseph Anton Koch, depicts Noah speaking to God after the Great Flood (Genesis 8-9), and God responding with a rainbow; a sign of his pledge. Rain is symbolic of the Earth Mother's tears. When it rains, we stay indoors, or run about with coats and umbrellas in a bid to avoid getting drenched. The dark skies and loaded clouds that accompany rain inspire heavy feelings similar to sadness and depression. As the Earth Mother's tears, the rain that falls during winter (in particular), the season of darkness, inspires hibernation and emotional cleansing. We are inspired to investigate who we truly are, both externally and internally, to purify our mind, body and spirit and to engage a symbolic death of sorts, or consciously banish our tired, familiar self forever. Trout Dreaming encourages us to contemplate our 'rainy times' when they come, and to bask in their glory and learn from them. It assures us that when they pass, a promised time of healing, new life and love will be heralded by the appearance of rainbows.

Tuna
Transience

Tuna are ocean-dwelling fish, although some also inhabit freshwater regions. Most fish have white flesh, but the flesh of Tuna is pink to dark red because of the higher levels of oxygen-binding molecules in their muscle tissue. Travelling vast distances and achieving speeds in excess of 70 kilometres per hour, the Tuna is a migratory species known to visit coastlines on opposite sides of the world. With such a wide territory, the larger species of Tuna are often referred to as being a 'fish without a country'.

A nomad of sorts, Tuna embodies the transient qualities and lifestyle mind-set of the gypsy. Once referred to as 'gipcyans' or 'gyptians' (a derivative of 'Egyptian'), 16th century gypsies were thought to have come from Egypt. Now, the word generically refers to roving folk living chiefly among non-roving folk. And like the gypsy, the Tuna rejects social demand to settle down and remain in one place for any amount of time. Instead, it champions the adage, 'wherever I lay my hat, that's my home'. With the spirit of adventure alive in his heart, Tuna Dreaming inspires us to leave the comfort and safety of home or the security of a steady job to explore the wider world. Most people live a mundane, repetitious life, waking in the morning, having breakfast, leaving for work, returning home from work, eating dinner, watching television, showering and then retiring for the night, only to do exactly the same thing the next day…and the next. By living the ordinary life of an ordinary person, we begin to realise how the White Mouse must feel as he pushes forward on his exercise wheel – though constantly on the move, he goes nowhere. Although by working hard your goal may be to build a solid basis on which to enjoy an abundant future, Tuna asks, 'Are you slowly starving your soul of spontaneity, adventure and the chance to grow in the process?' Tuna encourages us to consider expanding our view of the world and enriching our life by physically exploring the beauty that surrounds us globally. Take a holiday, travel, visit the Seven Wonders of the World, or better still – leave work, sell your house and move interstate or migrate abroad. Break the patterns, expectations and rules by which we subsist, and champion the fact that life should be lived, and that we should only ever work to live and not live to work. Life should be about adventure and the seeking of excitement and knowledge, not the drudgery and monotony that comes with repetition and duty.

Whale
Record Keeper

Whales are divided into two suborders: Baleen Whales and Toothed. Most of the smaller Whales, including Dolphins and Porpoises, belong to the toothed Whale family. Whales communicate with one another by means of low frequency sound. Family members are capable of calling to one another over great distances through rhythm and vibration.

There are many tales of heroes being swallowed by Whales in their quest for enlightenment. Their descent into the creature's belly more often than not representing man's spiral into the Underworld, marking his inevitable re-emergence after certain tests are passed; a journey emblematic of sacred rebirth and retrieval of the human spirit. Whale asks us to remember the Earth as our Mother and to reconnect with her and the soul connection we forged at the beginning of time. Whale is a keeper of the Earth Mother's sacred records. She witnesses the proceedings that collectively authenticate the spiritual makeup of the Earth; the memories of each and every event that has ever and will ever contribute to her shaping, and stores them within her Dreaming. Whale helps us remember the spiritual history of the areas most significant to our personal journey and offers ways to enhance our medicine, our lives and the planet as a whole. It is said that people who work with Whale hold within their DNA the ability to comprehend the sound frequencies encoded in the audible rhythms and vibrations emitted by the great mammal. The throbbing, metrical song of the Whale offers them the chance to reconnect with universal consciousness and the heartbeat of the Earth Mother, which is reminiscent of the double heartbeat we all heard as we grew in our mothers' wombs. Whale opens the vaults of creation, offering sacred access to the knowledge stored within. She journeys with us, guiding us back to the deep-core rhythms of nature and our instinctual connection to the cycles of life. She helps us remember our personal truth and wisdom and how to reconnect to the heartbeat of the Universal Mother. Whale wants you to rebirth your emotional body and to revive yourself physically by tapping into the knowledge of your own genetic memory and personal rhythm. In doing so you will remember the sacred bond you innately share with all things and, in doing so, you will ultimately find the knowledge to heal yourself and your family. You may even glean insight into how the rest of humanity may follow suit.

THE KINGDOM
OF THE
COLD-BLOODED
ONES

Most reptilian species shed their skin at certain times of the year, stripping away the old layers of skin to reveal a new, shiny one. Similarly, they teach us to strip away our old familiar self to reveal our true and authentic self. Carrying the keys to effective healing, reptiles are the ambassadors of new life, fertility and rebirth.

native / indigenous reptiles

Crocodile
Creative Force

Sharing their family with Alligators, Caimans and Gharials, the Crocodile has ancestry dating back to prehistoric times, changing little in appearance since the Dinosaurs ruled the Earth. Crocodiles are large aquatic reptiles common to the tropical regions of Africa, Asia, America and Australia. They inhabit freshwater rivers and wetlands, with some species adapting to salt water. The Saltwater Crocodile of Australia, for example, has been found swimming far out at sea. They predate fish, reptiles and mammals. According to Egyptian mythology, the Crocodile was sacred to Ammut who was known as 'the devourer of the dead', punishing evil-doers by eating their hearts. The Crocodile was also sacred to Sobek, portrayed as a human with the head of a Crocodile or as a Crocodile itself. The temples of Sobek usually had sacred lakes containing Crocodiles that were fed and cared for by specially trained priests.

Crocodile Dreaming is best described as a force capable of delivering both tenderness and annihilation. The female Crocodile, for example, brutally grabs her prey by the snout and drags it into the water, rolling it over and over until it is dead. She then tears it apart and eats it. With the next breath, she lovingly scoops her hatchlings up from their nest, and carries them – in her jaws – to the relative safety of the river. She is the embodiment of the goddess Kali, the one associated with loss, devastation, fear and the uncontrollable forces of life. She is death itself. According to the principles of Tanta Yoga, however, she is also a symbol of rebirth; a vehicle of salvation. Crocodile views the process of death and rebirth as vital stages of initiation. As such, it demands we close one door so that another may open. As an amphibious creature, Crocodile acts as a doorkeeper to both the mundane world and the Underworld; the embodiment of both life and death in their purest forms. With eyes positioned on the top of its head, Crocodile encourages us to see above and beyond physical and emotional limitation so that we may trust our intuition and our ability to manifest our heart's desire.

Lizard
Dreaming

Lizards are generally four-legged, scaly reptiles, with external ears and movable eyelids. Unable to create their own body warmth, Lizards must absorb the warmth of the sun to stimulate activity. Many Lizards are able to regenerate lost limbs or tails, while others can change their skin color in response to environmental factors or stress. Lizards eat fruit and plant foliage, eggs, insects, mammals and carrion.

Déjà vu occurs when we consciously 'bump into' vital details or aspects of daydreams had on earlier occasions. When we daydream, we energetically leave the present in order to astrally 'check out' our potential future. While physically doing something routine, we find our mind wandering and our conscious mind leaving the physical confines of our body on an astral level, exploring future aspects of our life. When our conscious mind realises that we have been daydreaming, we snap back and instantly forget what we have just experienced and the body of the daydream is expelled from our mind forever. Daydreams are Spirit's way of allowing us to consciously explore our future while remaining bodily alert. About a week or two after having your daydream, you will suddenly get the uncanny feeling that you have done this all before. Even though the conscious mind disagrees, the subconscious mind remembers visiting this time and space. It remembers you placing yourself in this setting – astrally – weeks before, with the subliminal intention of remembering the fact on your bodily arrival. The physical sensation is your wakeup call, meant to trigger a realisation that something in or around you offers a window of opportunity, that once acknowledged will initiate a great change of fortune in your life. What you vision in your daydreams, Spirit offers the map to find, and all that is left to do is follow the directions with intent and resolve. Lizard, a creature that spends its days basking in the sun, daydreams its future into reality. Lizard's wisdom is that of the dreamer. It bridges the worlds by actively participating in its dreams – both waking and sleeping. As such, it advises us to take serious note of what our dreams are trying to tell us. It encourages us to keep a journal. It wants you to look to your daydreams as viable messages from Spirit and veritable roadmaps to possibility that would normally remain faceless for eternity. Spirit gifted you with this life as a chance to make your mark on the world. Don't waste a single chance by choosing to ignore the unrealised but fertile potentials your dreams may be gathering and shaping for your future.

Rainbow Serpent
Shaping the Land through Legend

The Rainbow Serpent is a primary Ancestor to many of Australia's indigenous people, with many of the creation stories centring on it coming from the northern parts of Australia. Dreamtime stories tell how the Ancestors (in animal or human form) shaped the land. When time was new, it is said, the Earth was flat and grey, with no mountains or valleys. And then the Rainbow Serpent appeared from the ground and fashioned the mountains, valleys, ridges and canyons as it worked its way across the landscape. It made the waterways by filling the Earth's rips and tears with its urine. A teacher spirit who showed the people how to dig for food and how to breathe, Rainbow Serpent was the mightiest of the Dreamtime beings, so feared by the other creatures that they stayed well away from him. Every time he moved, his huge multicoloured body formed a new part of the virgin landscape. When he became tired of shaping the Earth he found a waterhole and sank into its depths. Each time the other animals visited the waterhole they were very careful not to disturb him until one day, after a rainstorm, they saw his rainbow body arching up from the waterhole, up over the trees and the plains, through the clouds and down into another waterhole. The Rainbow Serpent is not a creature with which to tempt fate.

Rainbow Serpent Dreaming is focused on 'shaping the land' – both inner and outer. It teaches us how to journey inward to meet our authentic self, to reshape the inner landscape that is our personal reality, and face, combat and transform our fears and limitations into gifts of strength and power. Although it is safe to acknowledge the superficial lessons of the Rainbow Serpent, we are advised never to invoke this powerful spirit without unmistakable permission of an Elder, traditional understanding or ancestral guidance. It is worth noting that even Australia's indigenous people are careful not to disturb the Rainbow Serpent as they see him spread across the sky.

Snake

Transmutation

Australia, also known as 'Snake Island' – a name respectfully used by some Tribal Elders in reference to the Great Rainbow Serpent – has probably the largest array of venomous Snakes than any other continent in the world, as well as a healthy range of non-venomous Pythons and Tree Snakes. It is not unusual to happen across a Snake while swimming in a waterhole, bushwalking or tending a country garden during the summer months. What is not generally known, though, is that Snakes are equally as common in metropolitan parks and gardens, feeding on the creatures that inhabit the side-streets and alleyways.

The ancient Celts saw the Snake as a powerful symbol of fertility, often depicting Serpents in their artwork with eggs lodged firmly in their mouths – emblematic depictions of creation, with the masculine seed meeting and joining with the female egg. While embracing the promise of new life, the Snake can be seen as a representative of the healing we must accept if we intend to move into the next phase of our life in a complete and fertile way. As a symbol now employed by the medical fraternity, the Caduceus is a stylised emblem incorporating a pair of Snakes entwined together in the sacred act of copulation, working themselves as one around a staff, taking a symbolic journey to the higher, mystical realms of creation. Before we can welcome what we yearn for into our lives, we must first be prepared to acknowledge the things we no longer want or need. It is a recognised fact that there is no such thing as a sick person who is not grieving for something. If we are grieving for some aspect of life that we feel is out of our reach, no matter how hard we twist and turn in a vain attempt to draw it closer to us, the grief we feel will eventually make us ill. We grieve because we love, and to stop grieving suggests that our love has gone. Grief however, can be turned into power because to have lived with grief is to have known love, a power that empowers us to teach others how to deal with grief and see beyond it. Snake points out that we need to look deep within ourselves and honour those aspects that pose the greatest threat of making us ill. We have to hand them over so that we may see clearly again, allowing us to move forward with confidence and a renewed sense of purpose. Snake suggests that we look at our baggage, our burdens and our pain and transmute them into new opportunity, new life and the chance to start our journey over again. She offers us the chance to physically rebirth ourselves by strengthening us emotionally and deepening our relationship with Spirit.

Turtle
Mother Earth

Freshwater Turtles are aquatic reptiles that have webbed feet and sharp claws, used to pull themselves onto rocks and half-submerged logs. Freshwater Turtles deprived of water will eventually dehydrate and starve to death. Marine Turtles have flippers; paddle like appendages that afford them efficient underwater locomotion, but make movement on land clumsy and slow. Marine Turtles sustain a solely aquatic lifestyle, only coming ashore to lay their eggs. They have been swimming the Earth's oceans for more than 150 million years. Barely changed since the reign of the Dinosaur, six of the world's seven species of Marine Turtle occur within Australia's Great Barrier Reef.

Even when surrounded by those we love and respect, we sometimes feel alone and isolated. We sometimes forget our connection to Spirit and the relationship we have with the Earth Mother and creation. We feel apart *from*, rather than a part *of*, nature. We feel disconnected from the Great Wheel of Life and believe ourselves to be alone. Turtle, however, reminds us that we are never alone – that the Earth is our Mother and that she loves, speaks, protects and provides for us every day. Due to their ancient heritage, Turtles have long been revered as symbols of the Earth Mother, longevity and protection. Turtle lays her eggs deep within the warm sands of Mother Earth, confiding in her the protection and nurturing of her offspring. She trusts that the Earth Mother will provide them with all they need to develop so that they may emerge as strong, independent representatives of her future generation. To hide something sacred within the dark abyss of Mother Earth, away from the light of the Grandfather Sun, is symbolic of the ritualistic death endured by individuals of many ancient cultures in their search for healing, ancestral wisdom and spiritual enlightenment. As the Turtle's young emerge from the sand, they are in fact rebirthing as if from the womb of the Earth Mother. Their first birth is symbolised by the laying of the egg into the Earth, with the rebirth symbolised by the breaking free of the coffin-like eggshell to re-emerge from the nurturing energy of Mother Earth into the light of Grandfather Sun. Turtle prepared us for profound change – in the form of healing (regarding family issues, secrets, etc), personal growth and an awakening of sorts. You are literally being prepared for rebirth, emergence and a return to clarity. You are also being reconnected in a sacred way to the creative force of the Earth Mother's womb, her heart and the inherent wisdom she yearns to impart. You are being reminded that we are 'all related' and that, even when you believe yourself forsaken, you are being cradled and nurtured by Mother Earth.

appendix

Meeting Your Power Animal - A Meditative Journey

Preparation: Smudging

A tradition recognised by many tribal cultures, but made popular by the philosophies of the Native American people, smudging uses the smoke from burning herbs or specially prepared incense to cleanse and strengthen the energy field or aura of a person before they participate in any journey work or spiritual activity.

Smoke is an etheric substance capable of penetrating the subtle veils of creation. Herbs most commonly used in the smudging ceremony are sweet-grass, white sage, cedar and tobacco, although lavender, frankincense, cinnamon and eucalyptus are also occasionally employed as viable alternatives.

Smudging draws in positive energy, while banishing negativity and cleansing or purifying the aura on a vibrational level. To smudge, choose one or a combination of the herbs listed above, dry them thoroughly and place them in a heatproof bowl or dish. Take a match and light the crushed herbs until they start to smoulder, keeping in mind that it is the smoke you ultimately want and not a healthy flame.

Brush the smoke, using your cupped hand or a feather, so that it surrounds and touches every part of your body, as you ask the spirit of the herbs to remove all negative energy.

Visualise this energy leaving your aura and returning to the Universe via the smoke. You are now ready to participate in your quest to find your totem animal.

The Journey

By slipping into a meditatively induced altered state and requesting the wisdom of the animal spirit world, you will inevitably meet your totem or power ally. This beast will be of a species with which you already feel a bond. This creature will become your friend, your teacher and your life partner.

Still your conscious mind and silence the inner chatter to ensure that your subconscious mind is receptive and alert. Wait for the moment when you intuitively feel the need to open your consciousness to the other realms. Allow visions and symbolic images to waft through your mind. Keep your focus within yourself. Let any thoughts just go by. When you catch yourself engaged in an external conscious thought, just take a deep breath and bring yourself back to your centre.

Picture yourself on a great grassy plain, dotted with the most beautiful wild flowers. From where you are standing you can see two different paths: one to your right, which leads up to a steep mountain peak, and another to your left leading down into a deep valley.

Visualise yourself taking the left path as it leads down into the deep valley. You walk until you are standing at the edge of a forest beside a huge standing stone that seems to be guarding the path that leads into the forest. On the side of the standing stone is a word, engraved into the surface. This is an affirmation word, which describes and represents your potential at present. Take note of this word.

You start down the path, and to your left you notice an animal standing at the edge of the path. It says nothing, and will follow you as you pass. It means you no harm, but rather, for this meditation, will act as your guardian to ensure your safe passage.

You carry on down the path, which, although the forest is pitch-dark, seems to self-illuminate, enabling you to see and not stumble. You see many things as you walk. Thick over-hanging branches; incredible, brightly coloured butterflies and birds, sweet smelling flowers and huge insects, like beetles and Spiders, all too beautiful to be afraid of. All the while you feel eyes watching you, from amongst the trees. They are not threatening eyes, but rather curious and caring eyes. You know you are safe, because your guardian is not far behind, keeping a close watch on you.

Continue to walk until you come to a great clearing. The area has been carefully cleared, and here and only here the forest floor is covered in a lush green lawn, perfectly manicured. In the centre of the clearing, surrounded by huge stones, is a massive fire. This fire is so big you cannot see the top of the flames. The glow is so intense, you can see perfectly, as if in daylight. You would think that with a fire this big, the trees would be scorched and the grass would be withered, but they are not. You would also think that with a fire this big, the heat being radiated out would be so ferocious it would be impossible to venture too close, but it is not. The flames of this magical fire are golden orange in colour, like any standard fire, but the flames are cool to the touch. The fuel under the fire is burning, yet it is not diminishing. This is a sacred fire, protected by the forest. This is the Father Fire, sent to Mother Earth by Grandfather Sun when time was new. It was sent as the original spark destined to ignite the fire of life and all new beginnings. It is the Fire of Spirit, the one thing that links our inner fires to the Great Fire of Spirit. This fire means you no harm, and even if you were to put your hand into the flames, you would never receive a burn. Put your hand in and see. Feel the flames licking your hand. Feel the sensation of the flames enveloping your fingers and your wrist, but without any heat.

You sit in front of the fire, cross-legged on the ground. You close your eyes and find your inner peace. Feel the glowing love of Spirit fill you to the core, sent to you by the raging flames of this gentle fire.

Open your eyes and stare into the flames, the whole time asking for your true and powerful totem animal to present itself to you, even for just a little while. Focus on this thought, and clear your mind of other things. Keep your intent pure and your eagerness at a minimum. As with all animals, you will not be approached if you are radiating urgent and unsettling energies.

As you stare, notice a pair of eyes staring back at you. They are not human eyes, and you know this, but you cannot, as yet, make out what sort of eyes they are.

Gradually a face forms around the eyes, and you notice a neck, followed by a body and legs. The animal is now whole and gingerly steps out of the flames and sits in front of you, perhaps to have a scratch or a stretch.

This animal is your totem animal; it may be a bird, a beast, a reptile or an insect. It may even be a fish, in which case your environment may have changed without you noticing.

Watch how the animal relates to you. Does it circle around you, or rub up against you? Does it sit in your lap, or touch you with its nose? Does it make any sound? Does it make any 'threatening', or sudden moves? If it has ears, are they upright or laid back? Does it have a tail? If so, is it upright, hanging down or tucked under its body? Take note of these things and any other obvious features.

After spending time with your animal/bird/reptile/insect, becoming accustomed with one another, and possibly communicating about this and that, say goodbye and allow the animal to return to the flames. It must not follow you out of the forest, so insist on it returning to the Father Fire. Wait patiently if you have to.

Once the animal has returned to the realm of Spirit, look down to the ground beside you; in the grass you will notice a word. A word of wisdom meant as a message to guide you and link you to this animal once you part. This word will open up the communication link between the animal and yourself, and will act as a symbol of its Dreaming to you.

Begin walking back up the path. You will notice that your guardian animal is still following you. You will also notice that it made no gesture towards your totem animal, as they have already met. Spend some time returning up the path. Notice the things you saw on the way in, and notice that although the forest is as black as pitch, the path continues to illuminate the way. At the end of the path, where the edge of the forest meets the grassy plain, your guardian will step back to the side of the path, where it met you, and nod a farewell. Make your way to the standing stone, and take note of the engraved word. You will notice that the original word is still there, but underneath another word has been added. This word symbolises your possible potential now that you have the power of your totem animal walking beside you. Take note of this word and add it to the other two words. You now have three words. Say them in your mind. Do they prompt any feelings, thoughts or emotions in you as you say them?

Take your time to walk across the grassy plain once more, again stopping to observe and enjoy the wild flowers.

Make a silent prayer to Spirit for a reason sacred to you and to offer thanks for the messages and visions experienced during the meditation. Ask Spirit to surround the Earth in a healing and protective green aura and focus it mainly on the animal kingdom. Wiggle your fingers and toes as you return to the physical room and open your eyes when you are ready.

Honouring your Power Animal

Once discovered, it is important to honour your totem animal and its Dreaming. Once the Dreaming has been shared and the trust of the animal gained, it is important to honour the presence of your animal and to show it the recognition it deserves. The animal must feel comfortable and welcome in your sacred space – your home, office and even your car. You must make it feel part of your life as you would a new pet. You must make the spirit animal feel as though it is free to treat you and yours as an extension of its own kingdom. If the animal is to work side by side with you, you must encourage it to stay. Allow it to become part of your essence.

Making the animal feel welcome is a relatively easy task. Maintaining this energy, on the other hand, requires conscious effort. One's intent can sometimes be taken for granted, and through laziness or as a result of the pressures of everyday life, may become a little slack. Simple steps can be taken, therefore, to ensure this does not happen.

Determine how you are going to welcome the animal into your space, and, once there, encourage it to stay. Some obvious suggestions include wearing jewellery representing your totem, hanging pictures of them in your home in a place you frequent on a regular basis, keeping a small statue on your desk or altar, or by donating to, visiting or volunteering your services to a cause that focuses on helping such animals. These are all simple things you can do that, even if for just a second, will help you deepen your relationship with your totem.

If you choose to hang pictures or display statues, do not think that by simply doing this your job is done. It is important to tend to these things by placing flowers nearby or by burning incense sacred to your totem animal, or simply dusting or polishing it regularly.

It should be noted, however, that this is not intended to imply that you should worship these images as idols. Instead, view them as physical representations of the animal spirit that is offering its help. Remember, if someone offers help, it is always polite to say thank you, or to acknowledge or reciprocate in some way. This is one such way.

about the author

Scott Alexander King is an animal spirit intuitive, psychic, teacher and practitioner of Earth Medicine, and holds a diploma in primary school education. After graduating from Victoria College, Toorak Campus in 1990, Scott realised his powerful ability to help children discover and harness their personal power and genuine nature. His commitment has led many children to overcome hardship and adversity, not only on an academic level but also on a physical, emotional and spiritual level. Today he is better known for his work with (among others) Indigo Warrior Children. He believes the empowerment of these young people is integral to healing our fractured community and his work now merges his two greatest passions: Earth Medicine and the enhancement of our children.

Scott's unique ability to communicate with the animal spirit realm and the energies of the Earth began when he was just eight years old. As a child, Scott realised he could see animal spirits (not 'dead' pets, but the inherent power of animals that walk with us: the power that was once incorporated into tribal lore and labelled as 'totem' energy). Although Australian by birth, Scott looks to the animals from a global perspective: his knowledge is not limited to the teachings of Australia's indigenous culture or Australian geography. He seems to have an inherent understanding of all animals – no matter which continent they inhabit. As a child, Scott relied heavily on his 'feelings' when it came to meeting new people. This energy warned him of deceit, rewarded him with promise and allowed him to successfully navigate his way through a very confusing childhood. As he grew, this 'energy' took form until he began to recognise it as being 'animal-like' in vibration – energy that he felt a natural bond with; energy that has never let him down.

With years of study and practice, Scott has refined his abilities and is today Australia's foremost Animal Spirit Intuitive, Psychic and Earth Medicine teacher. He currently lectures and offers experiential workshops Australia-wide. His work not only broadens awareness of humanity's ancient relationship with the Earth and the animals, it also offers a voice to the voiceless – namely our children and the endangered and threatened animals of the world. Scott's work includes: the wisdom of the animals, Earth Medicine, reading signs, omens and portents, psychic protection, divination, moon lore, natural magick, mediumship, meditation, genetic memory, soul purpose, personal power, the web of life and other spiritual topics. Those who participate in Scott's workshops and seminars come from all walks of life. Although most are everyday members of the general public, many are professionally trained in the areas of veterinary science, zoology, natural therapy (naturopathy, homeopathy, traditional herbal medicine etc), conventional medicine, psychology, child and adult education, social work and law.

Visit Scott's website at:
www.animaldreaming.com

bibliography

Andrews, T. *Animal Speak*. St. Paul: Llewellyn Publications, 1994

Andrews, T. *Animal Wise*. Jackson, TN: Dragonhawk Publishing, 1999

Beyerl, P. *The Master Book of Herbalism*. Washington: Phoenix Publishing, 1996

Berkovitch, S. *The Crystal Workbook*. Australia: Labrys, 1992

Carr-Gomm, P and S. *The Druid Animal Oracle*. Australia: Simon and Schuster, 1994

Cavendish, L. *White Magic*. California: Hay House, 2006

Conway, D.J. *Animal Magick*. St. Paul: Llewellyn Publications, 1997

Cooper, J C. *Symbolic and Mythological Animals*. London: Aquarian, 1992

Cunningham, S. *Encyclopedia of Magical Herbs*. St. Paul: Llewellyn, 1997

Elita, M. *The Miracle*. Australia: Blue Angel Gallery, 2006

Encyclopedia of Australian Wildlife. Readers Digest, Sydney. 1997

Grey, M. *Beasts of Albion*. London: Aquarian, 1994

Hicks, J and E. *The Law of Attraction: The Basics of the Teachings of Abraham*. California: Hay House, 2006

Meadows, K. *Earth Medicine*. Australia: Element, 1992

Morcombe, M. *The Great Australian Bird Finder*. Australia: Weldon Publishing, 1990

Oliver, S. *Hunting for Power: a Warrior's Guide to Freedom*, Australia: Fire Dragon, 2005

Sams, J. and Carson, D. *Medicine Cards*. New York: St. Martin's Press, 1988, 1999

Walker, B. *Woman's Dictionary of Myths and Secrets*. New York: Harper Collins, 1983

Walker, B. *Woman's Dictionary of Symbols & Sacred Objects*. London: Pandora, 1988

relevant websites

Anita Ryan-Revel – Australia's leading expert on the Chakras:
www.igoddess.com

Appin Hall – Ronnie and Maggie Burns' Children Foundation,
Tasmania: www.appinhall.com

Billie Dean – Australia's leading Animal Communicator:
www.billiedean.com

Judy Garrecht – Australia's favourite ambassador for the
empowerment of women: www.fromgrieftogoddess.com

Lucy Cavendish – Australia's favourite White Witch:
www.lucycavendish.com.au

Maria Elita – Australia's only Psychic Life Coach and creator of the
world's first Crystal Energy Bed: www.mariaelita.com

Susan Oliver – Australia's own inspiration for those yearning to
journey the Toltec Path to Power: www.impeccable.com.au

Toni Carmine Salerno – Australia's leading interpreter of Angelic
wisdom: www.tonicarminesalerno.com

The WA Conservation of Raptors – Two of Australia's most
passionate, dedicated people I know in the field of raptorial
rescue and rehabilitation: www.raptor.org.au

index

Also available from Blue Angel Publishing

Animal Dreaming Oracle
by Scott Alexander King
Illustrations by Karen Branchflower

In times past, it was not uncommon for a seeker of knowledge to request the advice of an Elder; someone skilled in the ability to commune with the energies of nature. Elders were seen as direct links between the people and Spirit, with their words held in high esteem.

When questions were raised, the Elder would take up a small pouch, perhaps containing claws, teeth, whiskers and bones of sacred animals which, after a quick shake, would be upended, the contents permitted to spill haphazardly onto the ground. Depending on where and how they fell, and the patterns they formed, the Elder would glean information relevant to the seeker by interpreting the messages offered by the animals represented by the claws and teeth.

Developed with the corresponding energies of the four directions in mind, the uniquely Australian *Animal Dreaming Oracle* embraces this ancient concept in a manner more befitting our times. Instead of the traditional claws and bones, it presents the animal energies to the people as beautifully illustrated portraits, with each animal's Dreaming clearly interpreted in the accompanying guidebook, allowing you to give and receive accurate and inspirational readings for yourself and others.

Features 45 cards & 132 page guidebook, packaged in a hard-cover box set.

Animal Dreaming Guided Meditative Journey CDs

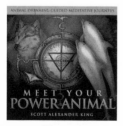

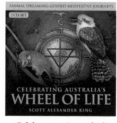

*Meet your
Power Animal*

*Celebrating Australia's
Wheel of Life (2 CD)*

*Healing with
the Animals*

Creature Teacher Cards
by Scott Alexander King
Illustrations by Sioux Dollman

Being a kid in this modern world can be difficult at times; confusing, overwhelming and even a little frightening. It's hard to know what decisions to make and what actions to take, because temptations, dares and opportunities lurk around every corner. There seems to be so much more for kids to be wary of, aware of and ready for these days - things that their parents, guardians and teachers never had to contend with when they were growing up.

Throughout the history of mankind, ancient cultures believed that we can communicate with and learn from the animals - that each animal offers its own unique insights and teachings, which can greatly enrich and deepen our lives, assisting us in communing with the forces of nature.

Taking this ancient principle and adapting it into an easy-to-use oracle card set, the *Creature Teacher Cards* and the accompanying guidebook offer daily guidance, nurturing and practical support from the animal kingdom, specifically catered towards today's young people, as they deal with real issues in a real and confronting world.

Drawing on the author's own life experiences as a child, and later as a father, school teacher and mentor to 'troubled' youth, this beautifully illustrated card set offers powerful, passionate and to-the-point wisdom to gently encourage young people to heal the past, stand confidently in the present and embrace the future as empowered and inspired individuals.

Features 45 circle-shaped cards & guidebook, packaged in a hard-cover box set.

For more information
or to purchase any
Blue Angel Publishing release,
please visit our website at:

www.blueangelonline.com